The foe claims in error that a philosopher I am.
God knows I am not what he says *I am.*
But, having endured this sorrow's nest, I ask:
Why should I not know at least what I am?

—Omar Khayyam

HUMAN ARCHITECTURE
Journal of the Sociology of Self-Knowledge

Editor:
Mohammad H. (Behrooz) Tamdgidi
Assistant Professor of Sociology
UMass Boston

Human Architecture: Journal of the Sociology of Self-Knowledge (ISSN # 1540-5699) is published by OKCIR: the Omar Khayyam Center for Integrative Research in Utopia, Mysticism, and Science (Utopystics) (www.okcir.com, info@okcir.com) and printed by the Okcir Press, an imprint of Ahead Publishing House (APH), located at 6 Hobbs Road, Medford, MA, 02155, U.S.A., tel/fax: 781.874.1448. Copyright © by Ahead Publishing House, 2002-6. All rights reserved. *Human Architecture* is indexed in CSA Illumina's *Sociological Abstracts*® and included in EBSCO's SocINDEX with Full-Text®.

Submissions: *Human Architecture* publishes both submitted and invited manuscripts as well as the working papers of OKCIR: the Omar Khayyam Center for Integrative Research in Utopia, Mysticism, and Science—an independent research and educational project. Contributors extend permission to *Human Architecture* for the publication of their work in the journal. They retain copyrights to their work and may publish them elsewhere. If the submitted manuscript has been published elsewhere before, written permission from both the author(s) and publication(s) where it earlier appeared should accompany submission to *Human Architecture*.

Editorial decisions: *Human Architecture* adheres to the peer reviewing principle for advancing scholarship—seeking innovative ways to meet the need in favor of liberatory scholarly practices most conducive to the aim and purpose of the journal. Selection of papers from submitted or invited manuscripts are based on their substantive relevance and the coherence and innovativeness of their argument in consideration of the mission of the journal. Views expressed in the journal by contributors are those of their authors and may not necessarily coincide with one another, or with the views of the editor, members of the Editorial Advisory Board, or the institutions with which any of the above are affiliated. Authors are responsible for the accuracy and integrity of factual, bibliographic, and referential materials used in their own articles, and for obtaining permissions for using copyrighted material in their manuscripts. Methodological, theoretical, historical, empirical, practical, as well as literary and artistic contributions relevant to the mission of the journal are all encouraged. The primary language used is English, but material in other languages may be included if relevant to the purpose of the journal.

What to submit: All manuscripts should be submitted in electronic format. They should preferably be double-spaced in Times 12 typeface., with 1 inch margins all around. In general, please follow a consistent bibliographic and citation style throughout the manuscript, following the ASA (American Sociological Association), MLA, or the University of Chicago style guides.

Where to submit: The Editor, *Human Architecture*, Okcir Press, 6 Hobbs Road, Medford, MA, 02155, U.S.A., tel/fax: 781.874.1448, e-mail: journal@okcir.com

Subscriptions: *Human Architecture* is a quarterly publication, usually published in two double-issues format (one regular Fall/Spring issue, and one special theme issue in Summer), both becoming available concurrently at the end of every Summer. *Individual and institutional single issues rates* are $30 (per double-issue) and $60 (per double-issue) respectively. *Individual and institutional subscription rates* per year beginning from the most recently published issue (when subscription order is received) are $60 and $120 respectively. Back issues or additional copies of the journal are available upon request at the same per single issue rates as indicated above. Rates include domestic shipping and sales tax, where applicable. For international or bulk orders please inquire for special rates & shipping charges. Make checks payable in U.S. dollars to Ahead Publishing House, and send payments to the Ahead Publishing House, 6 Hobbs Road, Medford, MA, 02155, U.S.A. Contributors each receive one free copy of the issue in which their articles appear. Rates are subjected to change without notice.

Advertisements: Current rates and specifications may be obtained by contacting the Okcir Press, 6 Hobbs Road, Medford, MA, 02155, U.S.A., tel/fax: 781.874.1448, e-mail: journal@okcir.com

Inquiries: Address all correspondence and requests to *Human Architecture*, Okcir Press, 6 Hobbs Road, Medford, MA, 02155, U.S.A., tel/fax: 781.874.1448, e-mail: journal@okcir.com

Changes of address: Six weeks' advance notice must be given when notifying change of address. Please include both the old and the new addresses in your request. **Postmaster:** Send address changes to Ahead Publishing House, 6 Hobbs Road, Medford, MA, 02155, U.S.A.

ISBN 1-888024-25-9

Human Architecture:
Journal of the Sociology of Self-Knowledge
Volume V, Issue 2, Spring 2007
ISSN: 1540-5699
ISBN: 1-888024-25-9

Editorial Advisory Board

Ayan Ahmed
B.A., Sociology
UMass Boston

David Baronov
Associate Professor of Sociology
St. John Fisher College

Anna Beckwith
Lecturer of Sociology
UMass Boston

Keilah Billings
Undergraduate Student of Sociology
UMass Boston

Bart Bonikowski
Doctoral Student of Sociology
Duke University

Milton Butts Jr.
Assistant Professor of Sociology
UMass Boston

Jorge Capetillo-Ponce
Assistant Professor of Sociology
UMass Boston

Arlene Dallalfar
Professor of Sociology & Women's Studies
Lesley College

Estelle Disch
Professor of Sociology
UMass Boston

Alicia Dowd
Assistant Professor of
Higher Education Administration
and Leadership
Graduate College of Education
UMass Boston

Benjamin Frymer
Assistant Professor of Sociology
Hutchins School of Liberal Studies
Sonoma State University

Bryan Gangemi
Graduate Student/ Activist
UMass Boston

Chris Gauthier
Doctoral Student of Sociology
University of Michigan

Michal Ginach
Psychoanalyst
The Institute for the Study of Violence
Boston Graduate School of Psychoanalysis

Panayota Gounari
Assistant Professor of Applied Linguistics
UMass Boston

Jenna Howard
Doctoral Student of Sociology
The State University of New Jersey at Rutgers

Tu Huynh
Doctoral Student of Sociology
SUNY-Binghamton

Glenn Jacobs
Associate Professor of Sociology
UMass Boston

Philip Kretsedemas
Assistant Professor of Sociology
UMass Boston

Winston Langley
Associate Provost for Academic Affairs
UMass Boston

Neil G. McLaughlin
Associate Professor of Sociology
McMaster University, Canada

Jennifer McFarlane-Harris
Doctoral Candidate
English and Women's Studies
University of Michigan, Ann Arbor

Emily Margulies
B.A., Sociology
SUNY-Oneonta

Jonathan Martin
Assistant Professor of Sociology
Framingham State College

Bruce Mazlish
Professor Emeritus of History
Massachusetts Institute of Technology

Askold Melnyczuk
Director, Creative Writing Program
UMass Boston

Aundra Saa Meroe
Postdoctoral Fellow
Institute for Urban and Minority Education
Teachers College
Columbia University

Martha Montero-Sieburth
Associate Professor of
Higher Education Administration
and Leadership
Graduate College of Education
UMass Boston

Anthony Nadler
Service-Learning and
Outreach Coordinator
Massachusetts Institute of Technology

Donna M. Rafferty
Undergraduate Student of Sociology
UMass Boston

Dylan Rodriguez
Assistant Professor
Department of Ethnic Studies
U.C. Riverside

Annie Roper
B.A., Sociology
UMass Boston

Khaldoun Samman
Assistant Professor of Sociology
Macalester College

Emmett Schaefer
Adjunct Assistant Professor of Sociology
UMass Boston

Frank Scherer
Doctoral Candidate
Social/Political Thought Program
York University, Toronto, Canada

Ingrid Semaan
Assistant Professor of Sociology
Mount Wachusett Community College

Tim Sieber
Professor of Anthropology
UMass Boston

Rajini Srikanth
Associate Professor of English
UMass Boston

Shirley Tang
Assistant Professor of
Asian American Studies
and American Studies
UMass Boston

Peter Van Do
M.A., American Studies
UMass-Boston

Aleksandra Wagner
BA Program Core Faculty, Sociology
The New School

Rika Yonemura
Doctoral Student of Sociology
U.C. San Diego

Reef Youngreen
Assistant Professor of Sociology
UMass Boston

Samuel Zalanga
Associate Professor of Sociology
Bethel University

In Honor of

Jesse Reichek (1916-2005)
Professor of Design
U. C. Berkeley

A Peer-Review*ing* Journal

Contributions to *Human Architecture: Journal of the Sociology of Self-Knowledge* pass through a rigorous selective process with respect to their fit, relevance, coherence of argument, and innovativeness in consideration of the scope, nature, and intended purpose of the journal. The journal adheres to the peer-reviewing principle for advancing scholarship, but aims to design and build new scholarly avenues to meet this requirement—seeking mechanisms that foster openness of inquiry and evaluation; mechanisms that invite constructive judgments subject to free, open, and mutually interactive, not blinded and one-sided, peer reviewing practices; mechanisms that can be employed as widely and dynamically as possible among specialist and interested scholars in the field who value the need for the proliferation of new, critical, and innovative personal and global insights and transformations.

To meet the highest standards of scholarship, liberatory editorial practices need to transition from static peer review*ed* to dynamic peer review*ing* models that de-couple publication from defective pre-publication peer review requirements, and engage in alternative peer review practices that remain open to all those wishing to review a manuscript at any time in the post-publication phase—encouraging expanded and deepening exchanges among scholars, authors and readers alike. They need to invite critical thinking about prevailing and dominant paradigms and inflame creative spirits to forge new scholarly horizons and intellectual landscapes. And they need to embrace the subaltern voices in the academia and beyond, voices of those who have been deprived of cultivating their sociological imaginations through formal scholarly publishing avenues.

Human Architecture warmly invites contributors and readers to peer review the articles herein and to openly share their critical and constructive insights with one another in the future chronicles of this journal.

Contents

HUMAN ARCHITECTURE
Journal of the Sociology of Self-Knowledge

Volume V　　　　　　　　Issue 2　　　　　　　　Spring 2007

vii　*Editor's Note: My Architect (1930-2007)*

1　**Identity Formation and Music: A Case Study of Croatian Experience**
　Miroslav Mavra and Lori McNeil, Long Island University, C. W. Post Campus

21　**The Nightmare of Clever Children: Civilization, Postmodernity, and the Birth of the Anxious Body**
　Sean Conroy, Boston Graduate School of Psychoanalysis

41　**Looking Inside Out: A Sociology of Knowledge and Ignorance of Geekness**
　Johnny Yu, University of Massachusetts Boston

51　**Parallel Dualisms: Understanding America's Apathy for the Homeless through the Sociological Imagination**
　Colin Allen, University of Massachusetts Boston

61　**Love and Marriage: Through the Lens of Sociological Theories**
　Ana Carolina Fowler, Tufts University

73　**Lifting the Fog: Finding Freedom in Light of the Sociological Imagination**
　Keyon Smith, University of Massachusetts Boston

83　**The Quinceñera Rising: Self-Discoveries on the Heels of City and Rural Town**
　Krystle Santana, University of Massachusetts Boston

91　**The Broken Path: Juvenile Violence and Delinquency in Light of Sociological Theories**
　Sylvia Khromina, University of Massachusetts Boston

101　**Why Do I Not Like Me?: Sociological Self-Reflections on Weight Issues and the American Culture**
　C. G., University of Massachusetts Boston

109　**Longing to Be Thin: Why I Wait Until Tomorrow to Change My Habits**
　Caitlin Boyle, University of Massachusetts Boston

117　**The Boston Irish Male: A Self Study**
　Anonymous, University of Massachusetts Boston

125　**A Family of Neglect and "Dysfunction": Personal Blames or Structural Constraints?**
　L. Z., University of Massachusetts Boston

137　**Exiting the Self-Destructive Highway: A Sociological Path Back to A Future Career**
　Paul Connor, University of Massachusetts Boston

145　**Beginnings**
　Arie Kupferwasser, Creative Art Therapist

149　**From the Cover Artist, Arie Kupferwasser**

Editor's Note:
My Architect (1930-2007)

Mohammad H. Tamdgidi

University of Massachusetts Boston

mohammad.tamdgidi@umb.edu

For years,
I was constructing myself to build a house.

And he was busy with his work.

In childhood,
Construction toys for building model houses,
Crafting boards, glue, and scissors,
Carpentry wood, saw, nails, and hammer,
Brushes, watercolors, oil paints, and canvasses
planted the joy of architecture in my heart.

And he was busy with his work.

In the primary and secondary schools,
And then in Tehran University's Technical College (of civil engineering),
    and U.C. Berkeley's Department of Architecture,
Arithmetic classes, and those on geometry and mathematics,
Classes on algebra and spatial geometry,
Design classes, and courses on drafting and architectural styles,
Planted the techniques of architecture in my hands.

And he was busy with his work.

The uprisings of homeless construction workers,
Raising new questions in my head,
    on the other side of the earth,
Planted the critique of architecture in my mind.

And he was busy with his work.

Advancements in industry and technology,
    in printing and computer systems,
Planted the art of architecture in my words.

And he was busy with his work.

Dialogue and research with professors
    in sociology, world-systems studies, and beyond,
Planted the notion of "human architecture" in my thoughts.

And he was busy with his work.

Following much curiosity, doubts, and uncertainties,
Following relentless toil, pains, and suffering,
I thought that I should separate my ways from his,
That I should separate my pocket from his coins,
So as not to remain a tool in his hands,
My heart and life dependent on his water and bread.

And he was busy with his work.

Yet, the more I struggled and searched within,
    To build a life apart from him,
The more I found all my heart, brain, and blood are his,
All my words, hands, life, and works are his.
How can I take pride in being independent of him,
When, from the cradle to the grave, I have been the house and he, the architect?

It was he who bought me the toys,
    And the crafting and painting tools.
It was he who bought me the education,
    And the tools for sharing my thoughts.

So, I kissed him and said:
"Dear father. You and I are parts of the same life-time.
"Either, divided, we become the means for the oppression of and by others,
"Or, as your name 'ahad' ('one') implies, together we can share in designing and building a better humanity."

And we got busy with our work.

(1995)

O Man, you think you own the world,
Yet, death is chasing you day and night.
What you ate were eaten by the ants, and what you took, taken by the grave.
Among the inheritance you leave, what you gave up is what you actually own.

The above short poem adorned the house of my beloved father, the late Mohammed (Ahad) Tamdjidi ... expressing the values of a pure heart. He passed away, quite unexpectely, on August 26, 2007, in Tehran, Iran. Despite his success at work, and his tireless diligence, my father always remembered the passing nature of life and the need to devote it and his resources to helping others in need. He was a father to many, and not just to us---a father to the young and the old, to relatives and non-relatives alike, to friends and strangers. He was an expression of fatherliness, that of giving to and helping anyone who approached him. His good deeds and name was known to many, and for many decades.

My late father loved life, and from the bottom of his heart believed one must live as long as one can, like a flower. However, even when approaching old age and critical illness, he thought of death in terms of how it could give life to others. Among the papers and notes we found on his desk, was the following quote in a newspaper clipping--expressing the extent to which, even when confronting death, he loved giving life to others:

> When the time comes, I do not want you to keep me alive using all kinds of wires and needles. Don't turn my bed to a place of death, and instead give it to one who is promised to live. Take my body from that bed and use it to give life to others. Give my sins to the devil, and my spirit to God. And instead of building an elaborate grave, lend a helping hand to a needy, or tell a soothing word to one who is thirsty for love and kindness. And know that if you do this, I will become immortal.

My beloved father left us. A great and free-spirited human being said good-bye and flew. He who had a big heart, with the majesty of his humbleness and conscientious devotion to others' well-being, left our presence. But his heart did not beat for himself, but for others, and for humanity and humanism. His heartbeat still echoes in the chests of many who were touched by his life, and he will be alive so long as he is remembered. His diligent and self-reliant spirit, his steadfastness and honor in keeping his words, his patience, forgivingness, and good deeds, will continue so long as we remember to do the same. And so, his heart will continue beating in what he left. As the Iranian poet Forough Farrokhzad wrote, important is to fly, for the bird always dies.

For those whose thoughts adorn the pages of this journal, and for those who read them, my father's passing and his remembrance may seem to be those of an outsider, of one whose life and death were simply matters having to do with the personal troubles of the editor of this journal. Yet, the very existence and continuty of this journal, for what it is worth, would really not have been possible without the life, the toils, and the joys and sorrows of this good man whose proud son I was. So, let's cherish more of the voices from our classrooms made possible by this, our common father, voices of those who have had the courage to move beyond insider/outsider dualisms dividing our common lives. "Other" is a product of false imagination, for we all are insiders, mirroring one another back and forth. And in this continual reciprocity, as Morrie Schwartz said, love always wins; and if it has not yet, it may perhaps be because the game is not still over.

Listen to how this reed is weiling,
About separations it's complaining.
From reedbed since parted was I,
Men, women, have cried from my cry.
Where is the heart, torn-torn, longing,
To hear my tales of belonging. ...
(Rumi, from the Song of the Reed)

UMass Boston Commencement, June 1, 2007

Identity Formation and Music
A Case Study of Croatian Experience

Miroslav Mavra and Lori McNeil

Long Island University, C.W. Post Campus

miromavra@yahoo.com • lori.mcneil@liu.edu

Abstract: Croatian national identity has undergone countless transformations, struggles and wars in an attempt to preserve its sense of self. The Balkan Peninsula has endured the brutish oppression of several empires, countless conquerors, two world wars and devastating civil wars. The result of this turmoil has produced cultural, political and economic changes that have all contributed to the erosion of each nation's sense of individual, regional and national identities. As the primary focus of this research, we use Croatia as a case study to supplement the understanding of identity generally and nationalism specifically. Grounding our work in both a historical analysis and theoretical framework of identity and nationalism, we conclude that music was used as a primary tool in a conscious effort to achieve the political and nationalistic goals separating Croatia from the larger Yugoslav Federation. We support our arguments by examining identity development as an ethnic and nationalistic influence on one's sense of self and also by locating and considering those forces used to establish and develop the identity of a nation in crisis.

INTRODUCTION

Across the centuries, Croatian national identity has undergone countless transformations, struggles and wars in an attempt to preserve its sense of self. The Balkan Peninsula has endured the brutish oppression of several empires, countless conquerors, two world wars and devastating civil wars. The result of this turmoil has produced cultural, political and economic changes that have all contributed to the erosion of each nation's sense of individual, regional and national identities.

It was in the late 1980's when the six republics comprising the Yugoslav Federation confronted the prospect of achieving national sovereignty. That is, the possibility of reconstructing a pure national identity in order to separate themselves from one another and essentially creating a clear image of the "other." Importantly, this possibility of national differentiation was quickly becoming recognized as an absolute necessity. This unofficial, yet powerful mandate in Croatia took many forms ranging from reconstructing the language to influencing the culture and traditions of all Croatians.

Miroslav Mavra completed his Bachelor of Arts degree in Sociology at Long Island University, C.W. Post Campus. He is currently pursuing his Master of Arts degree in Anthropology at CUNY Hunter College. Mavra's current research involves a comparative study of Roma communities in Central and Eastern Europe. **Lori McNeil** is an Assistant Professor of Sociology at Long Island University, C.W. Post Campus. The majority of McNeil's work focuses on issues typically related to women, children and other marginalized groups. Her recent work has been featured in the *Journal of Applied Sociology*, *Michigan Sociological Review* and *The Journal of Children & Poverty*.

Rarely do such contemporary examples of national identity formation exist providing potential sites for understanding this complex process. Thus, it is our goal to use Croatia as a case study, to supplement the understanding of identity generally and nationalism specifically as the primary focus on this research. As such, we will, first, examine identity development as an ethnic and nationalistic influence on one's sense of self, and, second, locate and consider those forces used to establish and develop the identity of a nation in crisis.

In order to achieve these goals, we will begin with a historical overview of what is known as modern day Croatia. This overview will be followed by a presentation of literature pertaining to identity of one's self as well as national identity. Next, the exercise of grounding this theoretical framework relating to identity will be employed. This application will occur by appropriating Croatia as a case study of both personal and national identity. This paper concludes with the weaving of the development of Croatian national identity together with the larger interdisciplinary theoretical framework on identity formation and nationalism. Based on the process described above, we will argue that music was used as a primary tool in a conscious effort to achieve the political and nationalistic goals separating Croatia from the larger Yugoslav Federation.

Historical Overview

Croatia is a small and underpopulated country. It is a nation that has held onto its existence by a thread. Because of its precarious geographic location and diverse geophysical area, the territory of modern day Croatia has been well sought after all through history. *Hrvatska*, or Croatia, encompasses the majority of the Adriatic coast to the south and shares borders with four Eastern European countries: Slovenia to the west, Hungary to the north, Bosnia-Herzegovina and Serbia and Montenegro to the east. All in all, 56,000 square kilometers of widely diverse landscape[1] make up the countries' current geographical composition.

The Balkan Peninsula,[2] for more than a thousand years, has been held, and accordingly regarded, as a crossroads between the East and West. The Balkans—of which Croatia is a significant constituent—having been a part of the Greek, Roman, Byzantine, Ottoman and Habsburg empires, has been devastated, rebuilt and continuously influenced by the confluence of divergent imperial forces and opposing tenets. In the summer of 1991, the self-proclaimed independent Republic of Croatia and the Yugoslav Federation found themselves in a war divided on ethnic lines; Serbs versus Croats, Catholics against Orthodox Christians, and neighbors killing neighbors. Although the worldwide general public, including the people of former Yugoslavia, seem convinced that Serbs and Croats are age old enemies, the fact remains that, until a series of events in the late 1920s[3]—which resulted in ethnic warfare during the Second World War—the South Slavs have lived peacefully and contemporaneously throughout history. Serbs and Croats have rarely thereafter been recognized for their striking similarities; instead it is the differences that stand between them that have become the main point of contention. Rather than finding a sense of unity in their shared development as people, it was

---

1. Croatia's relatively diminutive, yet heterogeneous land mass includes both the Julian and Dinaric Alps, 3,982 kilometers of coastline on the Adriatic Sea, the Pannonian Lowlands in the north, more than one thousand islands of varying size and five major rivers: the Sava, Krka, Drava, Mura and Danube rivers.

2. A landmass surrounded by the Black, Agean, Ionian and Adriatic seas constitute the five modern states of Albania, Bulgaria, Greece, Romania and the six former republics of Yugoslavia.

3. The assassination of Croat politicians in the parliament in Belgrade in 1928 is generally considered the point of initiation for the ethnic, political, religious and linguistic conflicts between Croats and Serbs.

the few differences that held the most importance in the minds of the people.

EXPLAINING IDENTITY FORMATION

Personal Identity

Comprehensively, the concept of an "other," in all its possible forms, invariably forges the construction of a self on levels ranging from individual to regional and national. An important application of our work is the notion of "social identity theory" developed by Henri Tajfel and J.C. Turner (1979). The central assertion stated by social identity theory is that an individual knowingly becomes part of a specific social group. That group's characteristics, or identity, are then internalized, thus acquiring an individualized social identity that depicts their particular role within the larger society. Turner (1987) terms this process, the "self-categorization theory." Tajfel and Turner (1986) demonstrated that by categorizing themselves as members of a group, the individuals would begin to display in/group favoritism. Moreover, individuals belonging to the in/group will begin to validate themselves, attempting to raise their self-esteem, by drawing comparisons between themselves, as a group, with an appropriate out/group; in other words, groups that have some relationship linking them together.

According to Tajfel and Turner (1986), "...the essential criteria for group membership, as they apply to large-scale social categories, are that the individuals concerned themselves and are defined by others as members of a group....Social categorization are conceived here as cognitive tools that segment, classify, and order the social environment, and thus enable the individual to undertake many forms of social action" (p. 15). The development of a shared social identity not only allows for collective action but also provides the basis for a dominant group to impose their power over more subordinate groups.

Another determining contribution to the understanding of identity formation is the concept of "narcissism of minor differences" presented in Freud's (1930) pivotal work, *Civilization and its Discontents*. Freud's (1930) construction and juxtaposition of "self" and "other" is perhaps best exemplified by the following statement: "It is always possible to bind together a considerable number of people in love, as long as there are people left over to receive the manifestations of their aggressiveness" (p. 61).

Continuing in the social psychological tradition, Mead (1934) suggests that a "self" is constructed, defined and refined by the eventual "taking the role of a generalized other." The "generalized other" involves the acquisition of those values and attitudes of a group or collected whole with whom one identifies. A complete self emerges only through the conscious effort of group identification. This practice of group affiliation can also be applied based on the concept of "groupism." Groupism "is the readiness to form groups around any observed or imagined differences in bodily or mental characteristic; almost anything will serve: ...age, sexual inclination, [and] eye colour..." (Allott, 1998, p. 4). National and regional identity can only exist, however, if the constituent group possesses certain shared essential qualities specific to that particular people and their culture, which tend to be an amalgamation of created, imagined, and existent elements. The uniqueness of one's identity is thus validated only when placed side by side an "other's cultural otherness" (Povrzanović, 1995).

National Identity

As was already suggested, social groups—such as those conceived on the basis of ethnic affiliation—construct, sustain and negotiate boundaries, those which define and maintain social identities of one group when opposed, and related, to another (Tajfel and Turner, 1979). Ethnicity, as described, is not a property of a group but rather an aspect of a social relationship between interacting groups that consider themselves different from one another. Cultural attributes thus assume an important role in the establishment of identity. Language, arts, religion, traditions and diet, for instance, must be well understood in terms of their development and 'authenticity.' Bloom (1990) introduces the centrality of symbols into national identity formation and authenticity explaining that it exists as a, "… paradigm condition in which a mass of people have made the same identification with the national symbols… so that they may act as one psychological group…" (p. 52).

As social scientists and scholars began to look at racial and ethnic relations, they observed how structural conditions played perhaps the most important role in developing prejudice among various groups and individuals. Out of this work arose several prominent theories, including group-threat theory, realistic group conflict theory, ethnic competition theory and ethnic segregation theory.

Group threat theory, stemming from Blumer (1958) and Blalock (1967), focuses on integration of minority groups based on two variables. First, the size of a minority population wishing to assimilate into dominant society influences the success of this process. Numerically smaller numbers of minority individuals are more positively received into a host society than are those whose numbers are larger. The second variable affecting assimilation is the state of the economy—stronger economies are more likely to again more readily and positively assimilate minority groups into dominant culture than are struggling economies. Group threat theory is often applied to the United States in order to examine regional and temporal variations of racial prejudice.

Realistic group conflict theory reflects the ideology of symbolic racism (Blumer, 1958; 1969). This framework attempts to explain the disparity between people's support for racial equality and their opposition to policies designed to increase integration and equality, such as affirmative action. Realistic group conflict theorists argue that "patterns of social inequality lead to competing objective interests between groups," thus leading to "perceptions of incompatible group interests, a sense of fraternal deprivation, and perceived threat, all of which affect attitudes toward racial policies" (Kunovich and Hodson, 2002, p. 189).

In order to explain contemporary ethnic political mobilization and ethnic conflict, scholars employ ethnic competition theory (Kunovich and Hodson, 2002). This body of work suggests that modernization promotes competition between ethnic groups and that, as competition increases, ethnic political mobilization and ethnic conflict arise. This theory was primarily developed as a response to the ideas set forth by modernization theory, which stated that through modernization ethnic distinctions would disappear.

Finally, ethnic segregation theory combines and offers refinements to the ideas presented by the previous theories (Kunovich and Hodson, 2002). This perspective suggests that modernization promotes ethnic segregation and inequality, and thus promotes ethnic solidarity, ethnic political mobilization and ethnic conflict. Ethnic segregation theorists point to the uneven development produced by both modernization and industrialization. In addition, they argue that, when one group perceives that their life chances are less than that of other groups, ethnic conflict and political mobilization occurs.

As a departure from the structural theories presented above, Michael Ignatieff (1993) utilizes Freud's framework to direct his work while simultaneously placing Freud's work into a macro perspective. In his book, *Blood and Belonging* (1993), Ignatieff begins with a general discourse on nationalism and canvasses six distinctive contexts in order to see how nationalism manifests itself in different regions and among different peoples. According to Ignatieff, nationalism can be broken down into three separate concepts. Nationalism, as a political doctrine, is the belief that the world is divided into nations—each with the right of self-governance and determination. As a cultural ideal, nationalism states that although individuals have many identities, the nation provides the people with their most important form of belonging. Lastly, nationalism as a moral idea is "an ethic of heroic sacrifices, justifying the use of violence in the defense of one's nation against enemies, internal or external" (p. 5). In addition, he introduces Freud's (1930) work of the *narcissism of minor difference*. The implied notion of Freud's theory is that a group of people necessitates amplification of the differences that separate them from others in order to preserve their sense of identity and individuality.

Therefore, individual, regional and national identity is often purposely rooted in ethnicity and nationalism—especially in societies where "authoritarian ethnic nationalism" (Ignatieff, 1993, p. 8) has been established. Ignatieff (1993) proposes that authoritarian ethnic nationalism takes root only where civic nationalism has never established itself. Ethnic nationalism, after forty years of single-party Communist hegemony—which destroyed all civic and democratic culture in the region—is therefore burgeoning in Eastern Europe. In addition to the three concepts of nationalism as identified by Ignatieff, it can further be broken down into two types: civic and ethnic nationalism. The former maintains that a nation should be united through a common political creed that all people, regardless of race, religion, gender, language or ethnicity can form a community of citizens with equal rights, brought together by their shared belief in a set of political values. On the other hand, ethnic nationalism is not based on shared rights that bind people together, but rather on people's ethnic characteristics—mainly their religion, language, customs and traditions. Ethnic nationalism asserts that it is not the state that creates the nation, but the nation itself that creates the state.[4]

CROATIA AND IDENTITY CONSTRUCTION THROUGH MUSIC

In a country of 4.7 million inhabitants, occupying a relatively small landmass, the overt diversity of cultural traditions, history, dialects and life-styles of modern day Croatia can only be described as, aberrant. The juxtaposition of Austrian architecture in Zagreb with the Roman coliseum in Istria; the sonorous tones of Dalmatian *klapa* singing with the high pitched plucks of the Slavonian *tamburica*[5], or the regional and sub-regional dialectal variants rampant in Croatia invites the query surrounding the nature of the people's identity. This work focuses not only on the complexity of identity formation through the use of music, but also under which specific social and political milieu does such a process occur.

Identity issues, we argue, were at the crux of the independence movement in Croatia. Reinforcing a national identity among the population created a distinct line between the two warring parties. Divided on every imaginable line, Croats and Serbs took to the rhetoric of nationalism and ethnic purity. No difference was too small to exploit in order to create an 'us' versus 'them' mentality.

Despite, or perhaps due to, the constant struggles, wars and ideological transformations diffused through the Balkan Peninsu-

---

4. While there are on-going debates and controversies as to the exact implications and meanings of the terms "nation" and "state," we have strictly interpreted these terms, in order to minimize confusion, to represent the people of a country and the political system by which it is-led, respectively.

5. A long-necked plucked lute that was most likely introduced in the 14th and 15th centuries by the Turks.

la, a strong sense of national, religious and ethnic identity and affiliation developed rapidly among the people. This was so specifically with the tribes and nations that eventually became the former Yugoslavian state. Whether referring to Macedonians, Serbs, Bosnians, Croats or Slovenians, each 'group' has evolved and acknowledged traditions, practices and beliefs that comprise their specific cultural history and identities.

Thus, the love for one's culture—coupled with their malleability and aptitude to acclimatize foreign elements—is a contributing factor for the survival of a people, their identities, nations and day-to-day practices. In her prefatory summation, Jelavich (1983) expresses a similar view:

> ...although Balkan societies, either willingly or under duress, have accepted much from the outside world, it must be emphasized that even where foreign institutions and ideas were adopted, they were subsequently molded and changed to fit national traditions and prejudices. (p. xii)

In general, the sentiments expressed above address all the nations of the Balkan Peninsula as a whole. Her words, however, also pertain to each nation specifically and may easily be applied to the people of Croatia.

In order to better understand the abstraction of identity in relation to Croatia, one must also examine the function of ethnicity and nationalism within a cultural and societal framework. Social relationships tend to acquire an ethnic element when cultural variants affect the interaction between members of different groups. In Croatia, acute ethnic awareness[6] essentially began in the late nineteenth century with instrumental national movements, such as Ljudevit Gaj's *Ilirski Pokret*, or Illyrian Movement. These campaigns promoted cultural awareness and propagated the development of an independent Croatian State. Elements such as music, media, literature and education were used and manipulated to result in ethnic socialization—the development of actions, attitudes, values and perceptions of different ethnic groups. The very same mediums were also instrumental for the creation of an imagined community essential for the solidarity of a revolutionary movement, be it of a cultural, political or militaristic nature. The creation of an imagined community successfully promotes the necessary ideology[7] by which one's reasoning and actions are rationalized and given a sense of greater purpose.

Through the closer examination of music within a social and political fabric, possibilities of understanding the national, as well as regional, identities present in the nation became more comprehensive due to the cultural and traditional ties inherent in artistic expressions of thought and emotion. In Croatia, music, literature, poetry, dance, theater, sculpture and painting, along with language, religion, national selfawareness and customs play a significant part in the lives of the people and their understanding of their personal and ethnic identities. These varied aspects of life have, since the arrival of the Slavs, played an important role not only in politics and the countless struggles for the creation of an independent Croatian state, but relative to the preservation of the people's culture, values, way of life and, most importantly, their need to determine their own fate as a distinct people and nation.

The following attempts to deliver a new perspective on the connection between music and national identity, thus better illuminating the process in which a nation's cul-

---

6. Ethnic awareness is the discernment of one's own as well as other's ethnic groups—involving their customs, defining traits, history, traditions and other

7. Ideology is defined as a system of discourses, beliefs, perceptions, rhetoric, ideas and practices which collectively serve the function to obscure what is real or truthful.

ture and ethnicity can be manipulated for political and social gain. It then becomes necessary to observe the utilization of music by social participants in specific local situations to institute boundaries, the justification of these boundaries and to maintain distinctions between 'us' and 'them.' Moreover, the role of ethnicity and nationalism in relation to identity and music must equally be examined. To inquire, 'When does ethnicity become important?' and, 'How is music used by political actors to propagate a sense of self based on terms of ethnicity and nationalist rhetoric?' is essential for the understanding of Croatian identity as perceived through, and supported by music.

Martin Stokes (1994) provides insight to begin this work. He persuasively argues that by simply examining your private musical collection, you will notice highly specialized sets of places and boundaries. A brief reflection on our own musical practices drives home the multitude of identities that we possess. He continues, "[m]usic is socially meaningful not entirely but largely because it provides means by which people recognize identities and places, and the boundaries which separate them" (p. 5). Interestingly, Stokes also points out that music presents a means for the unification of peoples, the breaking down of boundaries and promoting a sense of appreciation of different cultures and traditions.

Depending on how we are ordered by different social factors, music can either entrap us into a specific set of classifications, or it can leap across boundaries and actuate unexpected and expanding possibilities. The illimitable possibilities of music are significant to people's sense of identity because every individual can audibly recognize and identify with his or her notion of self by simply dancing to, performing, listening to, and thinking about music.

An important quality of music, as stated by Frith (1987), is that: "What music can do is put into play a sense of identity that may or may not fit the way we are placed by other social factors" (p. 147). Music therefore not only liberates people from certain social restrictions but allows people the propensity to choose and construct their own sense of identity…even if it does last only as long as a song.

This being the case, however, we suggest that the initial and primary goal for Croatia centered less on unity and liberation but rather on the issue of identity construction as tantamount. In fact, Jasna Čapo Žmegač in her 1999 essay, "Ethnology, Mediterranean Studies and Political Reticence in Croatia—From Mediterranean Constructs to Nation-Building," argues that a conscious decision was made to align Croatia with Mediterranean culture, while ignoring the Balkans, known also as the Dinaric cultural model. Efforts were focused on separating Croatian identity from the Balkan Peninsula, and more importantly, from the characteristics common to all South Slavic cultures. Creating a national identity based on regional identity, i.e., the Mediterranean, was quickly seen as problematic. megac states, "…the Croats do not relate their Mediterranean-ness with their national but rather with their regional identity" (p. 48). It was precisely the regionalism of the Mediterranean identity that prevented the development of a national identity. Thus, it is understandable that such a stance immediately triggered regionalisms and a failure at the incorporation of regional identities into the national identity.

Nonetheless, the political and social push to unify all of Croatia under a single identity through a transformation of a regional to a national identity referred to above was undertaken. This theme is of particular interest to Croatian ethnomusicologists, Jasna Čapo Žmegač, and Joško ?aleta. In "The Ethnomusicological Approach to the Concept of the Mediterranean in Music in Croatia," Čaleta (1999) points to the role of music and power in the context of the 1991 war and how such themes assisted in the construction of a new national and cultural identity. "With the rise of the new state of Croatia," he writes, "there was a need to re/define national identity. Mediterranean identity grew from a typically regionally-based identity to an important factor in the formation of the national identity of today's Croats" (p. 185). This process, while generally viewed as positive, did have some negative effects. A new national identity in some cases developed at the expense of other regional identities.

These general themes are also explored by other researchers including Martin Stokes (1994), Dušan Janic (1995), Chris Hedges (2002), and Naila Ceribašić (1995). The analysis put forth by Stokes (1994), in *Ethnicity, Identity and Music: The Musical Construction of Place*, deconstructs the relationship between ethnicity, place and music. He suggests that ethnicities are understood in terms of the construction, maintenance and negotiation of boundaries, and not the social or cultural characteristics within such a boundary. Ethnic boundaries, therefore, define and maintain social identities, which exist only in opposition and relativities to other groups. Accordingly, music can be used by social actors in specific situations in order to erect boundaries, and to maintain distinctions between two groups. Thus, Stokes (1994) postulates the view of music as intensely involved in the advancement of dominant classifications and social formations, particularly in new nation-states. Modern, burgeoning states place much importance on music because, when forms of communication are inadequate, radio becomes an important means of propagating a variety of messages, including those that promote social cohesion and national unity.

In sum, the viewpoints presented here are contrary to common historical models describing the development of the arts which generally coincide with times of peace. Instead, artists continued to steadily develop and influence the individuals' life in Croatia during political and economical hardships. With the ever-changing political and social climates in Croatia after the War(s), the arts were not always left to their own vices to develop organically. Instead, the arts—specifically music and dance—were forced to develop according to the needs and wants of the countries leaders and their socio-political goals. The following section serves as an exemplar of the manipulation process of contemporary Croatian identity to which we refer.

MUSIC AS AN INSTRUMENT OF UNIFICATION

One of the most important national symbols of Croatian identity is the *tamburica*,[8] sometimes called the *tambura*,[9] a plucked lute brought to Bosnia and Serbia in the 14th and 15th centuries (Bonifačić, 1998). *Tamburica* ensembles first began to form throughout the regions of former Yugoslavia during the 19th century, namely in the northeastern and central parts of Croatia called Slavonia. There are three major trends concerning *tamburica* ensemble.

The first trend, "*tamburica* folk ensembles" (Bonifačić), is characterized by few members in the ensemble, musical illiteracy, free and spontaneous performances and a weak connection with political events. The second trend includes "amateur *tamburica* ensembles/orchestras" (Bonifačić). They were very active in Croatia, and tended to be

---

8. The *tamburica* is a long-necked, pear-shaped plucked lute. The term for this instrument is a diminutive of "*tambura*," which is an ancient Persian instrument, estimated to have been brought to the Balkans during the fourteenth and fifteenth centuries by incursions of the Ottoman Empire. The instrument is reputed to have reached Croatia and Slavonia by the seventeenth and eighteenth centuries. Today, the instrument can be found across Croatia, existing in various shapes, with varying number of strings and in various tunings.

9. Although these terms are synonymous, *tambura* mainly refers to the solo practice of the instrument, while *tamburica* is used mostly in reference to ensemble or orchestral applications.

nationally aware and politically active. Formed in the mid 19th century, these ensembles became engaged promoters of the Croatian National Movement. The third trend, "professional, musically trained orchestras" (Bonifačić), came into being in the mid 20th century and was established by radio stations operating out of larger cultural centers in former Yugoslavia.

Croat ethnic awareness became tantamount to, and was embodied within, the Illyrian Movement in the early 1800s. The Illyrians'[10] strategy was to use the *tamburica* as the national symbol, that with which a native composer can write music based on traditional folk tunes, and the nature of the language in the lyrics could express national identity. This strategy was incorporated into most public events and performances. According to Bonifačić (1995), the *tamburica* was chosen for this purpose for two reasons: (1) the instruments diverse roles as both a rural and solo instrument and as an urban and rural ensemble instrument, and (2) Solo *tambura* and *tamburica* ensembles were so widely spread among the South Slavic groups that it was both convenient and easily recognizable. Due to both the Illyrian Movement and the Croatian National Movement, the Habsburg Empire subsequently banned the use of the instrument, thus giving rise to anti-assimilative ideology among the South Slavs, which provided the *tamburica* with a purpose. Playing the instrument as a means of resistance to the Austrians and Hungarians became prevalent until the beginning of World War One.

To support the glorification of the *tamburica*, a government-backed ensemble, *Zlatni Dukati*, was created. Ruža Bonifačić (1995), in an article published in *Collegium Antropologicum*, explores this relationship. The group originated in Slavonia in the mid 1980s releasing a recording of patriotic songs featuring the *tamburica*, based on the folk tradition of the Pannonian region.

Zlatni Dukati also formed a tight relationship with the Croatian Democratic Union (HDZ)—headed by Franjo Tuđman, who led Croatia into the war for independence in 1991. The group's participation in the party's advertising and campaigning broadened their popularity. Their public performances of patriotic songs became a meaningful symbol of the countries new, democratic future. After the war began, the official mass media aggressively promoted the group's recordings, which led to a wave of new patriotic songs being recorded by hundred of artists. This contributed heavily to the gradual formation of a new national identity in the newly independent nation of Croatia. Bonifačić (1995) credits *Zlatni Dukati* as having been "one of the initiators of the revival of Croatian patriotic songs, and even more—of the *tamburica* as a Croatian national symbol" (p. 75).

In the group's early years, they had a broad appeal to both Croats and Serbs because of their liveliness and high standard of performance. Although *Zlatni Dukati* was once very popular in Serbia, their new association with Croatian independence and identity in 1989 resulted in increased popularity in Croatia. Conversely, the possession of their cassettes by members of the Yugoslav Peoples' Army (JNA) became liable to punishment by Serb authorities.

In 1990, a period of great political tension among the republics of former Yugoslavia, a second album called Horvatska domovina (Croatian Homeland) was released. After the war began in 1991, most of the rousing, patriotic songs on the album became national hits. According to Ruža Bonifačić (1998), "[t]he members of the ensemble applied to volunteer in the Croatian Army. The rejection of their applications confirmed the awareness of the institutions in charge of the powerful propaganda role of patriotic songs and the activities of the Zatni Dukati in a war-time situation" (p. 138).

Several songs from their overall reper-

---

10. Referring to those involved in the Illyrian Movement (1830-43) which sought to unify the South Slavs on cultural, and political grounds.

toire stand out as having had achieved wide popularity. *Ne dirajte mi ravnicu* (Leave My Plains Alone) grew into a song of protest and resistance. The "plains" refer to the Slavonian flatlands where the war was at its fiercest, and from which the majority of Croatian refugees emigrated. When performed live, or aired on television, scenes of Slavonia's peaceful past were shown side-by-side with images of the war and refugees to further incite anger in the public. Another song, entitled *Vukovar, Vukovar*, addressed the embattled and besieged town of Vukovar, hoping to encourage not only the citizens of the town, but also the Croatian army to win back their land. This song became particularly important during the war due to the status of Vukovar as a symbol of Croatian resistance to Serbian domination. It was widely felt at the time that if Vukovar could be recovered, then the entire war could also be won.

The success of *Zlatni Dukati* inspired hundreds of groups, bands, and ensembles to form. The *tamburica* folk tradition permeated through most musical genres represented by the 1990's music scene. The *tamburica* has been used as a national symbol for decades and any group that employed the use of the instrument generally received the approval and support of the ruling party. Thus, we argue that the *tamburica* as a national symbol of Croatian identity is a forced political and social construction rather than an organic development— that which would be truly representative of the culture and heritage of Croatian ethnic identity.

Evidence supporting this claim is validated by the acknowledgement that almost immediately after the end of the war in 1995 the *tamburica*'s popularity became to rapidly wane. People's interest in the instrument and its particular musical tradition was only supported as long as there was reason. The instrument was nonetheless promoted as the national instrument, and accepted as such by people, until the death of Franjo Tuđman in 2000. Since then, it is still regarded as the official national instrument, but has virtually ceased to exist in the public sphere—giving way to the importation of music from Europe and America.

CREATING IMAGINED BOUNDARIES THROUGH MUSIC—AUTHENTICITY, WAR AND UNITY

A discussion of authenticity provides insight to the issue of music and identity. Thus, taking 'authenticity' as an example, we see how nomenclature is frequently applied to qualify the uniqueness and value of something or someone. In terms of organized sound, authenticity cannot be regarded as a property of music, musicians or their relationship with the listening public. All music is derived from the same source: artistic creativity, imagination and conscious effort, and therefore, cannot be 'inauthentic.' Folk music, for instance, is no more of a legitimate representation of people's cultural identity than is urban music. The usage and manipulation of such terminology, however, leads people to such assumptions—closely interlinking the notions of authenticity and identity.

The use of nomenclature in a digressive and figurative manner accords the term 'authenticity' great persuasive powers. In terms of music in Croatia, the labeling of styles, accompanying dances, instruments and themes as 'authentic' to Croatian culture, coupled with history strictly focuses on the dissimilarities inherent in the overall musical construction of Croatia. This forges and validates not only a unique sense of identity among the people, but also intense feelings of nationalism and ethnic differentiation. A classic example of such manifestations is the forced adoption of the *tamburica* as the national instrument of Croatia. It was during the recent period of warfare that the *tamburica* was importunately inducted into the daily lives of Croats throughout the country. *Tamburica* music was consistently played on the radio and orchestras were filmed for television. Bands wrote neo-traditional patriotic songs using the instrument causing its persistent incorporation into political, social and traditional rituals.

The *harmonika*, conversely, became an 'inauthentic' instrument due to its general association with Serbian music and popularity among the Serbs. This anti-popularization of the instrument occurred with complete disregard to the fact that it has been widely used in Croatian music for nearly two hundred years.[11] Tajfel and Turner (1986) refer to this instrument classification as part of a categorization process applied to an outgroup, that which often results in the construction of negative stereotypes. Although this instrument can be found throughout most of Croatia, namely Istria, Northern Littoral, Dalmatia and other areas in Northern Croatia, it has never been regarded as a characteristic attribute in Croatian music. In Serbia, however, it found a more significant status among their musical practices and is common to all regions. Consequently, the general Croatian populace regards the instrument as solely representative of Serbia music, culture and people. Thus, they have successfully created the image of the "other" and forged yet another ethnic differentiation to validate an imagined community of Croatianness.

This same differentiation process was undertaken with the *tamburica* and the *mandolina*, two traditional instruments commonly found in Croatia. As noted earlier, the *tamburica* was relegated to the status of being the national folk instrument and a symbol of resistance against the Federal state. It became an authentic symbol of a distinct Croatian identity. Paradoxically, the *mandolina* became inauthentic and was disregarded and widely ignored due to the fact that, along with the Croats, the Serbs too played the *mandolina*. The process of authenticity is further explained by Tajfel and Turner (1986) suggesting that society is characterized by flexibility and permeability and because of this we suggest that those symbols used for group representation also are imbued with these same attributes. In essence, this forced identity construction applied to the *mandolina* effectively relegated the *mandolina*, as with the *harmonika*, as symbolic expressions of the "other."

Down on the Mediterranean coast, a region called *Dalmacija*, a different model of identity formation through music can be found. Unlike the *tamburica*, however, the identity construction surrounding *klapa* developed organically. Within a Croatian framework, Bezić (1999; 1996; 1988), effectively puts national and regional musical trend into a historical context by examining the various and underlining aspects of how music interacts with people. Bezić accomplishes this through an examination of the connection between the ancient custom of kolenda singing and the more modern *klapa* singing pervasive throughout Dalmatia. The organic development of a singing style called *klapa*, and its subsequent role as a form of cultural representation, affords a different perspective on the question of identity and music. Bezić presents this example to demonstrate the process in which musical traditions evolve and influence culture and society.

Klapa singing offers a different course of development in music, which in turn, acts as a cohesive force binding not only regional identities, but extending out onto the national stage as a symbol of Croatian heritage. The evolution of *klapa* singing is representative of an organic, self-promulgating entity that came to depict a Croatian identity through its adoption, usage and acceptance by individual players, rather than by political institutions. Town by town, region by region, *klapa* singing first came to be a primary source of identity and pride for the Dalmatian coastline, and then later as a mu-

---

11. The *harmonika*, or accordion, was introduced to Croatia in the nineteenth century and was quickly accepted and adopted into traditional music practices.

sical genre endeared by Croatians. Although *klapa* did not play any prominent role in the 1991 war, it did help foster the definition of being a Croatian long before, and continues to do so even today.

Whereas the popularity of the *tamburica* has waned, there has been an explosion in folk festivals throughout Croatia featuring *klapa* singing, as well as other forms of traditional, usually local, musical forms. Because the latter developed along a natural and organic process, it found a place in people's practices. In 2004, *klapa* singing is seen as quintessentially Dalmatian, but also invokes images of Croatia as a whole, and is even enjoyed and appreciated once again in Serbia and Bosnia.

When examining the relation of ethnicity and identity, and how they are accordingly put into play through music, we must be aware that music is one of the less innocent ways these concepts are regulated, enforced and resisted. Although music is not as perceptible as outright violence, war and oppression, it is precisely the connection that music has with society that deems it a powerful and determinant force concerning these issues. In the 1990s, the predominate political situation—revealed through conflicting power relations, the disintegration of the federation, the establishment of new countries and the ensuing warfare— isolated the theme of music and dance within the context of ideological, social and political struggles and revolution. The role of music in the construction of identity thus became a pertinent matter in the political and daily lives of people on both national and regional levels.

In order to fully understand not just how but why music became a necessary and essential tool used by both political and social agents, it becomes imperative to illuminate the close relationship between ethnicity and nationalism, and that all attempts to recreate and reinforce a mythic Croatian identity are based almost solely on the ethnic composition of the nation. Because nationalism is usually ethnic in character, it can therefore be conceived of as a discourse of identity that is first culturally invented or reclaimed, and later geo-politically enhanced.

Importantly, Ceribašić (1995) asserts that popular music can become a powerful point of differentiation, one of "competing discourses and confronted states" (p. 94). He defines two main genre sub-groups of newly composed folk music. The first is comprised of music based on mainstream musical trends with quasi-patriotic lyrics. The second group relies on the musical content of past folk tunes, but rearranged to fit the sound of newly composed folk music. The author goes on to point out that the warlike image of Serbia and the feminine/ victim image of Croatia are portrayed in each nation's national instrument. In Serbia, the gusle, is seen as epitomizing the tribal and patriarchal nature of Balkan culture, while the *tamburica*, Croatia's national instrument, relates the image of the cooperative and peaceful laborer, or the hospitable and peaceful villager.

When one thinks of music in such a manner, music then becomes a tool, which not only acts as a form of entertainment and artistic expression, but also as an "extraterrestrial essence" (Stokes, 1994, p. 10) that manages, regulates and negotiates social and political relations. The often heard sentiments regarding music as a unifying force capable of bringing people together can and does exist—however, not to an extent that matches the relationship music has with opposite notions such as violence, propaganda, war and as a vital arm in the proliferation of state cultural policy.

Within the context of politics and war, Svanibor Pettan (1995), an ethnomusicologist and research scholar at the Institute of Ethnology and Folklore Institute in Zagreb, identifies three basic functions of music during this period: to provide encouragement for those fighting on the front lines and those hiding in bomb shelters; to provoke and humiliate the enemy; and to call for the involvement of the general public, the Diaspora and those in exile. Music also served as a means to express perceptions of, as well as experiences in, the war. In addition, it also served as a communication link between opposing sides. Many of the songs produced by one side generated a response by the other, usually with the purpose of being antagonistic. In one example, an incident confirmed by the International Human Rights Organization found that in the Keraterm detention camp in Bosnia- Herzegovina, prisoners were forced to sing Chetnik Songs by Serbian forces in order to humiliate and degrade them.

Pettan (1995) goes on to divide the entire war-related musical repertoire available on commercial recordings into two distinct categories: "official," and "alternative." The former consists of recordings produced by registered companies, sold in stores and having met high standards of sound quality. The latter recordings, in contrast, were of unknown authors, available only through street sellers and generally poor in sound quality. They were also, in some cases, political or lascivious in nature— generally aligned with radical ideology while the former shared and supported the views held by the Croatian government. Both repertoires did, however, include songs about famed political figures from Croatia's past, as well as victims of the war in progress at that time. This is not to imply that artists who began in one repertoire did not cross over to the other. The most well known example is the song Bojna Čavoglave (Čavoglave Battalion) by Marko Perković, more commonly known as "Thompson." A small company initially recorded it, gaining popularity through word of mouth until it was adopted by the "official" state sponsored music industry. Thompson's message, however, did not change and continued to appeal to the radical ideology of nationalism and rural values.

Since the onset of fighting in 1991, the two competing forces, Croatia and Serbia, adopted differing musical strategies both in the broadcast media and on the streets and battlefields throughout the region. While Serbia adopted music-making practices more similar to that of the Partisans of World War Two, under Marshal Tito, Croatia promoted more heterogeneous music genres. The diverse musical pieces found on Croatian media and at festivals, and concerts included domestic operas, rock, funk, punk, dance and rap, as well as the traditional, albeit polished, *tamburica* and *klapa* orchestras and ensembles. "As a reaction to the aggression against Croatia, a specific amalgam, a sort of "all-embracing" homeland music formed, with the objective of strengthening internal cohesion and national homogenization" (Ceribašić, 1998, p. 129).

Although many varieties of music were present in the country, the prevalence of the more traditional forms ultimately became the leading force in reconstructing regional and national identities and in achieving a sense of ethnic unity. These new traditional songs, often called newly composed folk songs, utilize traditional tunes combined with current messages in the text—often invoking traditional literary figures and vocabulary in order to celebrate heroic fighters battling their enemies. This genre began in 1943, but reemerged in 1991 as an influential focus of the wartime repertoire, mainly because of the promotion and elevation of the *tamburica* as a national instrument, symbolizing a unique Croatian identity.

Music as an Instrument of Reconciliation

Music is a potentially powerful element of culture that can act as both a unifying and separating force among people. This transfiguring quality of music can, in specific situations, be manipulated precisely because it is simultaneously a representation of people's identity, ethnicity, culture, traditions and history, as well as a product of these very constituents. Music is a social factor that influences and involves all members of society. The political and social realities of the past decade in Croatia show that music has been used to propagate feelings of nationalism, an image of the 'enemy—as other,' ethnic partitioning and even as a motivational tool for soldiers on the battlefield.[12]

Within the cultural boundaries of Croatia, however—especially after 1997 when the war in Bosnia came to a relative end—music was also used to aid and assist in the reconstruction of the nation, to ease suffering and develop understanding and unification among peoples. In most societies ravaged by war, verbal communication tends to break down, allowing music to be a critical unifying factor among the people. Music mitigates the pain brought about by violent struggles and often becomes the key to survival for individuals coping with post-traumatic stress, as well as for communities striving to reconstruct their cultural identity. Music has shown to even possess the capability to eventually promote greater understanding and tolerance between the very same peoples who once fought so vehemently against one another.

Tomislav Ivčić popular song, Stop the War in Croatia, adds to support to Ceribašić (1995) postulations. Ivčić's, *Stop the War in Croatia*,[13] quickly became the best selling song during the period of war in Croatia. Through lyric, Ivčić explicitly implores neighboring countries to mitigate the degenerating situation in Croatia. The expectation, or assumption, that Western European nations would interfere in the conflict existed merely as a faint glimmer of hope. Rather than calling for the armed intervention of an international military power, Ivčić's song called upon people to understand the devastating effects of nationalism and ethnic partitioning.

While an overwhelming number of patriotic songs urging people to fight emerged during the period of warfare in Croatia, attempts to use music as a means of curbing the forthcoming violence were made. Between the months of March and May in 1991, the *Hrvatski komorni* orkestar— The Croatian Chamber Orchestra— held several performances under the title, "Concerts of Peace and Hope." Among the musical pieces performed, the orchestra included Mozart's, Coronation Mass, and Mokranjac's, Divine Service of St. John Chrystom. By performing compositions related to the Catholic and Orthodox Christian faiths, the musicians hoped to unite both Serbs and Croats in their desire for a peaceful coexistence. Unfortunately, the events that unfolded shortly thereafter deemed their attempts ineffectual.

CROATION IDENTITY FORMATION AND MUSIC: A PERSONAL RETROSPECTIVE

As a first-generation Croatian born in the United States, my own name, Miroslav Mavra, serves as a marker of my "otherness." My dual identity served as the initial precept for undertaking the issue of identity, comprising both personal and national, and how, within the framework of war and politics, such constructions of self lend themselves to culture, intraand inter-ethnic group relations and politics. As a teenager, I was unaware of the intricacies of the conflict, nor did I care. Eventually, as the war passed and the years went by, I began to search for my

---

12. Marko Perković's song Bojna Čavoglave—inspired by his experiences defending his home village, Čavoglave—is a rock tune based on a seven beat meter common to traditional Balkan music. The lyrics encouraged soldiers to fight bravely and addressed the Serbian enemies in an aggressive and threatening manner. The video clip also portrays Croatian soldiers singing and simulating military exercises in a realistic manner. Interestingly, the songs popularity and increasing demands from Croatian soldiers on the front lines resulted in abnormally frequent airplay of the song and video clip by the state media.

13. Text: "Stop the war in the name of love/ Stop the war in the name of God/ Stop the war in the name of the children/ Stop the war in Croatia// We want to share the European dream/ We want democracy and peace/ Let Croatia be one of Europe's stars/ Europe, you can stop the war."

own sense of identity. I immediately turned to what I had once shunned away from in my younger years: my family's Croatian heritage. Weddings, festivals and other social gatherings involving Croatians had a whole new appeal to me. As I was slowly rediscovering my roots and my family's history, I was also searching for a place among my new community—a way that I could better understand and identify with a people, nation and culture that seemed so familiar and so different at the same time.

Since I was a small child, I have found peace and tranquility in music. I viewed my attachment to both modern and traditional Croatian music as a natural progression in my life. Furthermore, the music allowed me to find my natural place among my hereditary connection to the people of Croatia. I can still recall the countless festivals, family gatherings, weddings and even funerals where my heart swelled with a sense of pride and belonging when the band's song fired up the audience into a frenzy of dancing, spinning and drinking.

I was fourteen years old when the war in Croatia broke out in 1991. I did not experience the war first hand. Instead I watched the news stories on television from my parents' home in New York, and occasionally my family would receive some news from our relatives in Croatia. Memories of coming home from school, finding my parents and their friends cursing and yelling, with their fists in the air, at the CNN commentator as he explains the countless images of devastated villages still linger on in my mind. This is what I remember of the war.

I, myself, would argue that my personal desire for reunification with my lineage could lead to the recognition of my identity and place within the confines of Freud's "narcissism of minor differences" by simply creating divisional boundaries of an autochthonous nature amongst myself and those outside my hereditary ethnicity. The hope, however, remains that the resolution of my pursuits will rather be that of greater understanding, and repulsion from, the destructive nature of heightened nationalistic and ethnic contempt.

Although I have continuously visited Croatia throughout my life, it never occurred to me that my identity could be any more than that of a 'New Yorker.' This was the emergence of an intensive period of introspective analysis of the identity imparted to me by my family's extraction. The ensuing three years were a time of confusion and self-discovery. Aside from feeling a positive, renewed sense of being, as though my entire existence has been redefined, negative attitudes and views of the "other"— which in this case were the Serbs[14]— grew to be as important to my sense of identity as my initial acceptance of my cultural heritage. The uncompromising views of that time rather quickly transformed my perspective of the Serbs as people into 'my enemies.' They symbolized the direct opposites of me within the context of my newly redefined identity. To be against 'them' was to ratify one's sense of self.

Following a distant war in which a large portion of my family was directly involved, I fell victim to nationalistic sentiments spread among the larger Croatian community. A period of self-awareness and subsequent identity crises accentuated my sense of reality and, evidently, caused me to feel anger and disdain toward people that I have never met.

Today, I am still struggling with my identity.

Too young to have ever dealt with the complexities inherent to having been born in New York as a Yugoslav and a Croatian, instead, my search of a personal identity emerged in tandem with my native soil in the throws of its own identity crisis. Although aware that Croatia as a culture, as a people and as a defined group has existed for centuries, the dramatic events of the past century have forced the very notion of Croatianness to be questioned.

When I return to Croatia I wonder just how I fit into that society. Simple questions lack any discernible answers. What makes me Croatian?

---

14. Consequently, this personal phase coincided with the 1991 war between Serbia and Croatia, which heavily influenced feelings of indiscriminate animosity and hatred in myself, my family, as well as in most Croatian immigrants in America, by and large, towards the Serbian people.

Can it be as simple as the language, the traditions, and location? Empirical evidence points to similar questions arising in the thoughts of many Croatians themselves, as supported through news and magazine articles, artistic expressions and day-to-day conversations.

The people across former Yugoslavia have experienced numerous identity transformations over the last century, almost always with disastrous results. Efforts exerted either by an empire, kingdom, puppet state or federation to redefine and subjugate the local populations across the Balkans all failed. And now that each ethnic group has established their own sovereign states, I wait to see how they reconstruct their constituent characteristics as identifying markers of nationality.

In 2000, a Serbian friend came to visit me in Zagreb and stayed for several days. My family, friends and colleagues received her warmly. In public, however, our experiences were not the same. Because there is no way to disguise her accent, or dialect, her only option, when we would come upon a crowded tram or the occasional group of football hooligans, was to keep quite for fear that she would be identified as a Serb.

In recent years, this hostility has largely dissipated—although not forgotten among nationalists, and other hardliners—to where today it is not uncommon to see Serbian tourists during the summer season.

I share this growth and follow a path parallel to that of my country. Learning not only who you are, but also how to become what you are, is a process as arduous and endless as any noble pursuit. These are my personal reflections regarding the war time years in Croatia— this work not only serves as a personal journey, but also as an exercise in the demystification of ideological sentiment and the reification of the process of identity creation and sustenance.

Conclusions

In 1991, nationalistic politicians, both Croatian and Serbian, found ways to manipulate the *narcissism of minor differences* (Freud, 1930), making their own side appear as blameless victims, and the other side as callous murderers, thus setting the essential basis for the violence that ensued— thus giving rise to the development of an ethnic identity. In the words of Paul R. Brass (1991):

> …there is nothing inevitable about the rise of ethnic identity and its transformation into nationalism among the diverse peoples of the contemporary world. Rather, the conversion of cultural differences into bases for political differentiation between peoples arises only under specific circumstances, which need to be identified clearly. (p. 13)

In former Yugoslavia the stage was set for an ethnic based civil war through several decades of internal conflicts. As Tajfel and Turner (1966) hypothesized, years of discontent, political upheaval and a growing disparity between the rich and poor incited individuals to identify themselves with their ethnic group in favor of the national Yugoslav identity. Under Yugoslavia even identifying yourself as a Slovenian or a Croat first and a Yugoslav second was liable to draw a multitude of consequences. Thus, fueling feelings of dissent and revolt aimed at the notion of a unified South Slavic identity.

This left only the manipulation of Freud's (1930) narcissism of minor differences to spark the collapse of the nation-state and the dissemination of nationalistic paranoia among the population. The state of affairs in 1990[15] paralleled Brass's (1991) "specific circumstances," which prompted the political differentiation among similar peoples.

With the escalation of armed conflicts,

---

15. In 1990 the Socialist Republic of Croatia held their first multi-party elections, which brought Franjo Tuđman and his party, Hrvatska Demokratska Zajednica or the HDZ, into power and was followed by a referendum in which 94 percent of the voters chose independence from Yugoslavia.

fallible as well as politic, fear began to take hold in people's minds. They wanted to know who they could trust and rely on for their safety during the chaotic state of political and economic break down. Ethnic nationalism provided the safe haven people were looking for—one rooted in those of your own blood (Ignatieff, 1993). Nationalism and ethnicity as suggested by T. H. Erikson (1993), can thus be viewed as cognate notions and, therefore, conceived as culturally invented or reclaimed notions of identity.

When considering the complex nature of Croatia's interminable history, countless political modifications, struggles, spiced ethnic constitution and social relations, one cannot claim that music possesses either an overtly momentous, or instrumental role throughout the country's development. Yet, music cannot be written off as completely insignificant. Both popular and folk music in Croatia have been utilized and manipulated for a variety of purposes, ranging from instilling fear and allegiance in the hearts and minds of the populous to providing a source of hope and comfort during periods of economic hardship and warfare. The potential of music's politically and socially provocative nature was so highly recognized during Croatia's struggle for independence that musicians, politicians and citizens across the country were of the opinion that, "…music can under some circumstances be considered a 'weapon'" (Pettan, 1998, p. 910).

It is this very provocation and power which songs and poetry possess that has been underestimated and under-examined in the fields of social sciences that draws our attention to the topic. Perhaps the analysis of music in relation to nationalism, ethnic identities, war and politics will not provide answers as to why certain situations develop, are resolved, or could have been averted. Music, regardless of its effectiveness as an analytical tool, is, however– along with poetry, theater and visual arts–also a reflection of society, culture, traditions and history. It can provide an avenue to explore the humanist nature of people's lives and historical events. In the words of Theodor W. Adorno, taken from his 1961-62 lectures on the sociology of music, "…even quite distant cultures… have the capacity to understand one another musically" (Blum, 1994, p. 250).

Due to difficult historical progressions and adverse reactions to important social questions, the latter classification of music's use is a more accurate reflection of Croatia's contemporary realities. Although positive examples of the unifying characteristics of music are acknowledged and examined, our primary argument focuses on the relationship between music and people's sense of identity from the personal to national level. The underlining issues rest upon the 'use' of music in terms of reconstructing, preserving and disseminating people's sense of identity.

The importance of music in Croatia's distant and recent past should not be exaggerated, but should simultaneously be appreciated for its potential and ability to act as a powerful force in periods of both peace and war. The identity of Croats has many characteristics, each of which was influenced by a multitude of developments. By focusing on music, we do not intend to imply that other cultural phenomena and political influences played diminished roles in the process of identity formation. Language, the fine arts, dance, theater, religion, literature and many other societal and human elements equally contribute in creating the unique identities that comprise the regions, nations and ethnicities present across the globe. We look forward to additional contributions made to both the specific theme of Croatian identity, and the larger issue of identity formation, nationalism and ethnicity.

References

Allott, Robin. 1998. "Group Identity and Nation Identity." *Paper presented at conference of European Sociobiological Society*. Moscow.

Bezić, Jerko. 1988. "Contemporary Trends in the Folk Music of Yugoslavia." Pp. 49-73 in *Contributions to the Study of Contemporary Folklore in Croatia*, edited by Zorica Rajkovic. Zagreb: Institute of Folklore Research.

Bezić, Jerko. 1996. "Approaches to the People's Music-Life in Dalmatia (Croatia) in the Past and Present." *Narodna Umjetnost: Croatian Journal of Ethnology and Folklore Research* 33/1:75-88.

Bezić, Jerko. 1999. "The Dalmatian Islands—A Geographically Recognized Mediterranean Region—Showing Obvious Differ-ences in the Musical Expression of Their Inhabitants." *Narodna Umjetnost: Croatian Journal of Ethnology and Folklore Research* 36/1:157-172.

Blalock, Hubert, M. 1967. "Status Inconsistency, Social Mobility, Status Integration and Structural Effects." *American Sociological Review* 32/5:790-201.

Bloom, William. 1990. *Personal Identity, National Identity and International Relations*. Cambridge: Cambridge University Press.

Blum, Stephen. 1994. "Conclusion: Music in an Age of Cultural Confrontation." Pp. 250-277 in *Music Cultures in Contact: Conver-gences and Collisions*, edited by Margaret J. Kartomi & Stephen Blum. Sydney: Currency Press.

Blumer, Herbert. 1958. "Race prejudice as a sense of group position." *Pacific Sociological Review* 1:3-7.

Blumer, Herbert. 1969. *Symbolic Interactionism: Perspective and Method*. New Jersey: Prentice-Hall.

Bonifačić, Ruža. 1995. "Changing of Symbols: The Folk Instrument *Tamburica* as a Political and Cultural Phenomenon." *Collegium Antropologicum* 19/1:65-77.

Bonifačić, Ruža. 1998. "Regional and National Aspects of *Tamburica* Tradition: The Case of Zlatni Ducat." Pp. 131-150 in *Music, Politics, and War: Views From Croatia*, edited by Svanibor Pettan. Zagreb: Institute of Ethnology and Folklore Research.

Brass, Paul R. 1991. *Ethnicity and Nationalism—Theory and Comparison*. New Delhi, Newbury Park and London: Sage Publications.

Čaleta, Joško. 1999. "The Ethnomusicological Approach to the Concept of the Mediterranean in Music in Croatia." *Narodna Umjetnost: Croatian Journal of Ethnology and Folklore Research* 36/1:183-196.

Čapo Žmegač, Jasna. 1999. "Ethnology, Mediterranean Studies and Political Reticence in Croatia—From Mediterranean Constructs to Nation-Building." *Narodna Umjetnost: Croatian Journal of Ethnology and Folklore Research* 36/1:33-52.

Ceribašić, Naila. 1995. "Gender Roles During the War: Representations in Croatian and Serbian Popular Music 1991-1992." *Collegium Antropologicum* 19/1:91-101.

Ceribašić, Naila. 1998. "Heritage of the Second World War in Croatia: Identity Imposed upon and by Music." Pp. 109-130 in *Music, Politics, and War: Views From Croatia*, edited by Svanibor Pettan. Zagreb: Institute of Ethnology and Folklore Research.

Erikson, T. H. 1993. *Ethnicity and Nationalism*. London: Pluto Press.

Freud, Sigmund. 1930(1961). *Civilization and its Discontents*. New York: W. W. Norton and Company Inc.

Frith, S. 1987. "Towards an Aesthetic of Popular Music." Pp. 133-49 in *Music and Society: The Politics of Composition, Performance and Reception*, edited by Richard Leppert and Susan McClary. Cambridge: Cambridge University Press.

Hedges, Chris. 2002. *War is a Force That Gives Us Meaning*. New York/Toronto: Anchor Books.

Ignatieff, Michael. 1993. *Blood and Belonging: Journeys into the New Nationalism*. Canada: Penguin Books.

Janjić, Duan. 1995. "Resurgence of Ethnic Conflict in Yugoslavia: The Demise of Communism and the Rise of the "New Elites" of Nationalism." Pp. 29-44 in *Yugoslavia—the Former and Future*, edited by Payam Akhavan and Robert Howse. Geneva: The United Nations Research Institute for Social Development (UNRISD).

Jelavich, Barbara. 1983. *History of the Balkans: Eighteenth and Nineteenth Centuries Vol. 1*. Cambridge: Cambridge University Press.

Kunovich, R.M. and Hodson, R. 2002. "Ethnic Diversity, Segregation, and Inequality: A Structural Model of Ethnic Prejudice in Bosnia and Croatia." *The Sociological Quarterly* 43/2:185-212.

Mead, George Herbert. 1934. *Mind, Self, and Society: From the Standpoint of a Social Behaviorist*. Edited by Charles W. Morris. Chicago: University of Chicago Press.

Pettan, Svanibor, Edt. 1998. *Music, Politics, and War: Views From Croatia*. Zagreb: Institute of Ethnology and Folklore Research.

Povrzanović, M. 1995. "War Experience and Ethnic Identities: Croatian Children in the Nineties." *Collegium Antropologicum* 19/1.

Stokes, Martin. 1994. *Ethnicity, Identity and Music: The Musical Construction of Place*. Oxford, Providence: Berg Publishers.

Tajfel, H. and Turner, J. C. 1979. "An Integrative Theory of Inter-Group Conflict." In *The Social Psychology of Intergroup Relations*, edited by L. W. Austin. and S. Worchel. Monterey, CA: Brooks Cole.

Tajfel, H. and Turner, J. C. 1986. "The Social Identity Theory of Inter-group Behavior." In *Psychology of Intergroup Relations*, edited by S. Worchel and L. W. Austin. Chicago: Nelson-Hall.

Turner, J. C. 1987. "A Self-Categorization Theory." In *Rediscovering the Social Group: A Self-Categorization Theory*, by J. C. Turner, M. A. Hogg, P. J. Oakes, S. D. Reicher and M. S. Wetherell. Oxford: Blackwell.

The Nightmare of Clever Children
Civilization, Postmodernity, and the Birth of the Anxious Body

Sean Conroy

Boston Graduate School of Psychoanalysis

seaneconroy@gmail.com

Abstract: This paper is the culmination of my undergraduate studies and reflects the theoretical directions I was heading at the time of my graduation as well as my own personal struggles with anxiety. Through conversations with my professor and my contemporaries I began to have the sense that anxiety, and particularly that of a social nature concerning the ability to relate to others is a prominent feature of my generation. I attempt to trace a link between uncertainty and anxiety using pertinent sociological, psychoanalytic and medical literature in order to better understand the possible social causes of this anxiety, with a particular focus on postmodern renditions of uncertainty. I use illustrations from personal experience and psychoanalytic theory to attempt to understand the origins of anxiety. Finally I attempt a history of consciousness in the west as I subjectively understand it in order to better comprehend how the current global context contributes to the social anxieties and attachment disorders so prevalent in my generation.

Whether he is better or worse off there where he awoke after his death, whether he was disappointed or found there what he expected, we shall all soon learn.

—Leo Tolstoy

DISCLAIMER

I just received a terrible grade from a professor for using the pronoun "I" in an academic paper. Admittedly it is my style of writing to do so, and I am aware that professional research papers have always been absent of the subject. In modernity science is reason and the truth is authorless. Post-modernity, however, is reflexive (Giddens, in Beck, Giddens and Lash 1994) as are the personality types it produces (Lasch 1979) of which I am one. In the absence of the modern [and thus antique] idea of objective truth I will allow the ideas of this paper to be subjective. They are my ideas and the ideas of those I have read. Even objective reality, as best we can discern it, is subject to the limitations of humanity.

That said, I have bit off more than I can yet chew. The essay I am attempting to write is as difficult to write as its subject

---

Sean Conroy is a graduate student at the Boston Graduate School of Psychoanalysis. He graduated from UMass Boston, majoring in Sociology. He wrote this paper, equivalent of an undergraduate thesis, while enrolled in the course Soc. 480: "Senior Seminar: Sociology of the Body," instructed by Dr. Robin Gomolin during the Fall 2006 semester.

matter is to understand. Categorizations of times, or rather stages in human development which we label modern, post modern, radically modern, or any combination thereof, are explained, refuted, and disputed in different ways by different authors. Though the use of the term 'modern' would seem to denote a time-order, I believe this is a misnomer. Even antiquity had its modern and postmodern thought. I have to admit to a longstanding aversion to these topics altogether; a fact which has inevitably doomed me to a compulsion to understand them. I can always tell that a bitter distaste for a subject is certain evidence of its importance.

My distaste for the question of modernities could itself be a reflection of the postmodern condition. Epistemological concerns always drive me crazy for how unpractical and useless they seem. However, in a sense, epistemology is the very condition of humanity in postmodernity, or perhaps the ability/necessity that makes it inevitable. Chicken and egg arguments are also a source of angst for me!

My aversion stems from the difficulty and futility of trying to understand reality from within one human body which is merely an infinitesimal fraction of that reality, whatever it may be. The work of any thinker is his own take on reality, influenced by that of others. No matter how much empirical evidence he cites to make his claim it is *always* a reflection of himself. A theory can never be separated from its theorist. Her blood, sweat and *fears* always color whatever she calls *truth*. The same applies to all of the collective 'truths' which we call things such as science, sociology, psychology, etc. The empirical findings of our collective understanding are merely that which we collectively agree upon at any particular time. They are Kuhn's paradigms. They are as trapped by the confines of our social existence as our individual truths are trapped by our own bodies. So, in a preemptive defense of my own truth, before you come to the conclusion yourself, I will tell you one thing that has as much or more to do with the formation of my subjective reality than any other—I am afraid to die. And unless my findings are merely narcissistic generalizations—which they very likely may be—so are you.

TORMENTUM

Cheating death, achieving immortality, eternal youth … humanity has been obsessed with these pursuits as long as history and literature has been recorded. The epic of Gilgamesh, the oldest known piece of human literature dating back to the third millennium, B.C., is the story of Gilgamesh, whose "grief and fear of death are such that they lead him to undertake a quest for eternal life" (Sandars). Wars were waged during the crusades which were not unmotivated by a belief that the holy grail of Christ would lead to eternal life. Indeed, the Heaven of Judeo-Christianity is described as 'life everlasting.' Ponce DeLeon scrambled around the everglades early on in the European chapter of this continent's history searching for the fountain of youth. The list goes on forever.

Even in Shakespeare's sonnets we can discern that he proposed three ways of achieving immortality. "W. S. never said in so many words that there were three ways of defeating Time, but in his sonnets, you and I can draw the trio. If we look at sonnets 1-17, we see that procreation is the way. If we look at the majority of poems, 18-onwards, being the subject of poetry is the way. And if we look at 116, we see that finding a perfect spiritual partner certainly defeats Time's power" (John Tobin in a personal correspondence).[1] In Shakespeare we see some universal human defences against mortality: having children so that a piece of ourselves will continue on; being the sub-

---

[1] Thanks to Professor Tobin for this point.

ject or author of poetry or some lasting contribution to humanity as a life project; and the one we are obsessed with (and perhaps Shakespeare and his sonnets are partly to blame): finding true love the likes of which transcends life itself. Suffice it to say that at least as long as we have been able to record our thoughts, we have been aware of our mortality, and it has always been a problem for us. I argue that it is *the problem*.

UNCERTAINTY

> What is ... new about the postmodern rendition of uncertainty (by itself not exactly a newcomer in a world with the modern past) is that it is no longer seen as a mere temporary nuisance, which with due effort may be either mollified or altogether overcome. *The postmodern world is bracing itself for life under a condition of uncertainty which is permanent and irreducible.*
>
> —Zygmunt Bauman, *Postmodernity and its Discontents*, 1997

While the influence of parenting that psychoanalysis relies so strongly on is debated by many, it may have more to do with the way birth cohorts of a single family are both different in bodily makeup and how they will respond to the stimuli of parenting, and also different in how they receive and perceive this stimuli. Likewise it is with individuals of larger generational birth cohort. However, Twenge's meta-analytic study does suggest that the larger birth cohort of society does seem to share some common psychic formations in response to their shared environmental conditions, as Lasch (1979), Bordo (1985-1986) and Freud (in Gay 1989) also suggest when they connect particular mental health conditions to situated times and places. The fact that trends of similarity in response to environmental conditions are discernable in generational birth cohort and inconclusive in intra-familial sibling groups is likely a problem of sample size. A small handful of siblings is too small to be able to discern an average response to parents, whereas the shared experience of an entire society is a large enough sample to see a trend. Twenge has termed the latter part of the 20th century, "The age of anxiety" since anxiety disorders of various kinds seem more prevalent in current generations of children than of those in the 1950s (Twenge 2000).

It could be that the increased knowledge of global effects and awareness of the consequences of all our actions puts us in a position to self chastise so much in responsibility to our ego ideals which are largely internal. We look for some internal constancy with which to protect ourselves from an external environment of uncertainty.

There is some biological evidence of uncertainty and inconsistency in early rearing contributing to anxiety. Coplan (1998) has shown that groups of primates exposed in early life to mothers with manipulated inconsistent feeding conditions were shown to have higher levels of anxiety causing neurochemicals than those with consistent feeding conditions, even much later in life. It is a testament to the evolutionary survival necessity of anxiety. They needed to be anxious to survive.

It is thus death, as the need to survive, which is our first instinct—including the desire for food as sustenance and the conditions of its attainment from the earliest care giving objects. From there on it only grows more complex as the environment and social connections do, and the structures of our mind that arise in the service of our survival grow more complex as well. All that we do, think, and feel is in the service of our survival, however tangential and far-removed from the immediate necessities they may seem.

An Anxious Generation

Coplan and Twenge respectively showed us that the conditions of early life can have lasting effects on the biochemical conditions that affect personality and emotions later in life, and that trends in personality development and mental health can be discerned among members of generational birth cohort.

In their exposition of the emergence of global generations, June Edmunds and Bryan Turner (2005) urge sociologists to "establish a new research agenda for work on generations … members of generations are held together by the experience of historical events from the same or similar vantage point." Generations "also identify themselves in terms of historical or cultural trauma, which is necessarily a social process. Events that come to be seen as cultural trauma in the popular lexicon are created and recreated through a variety of social processes by members of a national, social (or global) group" (Edmunds and Turner 2005). This lends credence to the idea of a collective consciousness. Such an idea is not bound to be very controversial, for the character of nations , shared belief systems, etc., are easily described as collective consciousness.

Prior to world war two collective consciousnesses were arguably experienced on a national level at most. However, after WWII it can be said that we first began to experience trauma and consciousness on a global level. The need for an entity such as the United Nations is evidence that perhaps for the first time in our history we began to experience a collective consciousness as not merely individual nations and groups, but as a species. A world war in which so many were killed, and more poignantly the Holocaust and the American use of nuclear violence against Japanese citizens, were traumas experienced (at least eventually) on a global level—unless of course you're Mahmoud Ahmadinejad.

I would argue that the atrocious events of WWII forced the world to reckon with itself in a way it never had to before. Sigmund Freud and Friedrich Nietzsche among others were responding to a change in consciousness years before WWII and ushering in the advent of postmodernity. However, they were relegated to the areas of the intellectual elite at best [mind ghettos] and more often chastised by the traditional conventions of modernity, still very much in power, which they threatened. After the events of the Second World War there was a period of shock and denial. The 1950s was a period of retraditionalization. In the united states and Europe, at least, people craved stability and it can be said that postmodernity was still confined to the intellectual elite and the culturally disenfranchised like Kerouac and the Beatniks. But the trauma had been experienced, and in the 1960s the first global generation (as noted by Edmunds and Turner) and arguably the first postmodern generation came of age. The birth of postmodernity which came from the womb of global trauma, reminds me of Ferenczi's "Clever baby," for he observed that, "traumatized young children often had accelerated developmental characteristics, including highly acute sensitivities and intuitions—in short, wisdom beyond their years" (Fortune 2003). In the case of postmodern generations, their wisdom was beyond not so much their age, but their era, modernity. They were the children of the generation that experienced the great depression and WWII firsthand. They were the baby boomers and large in number, and comfortable in economy they had the luxury of questioning tradition. It was tradition that reproduced the inequalities and fear that allowed for the Holocaust, and with the 60s generation, the work of postmodern thinkers like Freud and Nietzsche was injected into the collective consciousness writ large.

My generation is arguably the first

truly postmodern generation, having been conceived, born of and raised by post moderns. Our parents intergenerationally absorbed the traumas of WWII, and we inherited the trauma of the death of God and all that represents: the end of tradition, credible authority, of security and trust.

It is true that modernity and tradition carried on through the 20th century and are not at all gone today. But the collective consciousness has changed and a type of postmodern malaise is rendering tradition and modernity obsolete before our very eyes. We are a godless generation—a generation without anchors adrift in a sea of information. Overburdened by knowledge of the world and its dangers and underprotected by the now fragmented normative structures and conflicting values, we are struggling for identity. Giddens tells us that a sense of linear biography is central to our survival (Groarke 2002). If I may be so bold as to speak for my generation (my global generation), we are scared.

We experienced our collective trauma with the events of 9/11. I am actually astounded at the coincidence, but as I write this very passage, with my sister watching CNN in the background, an advertisement for the television show "splinter cell" about fictional terrorist groups, just came on the TV. The screen went black and an ominous buzzing sound grew louder and louder to reveal images of fire, smoke and injured bodies. A scary, deep voice asks, "When the next attack happens, Where will you be?"

This is the world we live in. One where trauma is commodified and turned into a product and our fear is colonized and exacerbated for profit and power (control). The commercial ends and we are taken to a Baghdad Military hospital where a young soldier talks to his wife on a cell phone to let her know he survived an attack. His face is grossly encrusted with drying blood and doctors's and nurses are attending to wounds on every part of his body. The cell phone is interrupted and one can only imagine the panic his wife is experiencing at home.

It is not only fear that comes with information, but guilt as well. Both are good ingredients for anxiety. The effects of globalization, the increasing supply of information and awareness that comes at us constantly like the ticker at the bottom of the CNN screen, or news tidbits in our Gmail accounts or on our cell phones, have the effect of keeping us aware of the myriad consequences of our actions. With greater knowledge comes greater responsibility. Ignorance is indeed bliss. Given such information we are forced to be complicit contributors to global atrocity, or become paralyzed entirely. Again, I couldn't write the coincidence so well were I to try, but again as I write this my sister, wearing her brand new engagement ring is licking envelopes, getting all the wedding invitations ready, and on CNN comes a news story showing pictures of some of the thousands of men, women, and children, even infants, who have had limbs amputated by militant political terror factions seeking control of the diamond mines of Sierra Leone—once again power through fear. The broadcaster tells us that because diamonds are untraceable, many of those on the market were obtained from these terrorist factions. On the couch my sister is licking envelopes with a ring she just loves, while I'm on the easy chair scribbling this paper and on the TV a child in Sierra Leone is at his desk at school writing with a pencil tied to the stump where his hand used to be. I don't feel I need any kind of theory to justify this as a contributing factor to our collective anxiety.

POSTMODERNITY?

The radical discontinuity of modernity sweeps away the traditional certainties which characterized pre-modern societies and which provided people with a stable sense of self-identity. (Giddens 1991:154)

In the introduction to his quite impressive compilation of social theory, Charles Lemert (1992) quotes David Bradley when he says, "…when seeking to understand the culture or the history of a people, do not look at the precepts of the religion, the form of the government, the curricula of the schools, or the operations of businesses; flush the johns" (2). This corresponds quite well to what Anthony Giddens calls the radicalization of modernity. He uses similar language to describe what he means by radical modernity—albeit more delicate. "These are processes of evacuation, the disinterring and problematization of tradition" (Giddens 1991:57). It is as though society has consumed and accumulated so much in the way of tradition that there is a backup and at the turning of the millennium we are in need of an enema!

Giddens can be said to be the primary theorist when it comes to the definitions of modernities. His structuration theory of personality development incorporates the post-Freudian theories of Erickson, Lacan, and Winnicott to further reconcile the relationship between psychic structure and society.

The chronological location of modernity and postmodernity is ambiguous. For instance it has been over 100 years since Nietzsche heralded the obituary of God, smack dab the beginning of western modernity, and I'm here in the new millennium citing him as as one of the eminent thinkers of postmodernity, an era which some believe we are still entering into. What's more, psychoanalysis, my preferred method of analyzing the relationship between the individual and society and Giddens as well, is 117 years old! One of the problems I have always had with the terms 'modern' and 'post-modern' is their implied time sequence. Isn't what's modern what is here and now? I suppose in the long run the seeming misnomer is useful for how it forces us to question the tentative relationship between time, history, and consciousness.

Is 'postmodern' meant to be read post-tradition? Giddens will make the distinction clearer than I will:

Hasn't modern society long been 'post-traditional'? It has not, at least in the way in which I propose to speak of the 'post-traditional' society here. For most of its history, modernity has rebuilt tradition as it has dissolved it. Within western societies, the persistence and recreation of tradition was central to the legitimating of power, to the sense in which the state was able to impose itself upon relatively passive 'subjects'. For tradition places in stasis some core aspects of social life—not least the family and sexual identity—which were left largely untouched so far as 'radicalizing Enlightenment' was concerned. Most important, the continuing influence of tradition within modernity remained obscure so long as 'modern' meant 'Western'. Some one hundred years ago Nietzsche had already 'brought modernity to its senses', showing Enlightenment itself to be a myth and thereby posing disquieting questions about knowledge and power. Nietzsche's was, however, the lone voice of the heretic. Modernity has been forced to 'come to its senses today, not so much as a result of its internal dissenters as by its own generalization across the world. No longer the unexamined basis of western hegemony over other cultures, the precepts and social forms of modernity stand open to scrutiny. (Giddens, in Beck, Giddens, and Lash 1994: 57)

Globalization has been a catalyst of the ushering in of postmodernity. It is as though the larger a society gets, in this case the entire world, the more drastically its conventions fail and need to be questioned and reinvented. Globalization has arguably been taking place since our first ancestors began to walk away from the middle of the African continent. What is new is the speed and scale of globalization that technology and communication have engendered.

The radicalizing enlightenment of late modernity was threatening to traditional moderns, and indeed all of us, since it is human to need anchors. After all a life without any constancy is the fate of a madman. It is to the condition of having lost faith in all tradition, to having no comforting idea of what to replace tradition with (i.e., family, gender, identity, etc.) that I refer to as postmodernity. The conditions of human evolution which brought us the ability, and indeed necessity, to think keep growing in complexity. Postmodern, in the way I use it, refers to the coming period (or one already here) which is as yet uncertain. The future always is, however, a postmodern future is scarier than any old future, because I don't know exactly what we will be able to bring with us from modern tradition, if anything at all. When I quote Nietzsche and say "God is dead," I mean we are now alone, without God, tradition, and everything we were able to believe in order to secure our purposes. The human mind adapts and evolves structurally as well as biologically in response to the needs of survival in its situated civilization. Our situation is changing rapidly. It may be many decades since Freud started thinking up postmodern ideas and Nietzsche saw that God was dying, but Postmodernity is coming fast. Tradition and authority are losing credibility that was based on assumptions of modernity at an incredible rate. We find ourselves having to adapt and evolve (a process which happens best very slowly) almost immediately. Anxious bodies grasping at straws to know and enact their place in Goffman's interaction order, are a casualty of rapid transition.

The chronology is vague. I converse with Freud and Nietzsche as though they were on the phone with Giddens, Susan Bordo and I because time is irrelevant. The concept of modernities is about the structure of consciousness rather than time-order. Recently I attended a psychoanalytic conference where a young analyst declared her concern that the field of psychoanalysis was moving away from the unconscious. She observed that something "very serious" was going on. My professor took my pen and paper and wrote, "The serious thing is postmodernity." She was absolutely correct. The unconscious may not be disappearing, but the structures of the mind that Freud discerned were those that existed in modernity and were suited to those needs. Structure theories of the mind are merely cognitive attempts to organize and categorize the myriad functions of the part of the body that interacts with the environment which we call 'mind.' The young analyst who was so concerned may have been mourning the death of modernity and the structural theories from which she derives a comfortable 'understanding' of reality. Consciousness and mental structure are adaptable, plastic, entities which allow us to survive in an ever changing environment which includes the social life which we call civilization. Civilization is changing. Consciousness is changing.

Of course the potential for postmodern thinking was with us all along. So long as there was the ability to think, there was the ability to question. Reality testing is the human condition and on an individual as well as social level we are never done with it. So long as we could question we have been able to philosophize ourselves into oblivion. Forget for the moment that the ancient Greeks had philosophy, for even they and many before them were postmodern in drips and drabs. Even

Shakespeare, the pay for play author who wrote at the beginning of the European chapter of western civilization thought of life as "a tale told by an idiot and signifying nothing." Idiots and madmen abound, postmodernity has been with us all along. Our ability to rationalize made it an inevitability. We questioned and thought and thought and questioned and looked for meaning and looked deeper and deeper and lost all meaning only to recreate it until the postmodern uncertainty became the norm.

We are afraid of risk now that our contesting of tradition—whether it was the expected outcome or not, since our contestations of tradition themselves were a manifestation of the human need to feel a sense of control (the omnipotence once ascribed to God)—"have created greater uncertainties, of a very consequential kind, than ever existed before" (Giddens 1991:59). What we call postmodern thought is a reflection of the pushing of the envelope of human rationalization. Whether chicken or egg, the societies we cerate are both the cause and the effect of the mental (bodily) abilities and structures we are able to utilize for our survival and adaptation. It is no mistake that Nietzsche's protagonist is a madman, who "In the bright early morning lights a lantern and therewith first seeks God, calling out as he does, 'Where is God … I want to tell you we have killed him, you and I. We are all his murderers … God is dead; God remains dead, and we have killed him. How shall we console ourselves? … we the murderers among all murderers? The most holy and most powerful things, which the world had up to now, have been bloodied with our knives. Who will wash this blood from us? With what water can we clean ourselves? What atonement, what holy ceremony will we have to invent? Is not the magnitude of this deed too great for us? Must we not become God's ourselves to appear worthy of it?" (Pippin 1999:497). Enter Narcissism.

LOVE VS. THE APOCALYPSE

In *Civilization and It's Discontents* Freud says "Civilized man has exchanged a portion of his happiness for his security." In Bauman's *Postmodernity and Its Discontents*, a modification of Freud's title, he explained the reversal, "Postmodern men and women exchanged a portion of their possibilities for security for a portion of happiness."

Freud tells us that ego-libido and object-libido are antithetical. "The more of the one is employed the more the other becomes depleted". He tells us that being in love is the opposite of "fearing the end of the world."(Gay 1989:547) It is interesting that in modern times we are so preoccupied with intense romantic love (Lasch 1979) and also with the end of the world or similar such anticipations of doom and mortality. My peers, as well as my self, seem to be hell-bent on finding an other, "the one" even terrified of not finding one. Could there be a relationship between the obsession with romantic love and the anxious times we live in?

When I was young and rumors spread around school that the world was going to end on Thursday at 2:15, my father told me that every age thinks the world is going to end and the same thing happened when he was a kid, and again and again. Years later in a history of Christianity class my father's advice was confirmed. The bible, which was written so long ago, was written by people who thought the end, the apocalypse, was near. The Judeo-Christian bible is the earliest subjective history of the west. The apocalyptic undertone of the text was arguably a response to the anxiety that war after war conjured. Although it was so long ago, it was arguably the same anxiety that we experience today. During Biblical times they were experiencing the beginning of globalization. We were beginning to write, we could record our history, our narrative of who and what we are, and this helped to allow larger and larger groups to identify with each other as nations. Civilization occurred, we were no longer animals living in small bands, we were large-scale symbionts colliding on a global scale. The forms of communication we have now only make the relationship between time and space smaller and thus globalization much, much faster.

Civilization is an attempt at achieving security (Bauman 1997). Our current post-9/11 time is heavily laced with fear. We too may feel that the end is near. Our parents grew up with the fear of nuclear holocaust and a WWIII that promised to bring an end to civilization as we know it. One only has to watch ten minutes of CNN to feel like global conditions are escalating toward such an apocalypse. As I grew up in the 80s and 90s there was a *pax romana* of sorts. Sandwiched between the end of the cold war and 9/11, there was a comfortable period of rest wherein the country had the luxury of having little to be afraid of more than Ellen DeGeneres kissing another woman on national television. No doubt my memory is tainted by my age at the time, but these were quaint, insulated, consumeristic times as I recall them. We had forgotten about the bomb, while other's in far corners of the globe scrambled to figure out how to make them. Nestled comfortably in the shadow of Gorbachev's peace-prize and able to purchase souvenir chunks of the Berlin wall, I grew up feeling as though war was something from history. Even when Bush, the first, sent troops to Iraq, we tracked it on maps in school, there were desert storm trading cards, and no one I knew was a soldier. On TV you could watch live night vision feeds of green scud missiles trailing across the sky over Baghdad, but it didn't feel threatening.

I remember sitting at home alone watching TV by myself after elementary school let out when a special report came on the screen declaring war. I was exhilarated and terrified. War was something from history books, I pictured enemy soldiers filling our streets near our homes and fathers and sons picking up muskets like minutemen, defending their own homes. I was terrified, and I didn't know how long it would be before the enemy soldiers got here, so I called up my dad and told him what was happening. He calmed me down and told me that I didn't have to worry because wars didn't get fought on American soil. I could again feel safe, because just like before when war was something of the past (and hence fictional in a sense) war was again removed from my immediate reality; it was something foreign. I'll remind you again my history is very subjective, but it feels from my point of view that the nation and the western world grew up, and grew out of their comfort around the same time I was growing up.

9/11

I was a couple of short years out of high school and taking courses at night at a community college working part-time as a children's librarian when driving to school the song was interrupted so that the DJ could tell us that a plane had crashed into one of the WTC towers. Instantly I pictured an inexperienced Cessna pilot losing control of his twin engine prop plane, then the DJ said "a second plane has just hit the towers." *Reality* In the instant I heard the words 'second plane,' I knew it was an attack. No amount of rationalizing could make it a possible coincidence. I spent the morning, before they let us out of work early, getting internet news feeds for the ladies at the library. Some were crying, some were coming up with reasons why anyone would do this, others were cursing Muslims, some were doing all the three. I was comforting some of them, and I was trying to diffuse the racism of others, but really I was losing my innocence in a way I hadn't yet. I was picturing myself in a uniform, and not because I wanted to. I was realizing my age, and thinking that if this was what it seemed like, I was going to be drafted. All of the socialization, from Clint Eastwood, to my dad buying me toy pistols for successful potty training behind my mom's back, was being stimulated, and while I wanted no war, and wanted never to fight and was terrified, I felt equally that if there was a draft I couldn't let someone else die in my place. I went home and had the strangest impulse to hang a flag, more socialization maybe. I unfolded the moth hole filled triangle flag that had belonged to some dead veteran who nobody remembered and had been in our garage since I was born, and hung it straight up and down over our front door. I don't know what I thought, I thought maybe the neighborhood would feel safe if I reminded them where they were. I looked up and down the street and saw no one, my flag was all alone. When I woke up the next morning, there wasn't a house, car, or storefront without one. I had no idea everyone else would think the same thing.

That evening there were no jet planes crisscrossing double white lines across the sky in the flight pattern that goes straight over my house to Logan. There were, however, F14 fighter jets patrolling the sky. My sister, her boyfriend, and I sat in the yard, talking about the draft, and how this wouldn't be the kind we felt we could dodge. The flags slowed down eventually, and we stopped worrying about being drafted into WWIII. But the CNN ticker didn't get any more comforting. After a while it felt like our leaders were hell-bent on making sure of the coming of WWIII.

2012

I have heard more than a few of my contemporaries admit that they feel that 2012 may be the end of the world. This is an idea that has been disseminated by PBS and numerous documentaries about the Mayans. The Mayan calendar is considered to be the most accurate astronomical time piece created by man, and is a circle which ends in 2012. I recently heard a friend say, "No need to make any plans, we only have 6 years left, might as well live it up."

LOVE *ME* TENDER

Freud tells us that narcissism is a return of the object libido to the ego, self love, and represents "a happy love once more … a real happy love corresponds to the primal condition in which object-libido and ego-libido cannot be distinguished" (Gay 1989:561).

It seems we are constantly trying to reclaim our original state, that which we had as babies. Through some combination of the omnipotence of primary narcissism and the idealization of the original caregiver, who fed us and alleviated our first pain, we come to create an ego ideal.

Freud tells us "The ego ideal opens up an important avenue for the understanding of group psychology since the ideal has a social side." It is influenced by common ideals. When libido is turned back toward the ego in narcissism, in search of the ideal object, non-fulfillment of the ideal by the ego, as determined by the judgment of the superego, is transformed into a sense of guilt which Freud says is social anxiety. (Gay 1989)

The object of God, is the ultimate externalization of ego ideal, and in true chicken and egg fashion, is subsequently the ideal available for internalization. When Nietzsche tells us God is dead, I believe he is warning us—although warn is the wrong word, for you can only bring one's awareness to an event already taking place—about the unknown consequences of losing the external manifestation of the ego ideal. Narcissism, catering to the id, return of instinct, self-love, individualism, are all related to the return of the libido to the self in some way as a result of The death of God, or the fall of tradition and authority, the exchange of modernity for postmodernity, *se-*

curity for *happiness*. When Nietzsche tells us that "to have committed such a deed," "To have killed God," we must then be gods ourselves, he may be referring to the strictly internalized ego-ideal that results from a complete absence of the external ideal, God, who our own ability of rational scientific thought has rendered impossible. All we are left with is the internal remnants of a dying God, the impossible ideal we can never live up to, but by which we judge ourselves nonetheless. We have the ideal, but no longer any credible guidelines for its achievement. Nothing in postmodernity is credible. This is the result of being the antecedent of modernity which "institutionalizes the principle of radical doubt and insists that all knowledge takes the form of hypotheses; claims which very well may be true, but which are in principle always open to revision and may have at some point to be abandoned" (Giddens 1991).

For Freud "anxiety" is distinguished from "fright" and "fear." "*Fear* requires a definite object of which to be afraid … *Fright* however is the name we give to the state a person gets into when he has run into danger without being prepared for it; it emphasizes the factor of surprise … *Anxiety* describes a particular state of expecting the danger or preparing for it, even though it may be an unknown one"(Gay 1989:598).

Anxiety is a call to action, or to brace oneself for the need to act. The human condition is being aware of mortality—the greatest of uncertainties, and the root of all fears. Environment has a lot to do with how this anxiety is experienced. For the truly religious of modernity, the trust and love of god, which we call faith, provided an avenue for release of libido to combat this anxiety, in the same way that cathecting the mother object, or a lover, with one's libido soothes the individual. For the postmodern individual however, who is profoundly skeptical of rationalization and the problematic attachment to the reality principle; for the scientist, the social theorist, and the philosopher who can scarcely trust the veracity and existence of authority of institutions which have any real authority; or for the student of psychoanalysis whose postmodern reflexivity renders the idea of "true-love" unbelievable, much less the existence of God, the ability to cathect an external object sufficiently and permanently enough is impaired by an awareness of the transient nature of all things. For post-modernity is as Z. Bauman says, a recognition of a condition of uncertainty that is permanent and irreducible. Our ability to trust, which is one of the key ingredients in Anthony Giddens' structuration theory of human personality development, is impaired (Groarke 2002). We leap from love to love, religious experience to religious experience, because not a one will gratify our need for very long. We are pleasure seekers, and pleasure only exists at the moment of release of unpleasure. We derive great pleasure from the relinquishing of anxiety that arises from intense but fleeting attachments to other external objects (toward which we can temporarily direct our inwardly bound libidos before recoiling back into ourselves). If it sounds almost like a vaguely euphemistic description of sex, its probably not a coincidence.

If love really is the opposite of apocalyptic fear, or death anxiety as Freud supposes, increased fear of the end should lead to increased need for love, and paradoxically for the narcissistic child of postmodernity no such love exists as can successfully supplant his or her anxiety.

THE NARCISSISTS

A Muslim, a Jew, and a Christian walk into a bar and the bartender says, "God is dead. What should we do with the body?" "His or ours?", the holymen reply in chorus. A drunk at the end of the bar wakes up, lifts his head and asks, "There's a difference?"

Lasch (1979) writes, "Every age develops its own peculiar forms of pathology, which express in exaggerated form its underlying character structure. In Freud's time, hysteria and obsessional neurosis carried to extremes the personality traits associated with capitalist order at an earlier stage in its development-acquisitiveness, fanatical devotion to work, and a fierce repression of sexuality" (41). I have heard many times my own generation of Americans described as lazy. I regret to say that my own capacity for procrastination has illustrated this quite well. What kind of peculiar forms of pathology emerge from a generation whose capitalist ancestors have already acquired the resources of capital through the fanatical devotion that led to their own repressed neuroses? What sort of neuroses do we now harbor?

In 1979, one year before I was born, Christopher Lasch described a culture of narcissism. Rebelling against an increasingly common interpretation of narcissism as self-interested greed, he recalled the words of Sennet who told us "narcissism has more in common with self hatred than with self-admiration" (31). In the post-acquisitive capitalist period, our postmodern character disorders become the "most prominent form of psychiatric pathology ... [which] together with the change in personality structure this development reflects, derives from quite specific changes in our society and culture—from beauracracy, the proliferation of images, therapeutic ideologies, the rationalization of the inner life, the cult of consumption, and in the last analysis from changes in family life and from changing patterns of socialization." The detraditionalization and fragmentation of normative systems paves the way for the anxious body. The uncertainty of postmodernity is the social mother of anxiety, and if Bauman is right it is here to stay.

The narcissist, to whom the anxious body belongs, tells us much about the society that created her. As Lasch (1979) says, "the collective mind, if there is such a thing, reflects the needs of the group as a whole, not the psychic needs of the individual, which in fact have to be subordinated to the demands of collective living" (33). I would like to say that I do not exemplify many of the descriptions of the narcissistic personality Lasch points out. However, if I am at all representative of my generation, and the personality of my time, I must be brave enough to admit that I felt uncomfortably summed up by Lasch's description of the "character traits of pathological narcissism, which in less extreme form appear in such profusion in the everyday life of our age: dependence on the vicarious warmth provided by others combined with a fear of dependence, a sense of inner emptiness, boundless repressed rage, and unsatisfied oral cravings."(Lasch 1979:33)

A professor of mine once told me that alcohol and drug abuse seemed to be far more prevalent in my generation than in those before it. I reluctantly accepted this when confronted with the data. It is of personal importance to me to situate this substance abuse in context:

> Internalized images of others, buried in the unconscious mind at an early age, become self images as well. If later experience fails to qualify or to introduce elements of reality into the child's archaic fantasies about his parents, he finds it difficult to distinguish between images of self and of objects outside the self. These images fuse to form a defense against the bad representations of the self and of objects, similarly fused in a harsh, punishing superego. (Lasch 1979:39)

Here we find the seeds of self-hatred at the blurred intersection of self and society experienced by the narcissist. My interest in connecting this quote to the commonality of drinking and drug use in my generation is one of extreme concern for our future. In our attempts to quell the desires and in-turned rage of our anxious bodies we turn to drugs and alcohol at an early age. There is evidence that alcohol abuse occurs in comorbidity with anxiety quite often (Chartier 2003). If we do not find a way out of this paradox of avoidant behavior soon enough to have those later experiences which Lasch tells us could introduce elements of reality into our archaic fantasies, we may find ourselves fixed permanently within the prison of our anxious, narcissistic, self-hating bodies. It is in those bodies that it all begins, with that bedtime story told to us by Sigmund Freud, *The ego and the Id*. I will attempt to trace a possible historical context for western American psychic structure. It is a story of evolution and adaptation. Whether in the end it is a comedy or a tragedy I will let the reader decide. Shakespeare couldn't decide either, and he was there for the beginning of the western version of civilization.

CIVILIZATION: A BRIEF HISTORY OF CONSCIOUSNESS IN THE WEST

The structures of the mind Freud discerned were not facts, but ideas. Ideas which described portions of the human ability to think that made possible the ability to live socially. They were necessary structurations of mind for survival in the world he lived in. I don't yet have the answer to the question of why this ability to think exists at all; why natural selection would find it better to create an animal with something more than instinct. Natural selection, in and of itself, supposes that propagation and continuation are the primary purposes of all living things. I don't have the answer to why our particular mental ability helps us do this any better, especially when the burden of this ability causes so much misery and often threatens our existence as both individuals and as a species (i.e., suicide, holocaust, war, etc.). If you still believe in God, you can insert him here; I'm sure you will if you do. Life is about finding meaning to survive (Shilling 2003:153). Your meaning is as good as any other if it suits for you that purpose. And God Bless you if you can.

Peter Berger tells us, "…humans are a species whose very conditions of embodiment force them to act, and to invest themselves and their actions with meaning in order to survive. In this context, the prospect of death constitutes a threat to people's 'world-building' and 'self-building' activities which needs to be dealt with by society through the provision of shared meaning systems. The provision of such systems has become increasingly problematic in modernity, especially in the context of the shrinkage of space occupied by religion" (Shilling 2003:153). Berger also asserts:

> All reality is socially constructed, as a consequence of Man's incompleteness, but human beings require stable meanings and cannot live in permanent awareness of the socially constructed and precarious nature of everyday reality, and they are forced to clothe these certainties with permanent significance. (Ibid.)

He may very well be right. This seems to be the problem we are having in postmodernity. Our mental structures/apparatus are, while not unequipped, *ill*-equipped for the rapid transition into postmodernity—like the child growing up who is accustomed to the illusions of certainty provided by its mother and encounters reality with discomfort. Civilization and it's traditions were our consistent mother, our constant object. The structures of the ego and superego as they existed for Freud's discovery were suited for a particular purpose of survival in the modern and traditional world of civilization. They are the apparatus of mind, those webs of biochemical processes surging through our entire visceral bodies which allowed us, as a collection of ids, to live amongst one another in a certain order with a certain division of labor that allowed us to survive in a world we are physically too weak as mere animals to navigate without intelligence and cooperation.

"Consciousness precedes socialization … human beings can never be fully socialized into shared meanings" (Shilling 2003:155). No matter how intensely we are, or try to be, connected to one another we cannot be completely socialized into shared meanings. Each individual lives in a separate world, a separate reality. True understanding is impossible, empathy can be profound, but no one ever fully understands another's experience. Reality is, as I have said, always subjective. Shared meaning systems keep us connected. Canadians have a shared Canadian experience. Americans have theirs. But within any group each individual has her own experience of reality and she is utterly alone within it. Our mind perhaps began to form before our social connections did, and it will perhaps die apart from them as well. We cling to social connections like we cling to life itself, because they are one and the same. We will die and our fear of death extends to our loved ones for they too are aging and fragile. "When no great attachments are formed, no great losses can be experienced" (Shilling 2003:168). Susan Bordo (1985-1986) shows us how anorexia nervosa and hysteria are exaggerated manifestations of women's experience of civilization. As a symptom or defense social anxiety and anxiety disorders in general is an exaggerated manifestation of risk-diminishing. The narcissistic turn of the libido inward is a result of the unreliability of external objects in postmodernity. When everything is hypothesis waiting to be disproved, the only thing that is real and constant is one's own body. Attempts to anchor oneself in postmodern uncertainty are conducted within and upon the body in the form of body projects (Shilling 2003:4), tattooing, body modification (Sweetman 1999), and myriad other narcissistic endeavors. There is evidence of comorbidity of anxiety disorders and eating disorders. Though eating disorders are attributed to the oppressive conditions of modernity their path of control is through the self just as the narcissistic devices of postmodernity will be. Perhaps even the constant de-valuing of self is a narcissistic defense. This sounds antithetical, but if self is the only anchor and is cathected with the libido, the idea of death might become even more frightening. Valuing oneself under these conditions only makes the inevitable loss of the only thing we truly possess even more of an occasion for mourning.

People often tell me, when I declare that all anxiety is death anxiety, that they are not afraid to die. From within my own psychic structure it's difficult to believe. Keeping in mind the previous statements about the presence of the author in any theory, the reader of this essay must have a pretty good idea of how anxious my world/reality is. I tend to wonder if their seeming sureness that they are not afraid to die is not just the manifest portion of a greater defense which itself speaks to the fear of mortality. What would pain and discomfort be without death? It would still hurt, but would it be so terrifying if it was not often an indication of a possible threat to our existence?

When asked in class once what we were each afraid if no one said "terrorists" or "World War III." We all said something entirely more superficial or inwardly specific such as "failure," "loneliness," "getting fat." It was almost always a reflection of self and not an external threat. With the exception of myself, no one answered "Death" at all. I even amended my own answer. I did so because I only answered "death" because I do fear it terribly and I do believe it is the root of all anxiety. I changed it to fear of being invisible, unwanted and alone.

Failure, getting fat, what do these have in common with my fear [which I'm narcissistically assuming is *the* fear] of loneliness and death? In fact what does loneliness have in common with death? I think all the fears mentioned in class reflected aspects of the self one values, but more importantly one supposes others value. Arguably others' valuation of these traits are the very reason why they value them in the first place. It is others they are afraid of losing; those connections to others which we were conditioned to need from birth for our emotional and corporeal survival (also reflections of the same drive)—the emotional being a response that is meant to self indicate the activities that ensure survival, emotions like love and anxiety.

If I haven't convinced you in the preceding pages that death is the root of all anxiety I doubt I will. However, this portion of the essay is a subjective history of consciousness in western civilization, and civilization is about security, and security is about survival. Twice already in this essay fear was mentioned as a mechanism of social control. Fear of death made civilization possible.

The work of Norbert Elias gives us a good picture of the story if civilization.

> The uncivilized body was constrained by few behavioral norms, gave immediate physical expression to emotions, and sought to satisfy bodily desires without restraint or regard for the welfare of others ... the gradual civilizing of the body has taken place in the context of changes in the major *fears* facing individuals and the dominant mode of *social control* characteristic of societies. Fears of attack in relatively unregulated societies are increasingly replaced by social 'fears' of shame and embarrassment in modern societies, and from being forced on people externally, control comes to be self imposed. (Shilling 2003:132)

Elias uses the concept of 'symbol emancipation'—"a unique ability to learn and synthesize symbols, to develop these into a language marked by reflexivity, variability, precision, flexibility and a high degree of reality congruence"—to explain that "While human bodies remain irreducibly biological ... evolution has equipped them with capacities (for example, of speech and thought) which release them from dependence on further biological change" (Shilling 2003:133). Further,

> The development of the civilized body in Europe is not determined by the rise of modern capitalism, as a response to the demands of production and accumulation, but is related to the transformation of the warrior nobility of the early middle ages into a court aristocracy.

Capitalism did not invent civilization, war did. If unregulated societies are in fear of invasion, those who could protect would become "Noble." For people who lived in fear, the ability to protect or keep order is the most valuable form of social capital. This could even perhaps explain the early onset of males' gaining more social capital since in early society brute force was the language of diplomacy:

> In early medieval times, the personality structure was volatile, behavior was unpredictable and frequently fluctuated between extremes for apparently minor reasons. Life was short, food was often in irregular supply ... and violence was part of everyday life and was not seen as exceptional or

even undesirable. Pleasure was taken in torture, mutilation and killing, and people had to be ready to defend themselves and be prepared to give free reign to their emotions in order to safeguard their lives, property and possessions. […] The existence of extreme forms of asceticism and renunciation in medieval society does not contradict this general picture. Such restraint was also a flight into physicality. (Shilling 2003:134)

Here we see that at the beginning of civilization, as in the present, the body is paramount. Asceticism mirrors anorexia. Those who derive emotional soothing from food, especially where it is among the only means they have to employ, are usually more likely to become anorexics or bulimics. It is in this way that whatever the exact mechanism, asceticism and hedonism come from the same place as evidenced by the dichotomous practices of the middle ages.

There is a narcissistic service of the id in either case, antiquity or postmodernity, though for different reasons. In antiquity we were adjusting to civilization and emerging from an animal existence, and in postmodernity we are withdrawing from civilization in a different way since it no longer captures our trust since all is reduced to the transient and hypothetical. We must remember that psychic structure is not fixed. In antiquity we had not yet developed fully the same ego and superego which we are now beginning to experience as changing once again:

Court societies institutionalized highly detailed codes of body management which were used to differentiate between people on the basis of their relative worth. (Shilling 2003:135)

Relative worth here is another term for 'social capital':

In contrast to medieval times, court societies did not require individuals to be constantly ready to display a high level of aggression. Instead, physical battles were frequently replaced by courtly intrigues, and survival depended less on bodily strength than on adherence to behavioral codes and skills of impression management … The presentation of the body was more important for success than overcoming other bodies by force, and it became a necessity for court people to develop 'an extraordinarily sensitive feeling for the status and importance that should be attributed to a person in society on the basis of his bearing, speech, manner or appearance. (Shilling 2003:135)

In court societies we begin to see the beginnings of the necessary mental structures that we are familiar with in Modernity. All of this impression management as a necessary survival skill shows us where Goffman's interaction order began. Once the status had been gained and relative worths set, the dramaturgy began—although there would always have been an interaction order, primitive as it may have been in early antiquity. Even 'you hit me I hit you' is an interaction order, but in court societies we see the beginning of Goffman's presentation of self. When self presentation is so important to survival we need to develop a reliable self-concept. It was here that the ego was born, in the sense that Freud knew it. When 'bearing, speech, manner and appearance' became so important, we needed an ego to help us keep track of ourselves. Selves until then had been largely id.

"The search for distinction within court

society ... was ... behind the internalization of codes of behavior, and the increased attention given to the monitoring and control of the body ...[and] court competition ..." (Shilling 2003:139). This led to an increase in "the amount and frequency of mutual identification":

> ... preserving or improving one's social position within a competitive situation necessitated a more 'psychological' view of people which involved precise observations of both one's own and others' actions and expressions. Taking more conscious account of how one's behavior will be interpreted by others can also be seen as constituting a higher level of identification with others. People are forced to pay more attention to more people than was previously the case ... One implication of this is that mutual identification is conducive to promoting both a greater degree of sympathy and empathy with others. (Shilling 2003:139)

Here we see the beginning of the best and worst of society. Once we had the ability to mentalize the other we were capable of great deeds of empathy and love and others of inequality and hate. Elias further writes,

> The development of civilized bodies involves a progressive socialization, rationalization and individualization of the body ... [S]ocialization ... [is] ... the hiding away of natural functions and the transformation of bodies into a location for and an expression of the codes of behavior. (Shilling)

Rationalization strengthened the "boundaries between consciousness and drives.

> "The rationalization of the body also involves the progressive differentiation of the body: it is seen as less of a 'whole' and more as a phenomenon whose separate parts are amenable to control."

Here we see the beginning of the way we fracture in all of the ways we do. The ways we 'split' into ego and superego, multiple 'selves,' separation of the drives, etc. The superego is borne of the need to make sure the ego is in accordance with society's regulations:

> With the progression of the civilization process, life becomes less dangerous but also less exciting. As strategic thinking replaces immediacy of expression there is a trade-off between spontaneous pleasure and the security of controlled planning ... One effect of this is that the drives and passions that can no longer be displayed directly between people, often struggle just as violently *within* individuals against the supervising part of themselves. The strict moulding of children often leads to interpersonal conflicts which serve to pattern their personality structure and can have a detrimental effect on their relationships as adults ... The amount of violence in everyday life may have been reduced, but the battlefield is ... moved within ... the drives, the passionate affects, that can no longer manifest themselves in the relationships *between* people, often struggle no less violently *within* the individual against this supervising part of himself. (Shilling 2003:143)

Elias's history lesson has brought us up to the conditions of modernity and the conflicts which Freud discerned in his patients. He continues, "there is often no complete resolution between the supervising consciousness and the supervised drives of individuals. The balance between these is frequently subject to disturbances which range from revolts of one part of the person against the other, or a permanent atrophy…"(Shilling 2003:144)

Atrophy and revolt; the condition of the fragmentation of consciousness into psychic structures has caused us much pain. I have perhaps exhausted the reader with quotes from Elias by now, but I believe his is a brilliant description of the history of consciousness. Though he does not speak of psychoanalytic structures of the mind, his history has provided me a good idea of where the Freudian structures may have come from, and also a very good illustration of how fluid psychic structure is. How adaptive it is. We began as id, as animals, and our consciousness developed through social evolution, for our survival as a means of circumventing the fact that our biology doesn't evolve fast enough to do so on its own.

This historical account of the changes in psychic structure is presented as further support to the notion that social conditions do affect psychic formations and mental health, like Lasch's *narcissism*, Bordo's *anorexia*, and my *social anxiety*. It is also presented since a look at where we have been, may have something to say about where we are headed. In postmodernity only one thing's certain … nothing will ever be the same.

Conclusion

We are a clever species; able to reflexively observe our own experience, and cognizant of our own mortality. The chemical processes of our bodies form complex systems of response to external (environment) and internal (instinct/id) stimuli, which we call mind. One structure of the mind which Freud calls ego, is the self-concept. It was imperative to evolve an ego to live in groups, as well as a superego with which to mediate the experience, because group life in 'civilized' form requires an awareness of self so that one's actions can be molded in accordance with the demands of social life. The ego and consciousness started out small, it needed to know very little and in primitive more animalistic social formations the id and instinct were superior to the ego, just as the instincts of most animals exist in almost complete absence of an ego. Perhaps with further study of the more social animals, primitive versions of the ego could be observed. If you've ever held a snake or a lizard, much less an insect, it is apparent that they have virtually no concept of self or other but seem to act solely on impulse. Those of us with dogs may observe a higher degree of self-awareness. It is all just stimulus and response at its core, however simple or complex, even for humans, but dogs seem to have a higher capacity for recognizing the desires of the other in service of their own instinctual gratification—even to the point of regulating their own behavior in the presence of their owners.

Anxiety is a call to act, whether fight, flight, or repress, and it is a part consequence of the management of libido. In early western civilization, the court society demanded an awareness of self, a greater capacity of ego, for our survival through the successful performance in Goffman's interaction order. After all as social animals we need each other and our division of labor to survive. The work of Goffman illustrates quite well how much of our behavior is in the service of maintaining social status.

In late modern and postmodern civilization the authoritative structures which determine norms of behavior are increasingly debased and fragmented and the interaction order is confused. The management of our bodies, through the use of the ego and superego is problematized. The interaction order gets confused and confusing. The ego and consciousness need to be quite large to accommodate the complexity of an information-packed postmodern environment and the reflexivity coupled with the rationalization of modernity that reduces all truth to hypotheses which can be proven or disprovenat any time. This complicates one's satisfaction with his ego. The conditions are so uncertain that it is very difficult to always behave in a way that lends itself to a feeling of security. The ego ideal which is a product of both the original omnipotence of the infant self and the idealized omnipotence of the first providing object and is symbolized by Nietzsche as the internalization of a dead God in rationalized modernity, and is indeed the origin of that God, is impossible to achieve under even the most simple of environmental conditions

In postmodernity it is even more impossibly so and one attempt to deal with the impossibility—which is a result of the ensuing anxiety whether it be the energy of guilt or fear—is the paradoxical risk-diminishing of social anxiety, and narcissistic impossibility of external libido cathexis. If we are obsessed with romantic love, and leap to and from such experiences in order to seek gratification, it is truly because only in the instant of intense emotional intimacy is our death anxiety, which Freud posited as the antithesis of object-love, supplanted and soothed. An experience of this intensity is impossible to sustain since pleasure, as Freud said, is merely the experience at the moment of release/renunciation of unpleasure (ego and id).

In modernity, the psychic malformations of hysteria and obsessional neuroses were a result of the repression of the id in the service of social security. In postmodernity the psychic malformations of social anxiety are problems of the ego in that security is sacrificed in service of the id since the repressive structures of modernity, while causing us unpleasure, failed to provide us with security and are failing even more as we grow more postmodern and our egos are struggling to create in themselves some measure of security. The ego sustains a few blows. It is bombarded with information, and postmodern self discovery such as psychoanalysis, so the consciousness needs to be quite large. The amount of information increases the number of dissonances the superego needs to balance, and, likewise, the fragmentation of authoritative structures and normative systems also increases the amount of dissonance the mind needs to balance (i.e., CNN, all the global responsibilities, etc.)

As a postmodernist, I can no longer sustain utopian visions and I wonder if there is ever an ideal balance between security and happiness or if we are destined to continuously bounce back and forth in the service of one or the other, the way the political climate of the United States seems to wax and wane from liberal to conservative whenever we get tired of whichever one we have had for too long.

The nightmare of clever children, as my title calls it, is precisely the awareness that Bauman recognizes. We are outgrowing certainty. We are aware that we will die, and our intellectual ability has led us to a point in history where "God," or the comforts of tradition, have died. It is as though humanity grows up on a social level, as a species we seem to travel, though much more slowly, a similar trajectory to a maturing child. We acquire the reality principle in varying degrees as to suit our needs, likewise with the shedding of the pleasure principle.

We are left to find our own meaning for an existence we continue to prove meaningless, we are anxious about our own demise, and on a civilization level we seem to be hurdling towards it at an incredible rate. Under conditions where meaning is hard to believe in, the body and the id and its instincts are once again becoming paramount to our personal meaning. It appears that now, in more "educated" form, we are regressing back to the conditions of pre-civilized life, where our instinct is king. This time it is different, however, and we are not back where we started as animals, but remain regulated. It seems that we are stuck between a rock (happiness) and a hard place (security) and the only avenues of achievement of either come through the self.

We are an anxious and self-punishing generation. We are not only bracing ourselves for a condition of permanent and irreducible uncertainty, We are living it. We are its products, the anxious bodies of Postmodernity.

REFERENCES

Bauman, Z (1997). *Postmodernity And Its Discontents*. Cambridge, UK: Polity Press.

Bauman, Z (1992).Survival as a Social Construct. *Theory, Culrture & Society.* 9, 1-36.

Beck, U., Giddens, A., Lash, S. *Reflexive Modernization: Politics, Tradition and Aethetics in the Modern Social Order* Chapter 2: Giddens, A. *Living in a Post-Traditional Society* Polity Press

Bordo, S. "Material Girl": The Effacements of Postmodern Culture

Bordo Susan (1997) The Body and the Reproduction of Femininity in Writing on the Body. Columbia University Press.

Bordo Susan (1985-1986) *Anorexia Nervosa: Psychopathology as the Crystallization of Culture*. The Philosophical Forum. Vol. 17, No.2.

Borossa, J (1999). *Selected andor Ferenczi*. London: Penguin Books.

Cash, T (2004).Body Image in an Interpersonal Context: Adult Attachment, Fear of Intimacy, and Social Anxiety. *Journal of Social and Clinical Psychology.* 23, 89-103.

Chartier, M (2003).Considering Comorbidity in Social Phobia. *Social Psychpidemiology.* 38, 728-734.

Coplan, J (1998).Cerebrospinal Fluid Concentrations of Somatostatin and Biogenic Amines in Grown Primates Reared by Mothers Exposed to Manipulated Foraging Conditions. *Archives of General Psychiatry.* 55, 473-477.

Elias, N (1985). *The Loneliness of the Dying.* Oxford: Basil Blackwell.

Edmunds,J. & Turner, B., (2005).Global Generations: Social Change in the Twentieth Century. *The British Journal of Sociology.* 56 Iss.4, 559-577.

Fortune, C (2003).The Analytic Nursery: Ferenczi's 'Wise Baby' meets Jung's 'Divine Child'. *Journal of Analytical Psychology.* 48, 457-466.

Gay, P (1989). *The Freud Reader*. New York, NY: W.W. Norton & Company.

Giddens, A (1991). *Modernity and Self-Identity.* Stanford: Stanford University Press.

Groarke, S (2002).Psychoanalysis and Structuration Theory: The Social Logic of Identity. *Sociology.* 36(3), 559-576.

Hughes, K (2005).The Adult Children of Divorce: Pure Relationships and Family Values?. *Journal of Sociology.* 41(1), 69-86.

Lasch, C (1979). *The Culture of Narcissism.* Norton $ Co..

Lemert, C (1999). *Social Theory: The Multicultural and Classic Readings*. Boulder, Co: Westview Press.

Merikangas, K.R. (2003).Family and High-Risk Studies of Social Anxiety D. *ACTA Psychiatrica Scandinavica.* 108(Suppl.417), 28-37.

Nettleton, S (2006).'I Just Want Permission to be Ill': Towrds a Sociology of Medically Unexplained Symptoms. *Social Science and Medecine.* 62, 1167-1178.

Pippin, R (1999).Nietzche and the Melancholy of Modernity. *Social Research.* 66 No. 2, 495-520.

Rector, N (2006).Social Anxiety and the Fear of Causing Discomfort to Others: Conceptualization and Treatment. *Journal of Social and Clinical Psychology of S.* 25, 906-918.

Sandars, N.K. (1960). *The Epic of Gilgamesh*. London: Penguin Books.

Shilling, C (2003). *The Body and Social Theory.* London: Sage.

Strachey, J (Ed.). *The Standard Edition of the Complete Psychological Works of Sigmund Freud.* London: The Hogarth Press and the Institute of Psycho-Analysis.

Sweetman, P (1999).Anchoring the (Postmodern) Self? Body Modification, Fashion and Identity. *Body and Society.* 5(2-3), 51-76.

Tolstoy, L (1960). *The Death of Ivan Ilyich and Other Stories*. New York, NY: Penguin Putnam.

Twenge, J (2000).The Age of Anxiety? Birth Cohort Change in Anxiety and Neuroticism, 1952-1993. *Journal of Personality and Socoal Psychology.* 79 No. 6, 1007-1021.

Looking Inside Out
A Sociology of Knowledge and Ignorance of Geekness

Johnny Yu

University of Massachusetts Boston

johnny.yu001@umb.edu

Abstract: Geek. Nerd. Dork. Outsider. Anti-social. Outcast. Non-mainstream. No life. All of these words have been used to describe me, and all of them are true to some degree. These are terms used for people who have interests that are outside of popular culture. When a person falls out of the "in" group due to different interests, whether it be from liking things that the dominant group does not approve of or from *not* liking things that the dominant group likes, he gets branded with one (or all) of the above terms. This categorization is a way to separate the insiders and the outsiders, and a hierarchy is established. It is obvious that the outsiders are at the bottom of that arrangement, since all of the terms used to describe them bear a negative connotation. I open this discussion by first looking at myself. I do this because, according to the works of G.I. Gurdjieff, the process of knowing has to start with self-awareness. "The only person who can know myself is *myself* ... no amount of fantasizing about who or what I am will substitute for a direct, dispassionate look at the data" (Speeth). To look at this with such a narrow scope is not good enough, however. The problem of separating popular and geek culture lies far beyond just me or the groups of people I associate with. I move on then to gain a better understanding of the situation by reading the work of Elizabeth Minnich. She explains how divisions have formed, and how groups are excluded. This exclusion is necessary so that the dominant group can de-legitimize all other groups. The root of our problems with knowledge is that we have separated people into groups, or "kinds," as she calls them, and then taken the words of one group as having more significance than all other groups. Minnich goes on to explain that the root problem has led to errors in the way that we construct knowledge, and that there are four main areas where errors occur. She calls them faulty generalization, circular reasoning, mystified concepts, and partial knowledge. The four errors have a tendency to overlap, and they perpetuate each other as well as perpetuate the root problem itself. Looking inside out, and drawing upon Gurdjieff and Minnich, I then try to develop a sociological approach to the knowledge and ignorance of geekness.

Geek. Nerd. Dork. Outsider. Anti-social. Outcast. Non-mainstream. No life.

All of these words have been used to describe me, and all of them are true to some degree. These are terms used for people who have interests that are outside of popular culture. When a person falls out of the "in" group due to different interests, whether it be from liking things that the dominant group does not approve of or from *not* liking things that the dominant group likes, he gets branded with one (or

---

Johnny Yu graduated from UMass Boston, majoring in Social Psychology. He wrote this paper while enrolled in the course Soc. 440: "Sociology of Knowledge and Ignorance," instructed by Mohammad H. Tamdgidi (Assistant Professor of Sociology at UMass Boston) during the Fall 2006 semester.

all) of the above terms. This categorization is a way to separate the insiders and the outsiders, and a hierarchy is established. It is obvious that the outsiders are at the bottom of that arrangement, since all of the terms used to describe them bear a negative connotation.

This system of branding is a problem for many reasons. For one thing, it is a system that turns a difference in the preference of trivial interests, such as what kind of music people listen to and what forms of entertainment they enjoy, into marked divisions. With people thusly divided, it establishes that one particular culture, the "popular culture," is superior and more acceptable than the unpopular culture. Finally, the people who aren't in the "in" group find it impossible to break out of their ascribed identities. They find that they need to conform and change what their interests are to avoid being labeled as anti-social or geeky, even if the terms are not accurate descriptions of their characters.

I personally relate to this issue because I am a geek, in many ways. I have an interest in and work well with computers and the internet. I entertain myself with video games and trading card games. Much of the music in my collection is made by non-American artists, with names that few people have ever even heard of. I do not go to clubs, I do not actively date, and I do not watch sports. These are all trivial things, yet it's enough for people to describe me as anti-social, an outsider, and someone who has no life. I could never figure out why my choice in entertainment had so much bearing on my character, and why it is such a source of division.

I will open this discussion by first looking at myself. I do this because, according to the works of G.I. Gurdjieff, the process of knowing has to start with self-awareness. "The only person who can know myself is *myself* ... no amount of fantasizing about who or what I am will substitute for a direct, dispassionate look at the data" (Speeth 73). It is a difficult, and perhaps impossible, task, but looking at my experiences without bias and questioning my impressions and memories help me draw as clear a picture as I can possibly draw.

One of the important concepts from Gurdjieff's work is that of questioning how you think. "Judge everything from the point of view of your common sense. Become the possessor of your own sound idea, and don't accept anything on faith; and when you, yourself, by way of sound reasoning and argument, come to an unshakable persuasion, to a full understanding of something, you will have achieved a certain degree of initiation" (Gurdjieff 27). Looking deeply into how I formed my own thoughts, I can begin to see how muddled they are. My identity isn't as much based on how I see myself as it is on how I present myself to the world. I am only a geek because other people have told me I am a geek. With that in mind, I have conformed to their definition of what a geek is.

Recognizing that my own thoughts could interfere with my quest for the truth is the first, and most difficult, step. "Sometimes subconscious barriers need to be broken before a person can become aware" (Cohen 10). The problem with subconscious barriers is that it's difficult to know that they even exist. My preference for geek culture, for gaming, and for associating with that group could be caused by unconscious spite. Perhaps my years in high school being out of the "in" group have nurtured a sort of disdain for all things mainstream. This may have evolved over time into a tendency to "go against the flow." While this would be a logical explanation, it is not complete. I do conform to mainstream things if they fit within my realm of reason.

Thinking critically about my own thoughts brought me to a realization. I was thinking of myself as my ascribed character and using the definition that the dominant culture had given. I had always assumed that that definition was correct. So while I have thought of myself as anti-social, closer analysis of my everyday dealings reveal that nothing could be farther from the truth. Much of my time is spent interacting with people, whether it is with classmates and friends at school or through instant messaging over the internet. Most of the games I play involve other people, and in the case of games over the internet, there are even social interactions with people I have never been in the same physical room with. This *is* being social, but because it is not the mainstream way of socializing (going to clubs, bars, "hanging out"), it becomes invalid.

I had always seen myself as an outsider, but again, I've come to realize that that is also a flawed term. I am outside of popular culture, but I am inside of the geek culture. If simple things such as liking *Lord of the Rings* or *Star Wars* is enough to label someone a geek, then the geek culture has a rather sizable population. It is this population that I end up associating with when I play my games. This shows that "outsider" is a relative term, and is not an accurate way to describe me. It was my own fault for believing that I didn't "fit in," when it would have been more accurate to say that I merely did not fit in with popular culture. I do fit in somewhere, and that does not make me an outsider.

The "problem" of being a geek is not my fault. I have become pushed into that category by others, and my belief in the validity of the labeling system helped influence my preferences. This situation bears a striking similarity to a SUNY-Oneonta student's discovery of the sociological imagination. When talking about her social anxiety disorder, Murray writes, "I alone am not the cause of my anxieties and phobias ... The world around me influences my everyday behaviors" (Murray 52). I did not arrive at my geek identity by myself. The world around me labeled me a particular way due to my activities. There are certain criteria that give people the geek label, and I happened to fulfill enough of them.

I have no reason to feel like the geek community is somehow a "lesser" community. My experiences with the trading card game *Magic: the Gathering* has taught me that communities centered around a simple game can be very strong. When I first started the game, it was at a friend's suggestion. I had never played a trading card game before, and I didn't know what it would be like. The owner of the store, who sold me the cards, thought I was already into the game, and informed me that Saturday is "open gaming night." I asked him what that meant, and he said that that was when the tables in the store were free for anyone to come in to use for gaming, completely free of charge. He also said that they have a regular group of about twenty people who show up every weekend just to play.

I had no idea that *Magic* was such a social game at first. The fact that so many people from so many places would gather at this cramped Hobby Bunker store just to play this game fascinated me. After learning as much of the game as I could on my own, I went back to Hobby Bunker one Saturday and was astounded. In the back were about twenty people, separated into groups of four or so depending on who got there with whom. These people were all talking, laughing, playing, trading, and overall enjoying themselves. I didn't immediately feel like I belonged, newcomer as I was to the game, and found it difficult to approach and sit. One of them took notice of me and introduced himself as "John." He and his play group were from Everett, a town bordering Malden, my hometown. He had to travel to the store by bus for a half-hour. I introduced myself and told him I was new to the game. He demonstrated a few matches against a friend, explaining everything along the way to help me get a feel for the general flow of the game. Just before the store closed, John handed me a pile of common cards and told me I could have them. I went home looking forward to the next weekend, eager to play the game more often with my newfound friends.

The game was very fresh and exciting to me at the time. I could never figure out what it is about Magic that is so exciting. Perhaps it is the way the cards can interact with each other, allowing a strategic player to combine several cards for devastating effects. Perhaps it is the competition of seeing who can build a better deck or pilot their decks better. Perhaps it is the mystery of going against a new opponent, or someone who secretly built a new deck and wants to put it to the test. Whatever it was, Magic drew me in quite quickly, and I found myself wanting to build unique decks to pummel my opponents with.

I noticed over the weekends following that different people from different towns started showing up. Some faces I saw in previous weeks disappeared, as well. It wasn't until three weeks later that I saw John again, but during that time, I was playing duels with those strangers from other towns. The way I was accepted and how I accepted them was something I never truly gave much thought to until now. We were total, complete strangers, but because we played Magic, we were friends. Instantly, we were a community. We would make trades, discuss the cards, or help tune each others' decks. It didn't even matter if the following week a different group walked in. There would be the same friendliness and sense of community. Someone who is not inside this community would not necessarily be able to see that it even exists.

In order to stay in any group, I would have had to exhibit certain qualities. Erving Goffman calls this "impression management," and the term is rather self-explanatory. If I at least pretended that I liked sports or listened to popular music, and hid my true preferences, I would still be in the popular group. But as Sheerin Hosseini, a student at UMass Boston, described it, "I know that almost everyone engages in impression management at one time or another, to influence society. Still, I feel that something is wrong in our society that everyone has to alter their true selves to show themselves in a more favorable light" (31). The problem is not my inability to manage my image to the liking of the popular group. Rather, it is a problem with popular culture for finding my differences to be problematic.

A certain level of impression management would be needed in order to stay in the geek culture as well, but it does not seem as strict as in popular culture. Being in an outcast group, someone would probably find it harder to get *out* of geek culture than to get into it. The geek community can be broken down into subgroups, but they still share something in common. Whether you are a gamer geek, a computer geek, or a goth geek, you are a geek simply because you are not mainstream enough to be in the larger popular group. Whatever group you've chosen to identify with, you would need to tailor your image so that you fit into it.

To get at my motivation for being a gamer and a geek, I want to go back to Gurdjieff. "It is not enough to understand with the mind, it is necessary to feel with your being the absolute truth and immutability of this fact; only then will you be able, consciously and with conviction, to say 'I know'" (Gurdjieff 15). It is one thing to use sociological theory to say that I am managing my impression and whatnot, but it is something entirely different when I try to come up with my own conclusion. I do think that I get a genuine feeling of satisfaction when my geek identity is affirmed. I like being different from mainstream culture. Knowing this, though, it's hard to say that it is my only motivation. Still, it is good that I can even point this out.

Being self-aware is only the first step, but it is crucial. Instead of being trapped in the role of the geek, I can choose to break out of it or not at my discretion. Just by knowing that I gain satisfaction from being different, and being able to objectively see myself as being motivated by something so simple, I can consciously make better choices. Gurdjieff describes this consciousness as being "awake." The opposite would be being "asleep," where a person goes about his life without questioning what motivates him. It is a sort of prison, and if someone is not aware that he is trapped, he can never get out of it. The main difference between the awake and the asleep is that a person who is asleep does everything as an unconscious reaction to the world, while a person who is awake would be able to observe his reactions consciously and then choose whether or not to react.

To look at this with such a narrow scope is not good enough, however. The problem of separating popular and geek culture lies far beyond just me or the groups of people I associate with. I have gained a better understanding of the situation after reading the work of Elizabeth Minnich. She explains how divisions have formed, and how groups are excluded. This exclusion is necessary so that the dominant group can de-legitimize all other groups. The root of our problems with knowledge is that we have separated people into groups, or "kinds," as she calls them, and then taken the words of one group as having more significance than all other groups. "It is about changing *what* and, just as important, *how* we think so that we no longer perpetuate the old exclusions and devaluations of the majority of humankind that have pervaded informal as well as formal schooling in the United States and around the world" (Minnich 49). To fix the problem means changing the way we think. It is not a path of choosing not to acknowledge the differences in people's preferences for entertainment. Rather, it is the path of not letting those differences become divisions.

Minnich goes on to explain that the root problem has led to errors in the way that we construct knowledge, and that there are four main areas where errors occur. "Four basic kinds of errors derive from and lock in the root problem of turning *distinctions* among groupings of particular people into abstract, hierarchical *divisions* by 'kind' such that a particular few emerge as the imperially inclusive 'kind' or term, the norm, and the ideal for all" (Minnich 104). She calls them faulty generalization, circular reasoning, mystified concepts, and partial knowledge. The four errors have a tendency to overlap, and they perpetuate each other as well as perpetuate the root problem itself.

The first of these errors, termed faulty generalizations, is a relatively simple concept. It is taking a narrow view and using it as a representation of the entire picture. She also calls this "universalization," which may help clarify her meaning of this term. It is the process of changing the meaning of all-inclusive terms to actually refer to a small population. She uses examples such as "religion" usually being generalized to "Christianity" and "philosophy" being generalized to "Western philosophy." What this does is it excludes different groups, and makes it so that one group is more legitimate and more valid than others. We make faulty generalizations subconsciously. For example, if I told you I was deeply religious, chances are that you would think I believed in God. The fact that "religion" and "Christianity" have become synonymous in many American minds is a symptom of this error in thinking.

Faulty generalizations serve to set a norm, usually on the basis of majority. It establishes that a particular group, like Christians as an example, is the normal and default, with all other religions being deviations. This line of thinking, when applied to something like culture, serves to make one group more correct while labeling all others as deviant. This is what causes geeks to be looked down upon. From this error is born the idea that there are such things as normal choices of entertainment. Anyone who chooses to enjoy different things is a deviant.

Circular reasoning is the second error, and ties in very closely with the first. A circular statement is one that proves itself by referring to itself, which is logically unsound. The problem of separating people into different "kinds," leads to having to set boundaries and to patrol them. Setting boundaries means defining the different kinds so that accurate categorization can happen. Circular reasoning comes from attempting to set up these boundaries. Assertions such as "Females are more intuitive than rational" and "Blacks have rhythm" are examples of this circular way of thinking. They look, on the surface, like descriptive statements, but they are, in reality, *prescriptive* statements (Minnich 154). Rather than being statements that generalize a particular population's properties, they are descriptions of what those groups are *supposed* to be (or not supposed to be). It is, in a sense, working backwards. You could take a group of geeks and make a statement that describes them, or you could make a statement first and then categorize everyone who fits that statement as a geek. Looking at it rationally, the first method would be more accurate for categorizing different "kinds" of people, but circular reasoning will more often involve the second method.

This error is problematic because it leads to statements that cannot be contradicted. An example of circular reasoning would be if I took a common stereotype like "Gamers are anti-social." One would think that contradicting this statement would be as simple as finding a gamer who likes to socialize. However, because of the circular reasoning, this is not the case. If I find a gamer who has many friends, goes to parties, and is sociable overall, then the usual counter-argument would be that this person is not a gamer. The original statement was disguised as a description of gamers, but it really is just a way of "diagnosing" a gamer. It is really saying, "If you are social, then you are *not* a gamer."

The third error that Minnich describes is mystified concepts. This refers to the way certain ideas are given monolithic, exaggerated status so that they take on their own meaning. This meaning is usually some sort of distortion of the literal definition of the concept. Examples that Minnich uses are "gender," "sex," and "equality." In the dominant U.S. culture, Minnich claims that "equality" has been historically confused with "sameness" (Minnich 179). When minorities and women are fighting for equality, they are not looking for this "sameness." It is not enough that these oppressed groups have the "same" opportunities as the white, male, dominant groups. Yet, it is often cited that the fact that women and blacks can attend colleges is proof of "equality," and then the argument ends there. Equality is a mystified concept because it is a distortion. It is not aiming for sameness, because sameness is impossible. Individuals and groups of individuals cannot be completely same nor completely different from each other. In addition to that, oppressed and excluded groups already have a history of being outside of the norm. Having already been branded deviant, "sameness" for them means they have to prove they are "as good as" the dominant group.

This becomes relevant to geek culture because geeks are the oppressed group versus the popular culture. The statements on equality brings up one very important property of the oppressed groups. They are always on the defensive. As a geek, I have to prove myself to be as good as those in popular culture. I have to justify that my form of socializing is at least as good as their form of socializing. I am defending the artists of the music I listen to by citing their other works and what their fame is in countries outside of the United States.

Someone within popular culture does not need to defend his choices of preference. His choices are already perceived as the norm, and are therefore already correct. Only the deviants need to prove that they have merit.

The last of Minnich's four errors is what she calls "partial knowledge." The term "partial" does not mean only knowing a piece of the full picture, as it might suggest. She is instead referring to partiality—the idea that knowledge can be and actually is biased. She exemplifies this concept when she talks about religion, or more specifically, Christianity. "We have had histories that tell of the 'martyrs' who died for the faith that ultimately won, while the martyrs among those who lost have been called 'heretics,' 'infidels,' 'unbelievers,' 'superstitious Natives'" (Minnich 232). The winning side tells the story, and it tells it in a very particular way. This statement points out that the winners are always put in a good light, such as these martyrs who have given their lives to what is undeniably the "right" cause. The losers, who had also given their lives, only got what they deserved.

Why partial knowledge is a problem lies in the fact that it is always disguised as impartial knowledge. It is impossible for knowledge coming from human minds to not be tainted by human bias. The problem here is not to say that we should be aiming for knowledge that is completely objective, as that would be an impossible task. The problem lies in our false claim that some of our knowledge is absolutely free of bias. We have to get away from that lofty claim because it simply is not true. The result of believing that something is impartial when it really is not is that we take that knowledge for granted. It becomes something that cannot be challenged, in a sense, morphing into a monolithic, "mystified" concept. If the story of the winner is already taken as objective truth, then the losers' view of the situation would already be seen as "the other side of the story." The "other" already implies that it is biased, and inherently incorrect, when compared to the "objective," unbiased point of view.

The concept of partial knowledge serves the dominant group, and this is how it ties into my situation. Popular culture already establishes that certain trends are correct. This extends beyond just geeks and gamers; it applies to all people outside of the established norm. Certain activities, whether it be watching sports, eating meat, or drinking alcohol, are considered socially healthy. Even if groups outside of the norm such as vegetarians do not see things this way, they are considered to be wrong. Their point of view has been tainted by any number of things, whether it be because they are environmentalists or lovers of animals. If you are a part of the meat-eating "norm," though, your view is not considered tainted. The benefit and the downfall of the dominant group is its refusal to self-criticize.

Groups are separated into insiders and outsiders, oppressors and the oppressed, the dominant and the submissive, haves and haves not. Looking at the situation this way, using a wider scope than just my own personal experiences, it is easier to understand exactly what being a geek is. It explains why even though my own feelings are that I am correct, I still feel like I am wrong. There has always been this looming suspicion that even though I am enjoying being different from the norm and cannot imagine being a part of the larger crowd, I am somehow going down the wrong path. If the majority is acting differently from me, then wouldn't it make more sense that *I* am incorrect? It turns out, though, that my looming suspicious are probably because of what Minnich calls the root problem and her four main errors. I am one of the deviant "kinds." Therefore, the dominant culture has set up a system to make all other kinds illegitimate. I, being a part of this vast system, am feeling its effects. Even if through self-reflection I find that I am comfortable with the way I live, the bigger society is working to make me conform. It attacks me, and all outsiders at a deep level—it make us doubt our lifestyles. It constantly reminds us that we are wrong, and they are right. It makes us measure rightness and wrongness by their scale, which is arbitrary, and we always find ourselves ending up at the bottom of that scale.

In the David Yates film *The Girl in the Cafe*, the female protagonist is an example of the personal effects of being an outcast. My experiences as an outsider are similar to hers. She is regarded as a simple-minded, uneducated girl who does not know what she is talking about at the G8 Summit, and the people there did not initially take her seriously. She did not sum up her knowledge in statistics and numbers and bars and graphs, nor did she have a list of references to cite. She did not follow the format of what was considered correct knowledge, and so her ideas were seen as too simplistic. She was thus seeing herself as already dead, because her voice meant nothing to anyone. Her ideas were not bad, and they made perfect sense to her, but all that mattered was that they did not make sense to the leaders at the G8 summit—the people who have already defined what "true" knowledge should be.

As an outsider, I find myself feeling dead as well sometimes. There are things that I cannot say about myself when I'm with particular crowds. I cannot be taken seriously as a scholar if I admit that many of my hobbies are games. If I say that I am a gamer, and that my thoughts are constantly occupied by ways to strategize in all of these games that I play, I will somehow become less of a person. I would be discredited, because even if I have salient and profound things to say, I will be seen as childish—a grown man who still likes to play with cardboard, dice, controllers, and joysticks.

Another issue that the Yates film brought up also relates to Gina's feeling dead inside. In the film, she went to prison for harming or perhaps killing a man who abused a child. In her mind, it is wrong for anyone to harm a child. That was her logic and her reasoning, and the action that she took was justified as far as she determined. However, society punished her for harming the man who harmed the child. The justice system set up its own code of rightness and wrongness, and found her guilty. She was poor, she was a woman, and she harmed a man. As far as the dominant group was concerned, she was wrong, on many counts. It did not matter what her justification was, because her judgment was clearly not as unbiased, objective, and just as that of the judicial system.

I had an interesting thought as I was watching the 1999 film *Tuesdays with Morrie*. In it, the character Morrie, based on the real life story of the sociologist Morrie Schwartz who taught at Brandeis, is slowly dying of Lou Gherig's disease. The whole film centers around one of his former students coming to grips with his relationships to people, and to Morrie in particular. Morrie mentions as he is dying that there are certain things that people do not talk about because they are afraid to talk about it. Death is one of those things. Death is the failure of the body, and inevitably leads to the idea that the body will cease to function. The reason why people fear death is because it reflects a life that is not fulfilled. The fear of death mirrors an unsatisfied life. Talking about it means confronting it, and many people are not ready to accept the inevitability of death.

This relates to my situation because it lends me a small bit of insight on what is going on inside the insider. The insider conforms because he does not want to confront himself. He does not want to go through a process of self-criticizing, of doing something different, and of possibly being wrong. He is taking for granted the information provided to him by other insiders, and not questioning their rightness or wrongness because doing so would force him to question himself. He wants to go along with the notion that he is different and superior from those on the outside. Otherwise, it would open up the possibility that the insiders and the outsiders are one and the same, and perhaps that is the scariest thought of all. Once you are in the dominant group, you should be concerned with differentiating yourself from the outside groups.

At this point, I do not know if I am settled with this issue. It seems that even if I understand the system of oppression at a cognitive level, there is little I can do about the emotional level. I still feel like I should be ashamed and should be cautious with whom I share with. As comfortable and satisfied as I am with my deviations from the norm, there are still times where I feel like I'm doing something wrong, and that I should aim for the comfort of conformity. Social life would certainly be much easier if I conformed. I would be legitimate, I would be taken seriously, and I would be alive. But then I would not be me.

REFERENCES

Cohen, Samara. 2002. "I Only *thought* I Knew it All: Society and the Individual" in Vol. I, Issue 1, of *Human Architecture: Journal of the Sociology of Self-Knowledge*, 9-17.

Gurdjieff, George Ivanovitch. *Views from the Real World*. New York and Chicago (Arkana S.).

Hosseini, Sheerin. 2005. "Accepting Myself: Negotiating Self-Esteem and Conformity in Light of Sociological Theories" in Vol. IV, Issue 1&2, of *Human Architecture: Journal of the Sociology of Self-Knowledge*, 29-43.

Minnich, Elizabeth Kamarck. 2004. *Transforming Knowledge*. Temple University Press; 2nd edition. ISBN: 159213131X

Murray, Megan. 2003. "Treading Water: Self-Reflections on Generalized Anxiety Disorder" in Vol. II, Issue 1, of *Human Architecture: Journal of the Sociology of Self-Knowledge*, 50-57.

Speeth, Kathleen Riordan. *The Gurdjieff Work*. ISBN: 0874774926

Films:

"The Girl in the Cafe." HBO Home Video, 2005.
"Tuesdays with Morrie." Touchstone, 1999.

Parallel Dualisms
Understanding America's Apathy for the Homeless through the Sociological Imagination

Colin Allen

University of Massachusetts Boston

colin.james.allen@gmail.com

Abstract: Drawing various sources in Spencer E. Cahill's anthology, *Inside Social Life* (2004), the author, a First Year Seminar student at UMass Boston and an honor student, contrasts the contradiction found in his own personal life between what one thinks of oneself and what one actually does, with the contradiction at the societal level between sympathy offered to the homeless and what the society does about it. Such parallel dualisms experienced via the author's sociological imagination then leads him to explore, from a social psychological standpoint, various facets of the American culture and society as they relate to the problem of homelessness.

When the professor spoke about how dualism has become ingrained in much of our thinking and personalities, I initially shrugged off the idea as merely rhetoric. I knew that distinct dualisms existed in people, responsible for their inner fragmentation, such as in the case of people with Multiple Personality Disorder and perhaps with Manic Depression. Everyone would recognize the profound dualisms and fragmentations in people diagnosed with these disorders. Yet, we rarely acknowledge the subtle dualisms and fragmentations we all carry within ourselves. These dualisms may also be observed in society at large, in this case, the American culture and social policy. One dualism that pervades our lives in modern urban America is that of the dualism in our attitude toward the homeless: how we think about them vs. what actions we take on those feelings.

A quick look at one dualism experienced in my own life can be a good window for understanding the dualisms populating the American culture. My experience throughout grade school and high school was fairly consistent. Much of it revolved around the "potential" I showed, which I was constantly reminded of by my parents and teachers, and one which I rarely fully achieved. However, in college, the structure in my life was pulled out from under me, and suddenly the only one reminding me of my potential was me, and needless to say I was not achieving it. I think "potential" is one of the most important, and somewhat abstract, concepts in life. The disconnect between who I was and who I

Colin Allen is an undergraduate student at UMass Boston, majoring in Business. He wrote this paper while enrolled in the First Year, Seminar Soc. 110G-1: "Insiders/Outsiders," instructed by Mohammad H. Tamdgidi (Assistant Professor of Sociology at UMass Boston) during the Fall 2006 semester.

knew that I could be was shocking, and it sent me into a deep depression. I knew I could be getting A's, I wasn't. I knew I could work out in the gym and it would boost my confidence, I didn't. I knew that I should go to class and not just sleep all day, I didn't. It was not what I was doing; it was the fact that I knew what I was doing wrong and I simply continued to do it. I also knew that turning my life around and lining up my inner desires to achieve with my outward actions would make me a very content person; but I didn't.

I feel my situation is analogous to the United States and its stance on homelessness. For over 50 years, the problem of hunger and homelessness in America has not been a problem of resources, but a problem of inaction. It is an established fact that we have the resources to feed everyone in this country. And I'm also fairly sure that if I asked 100 people on the street whether or not they would want America to eliminate hunger and homelessness in our own country, nearly 100 people would respond with "yes." It's basically a no-brainer. So if we have the resources, and we definitely have the desire, why does it not happen? I would submit that it doesn't happen mainly for the same reason that I do not work out and I don't necessarily do all of my homework. It simply needs to be a priority, and yet it is certainly not. This contrast in what we do and what we ought to do is a dualism that pervades not only much of our everyday lives, but also the social structures and institutions with which we identify ourselves.

I would submit that one's initial reaction to the sight of a homeless person or persons is one of sympathy, and this initial reaction cannot simply be discarded because that sympathy is not acted upon. Rather, we must look at the profound disconnect between that initial reaction and the subsequent reflection. Oliver Sacks popularized this **dualistic conception of perception/reflection** when he wrote about the experience of his catatonic patients which was subsequently turned into a motion picture called *Awakenings*; Robin Williams played his role in the film. Sacks's patients looked like stone statues, with little to offer in the way of interaction, and thus were overlooked by other doctors, but Sacks did not judge solely based on his initial perception. He reasoned that there must be some way to cure these people of their ailment, and he would have never been able to help them had he not continued to reflect past the stage of initial perception. Similarly, the impetus to *not* react on the initial sympathy that one feels towards homeless people must have been caused during the reflection stage of thinking, and must be powerful enough to override the initial **sympathetic sentiment of the observer to another individual**.

There are a few reasons why, upon reflection, the feeling of sympathy becomes diluted or simply changes to a different feeling, almost always one less sympathetic than at first. From the sociologist Charles Horton Cooley we learn that a specific self that people often identify with is **the self as a feeling of possession or appropriation**. Within the framework of this specific self, people feel as though they are defined (and define themselves) by the materials that they possess. But this self may not be as "natural" a process in one's upbringing as one may think, and certainly not limited to an initial stage in development of our selves. As seen in the movie *Affluenza*, this problem has increasingly reached near epidemic proportions in the U.S. As a result of living in a capitalist, profit-driven society like ours, where material possessions often define the man or woman, the sight of a man or woman with literally almost no possessions is not normal to say the least. As people strive for the higher paycheck, the nicer car, the bigger house, they cannot imagine the feeling of having nothing to one's own name. Although sympathy can be derived from this, a feeling of implied responsibility is placed on the homeless, the thought that that person is in that situation because of what he or she did, and if the observer had been in his or her shoes, he or she never would have ended up there in the first place. Many people who pass by the homeless truly believe that s/he must have done something wrong along the way to somehow deserve or at least cause the situation that s/he is now faced with. Affluent businesspersons may believe that regardless of where they had grown up or what situation they had been born into, they still would have achieved their current level of success, overcoming whatever obstacles were in their way to get there. Though this logic is clearly not correct in many cases, I would submit that it is wholly irrelevant to the problem of homelessness, and should not affect one's desire, or lack thereof, to help those in need.

The work of the philosopher and sociologist George Herbert Mead can also be useful in interpreting how we can account for the public's behavior relating to the homeless. Mead agreed with the proposition that **in all of us multiple selves** exist, a state which is, in most cases, a normal occurrence (Mead 1962). Two "selves" that I think are most pertinent are (what one may awkwardly call) the self-defined self---i.e., the internal conception of oneself, and how one would like to be portrayed to others---and **the empirical self,** or the person we actually are as determined by our actions (Mead 1962). Another way of distinguishing this is that of contrasting between who we think we are, and who we actually are. In this case, these two identities clash. Most people define themselves as somewhat compassionate people who care for the wellbeing of others, regardless of their social-economic, racial, or cultural background. But in practice the empirical self does not live up to the high ideals that the self-defined self sets. In short, people are generally worse people than they say or think they are, and rarely the other way around. This dualistic nature of the individual's thinking/acting naturally applies to the society in which the individual was cultivated. Jerome Bruner expresses this social dualism: "For all our power to construct symbolic cultures and to set in place the institutional forces needed for their execution, we do not seem very adept at steering our creations toward the ends we profess to desire" (Bruner 1990:13).

This duality is also seen through other traditions with which people tend to identify. Take religion for example. In 2001, 79.8% of Americans identified themselves as Christian (Wikipedia 2006). Increasingly, however, people are straying from the true meaning and spirit behind Christianity. This can be seen in people's lack of care for the problem of homelessness and in people's subscription to the "just war theory," which are in quite a contrast to Jesus's clearly caring and non-violence teaching.

There must be other reasons that the homeless, who account for about 1% of the population in the U.S. (Washington Profile 2006), receive a disproportionately small degree of attention. One reason is the media. Mead introduced the concept of the "**generalized other**," and Melissa Milkie, in her article on the media's influence on adolescent girls, took that concept one step further by saying that the "media may have become a significant part of the generalized other---that is, the 'society' we know" (Milkie 1999:48). The generalized other, especially in the media, is suspiciously lacking of the most unfortunate members of our society. In the movie *Affluenza*, it is stated that the average child will have seen 1 million TV ads by the age of 20. I would submit that the amount of ads that pertain to the homeless or the problem of homelessness account for less than .01% of those ads, disproportionate to the percentage of society that they represent. In TV shows also, the homeless are shockingly absent from the "culture" that the media has fabricated.

Only with true observation and understanding of our inner reactions to the homeless can we see why little action is taken on the subject. The problem is so easily avoidable, one may think. Because the issue of homelessness is never on the front burner, and people are never forced to align their internal sympathy with their empirical self, if everyone were made to reflect on the subject, perhaps to write about it, people may understand better the cavernous gap between what they claim they would do and whether or not they actually take action. As Louise DeSalvo states in her book *Writing as a Way of Healing*, writing and reflecting would "force us into an awareness about ourselves and our relationship to others and our place in the world that we wouldn't have otherwise had" (1999:5). With the help of this cathartic and illuminating thought, the public may realize the situation that our society is in.

However, the problem lies in the fact that we have **reified the concept of homelessness**: we have accepted the phenomenon of homelessness as a true, natural thing when it is our very system that has created it. In doing so, we have not only forgotten the millions left homeless, but we have also made the classic blunder of accepting a socially created problem as a natural occurrence, and thus stifled our ability to progress. And because, as Clifford Geertz put it, **"there is no such thing as human nature independent of culture"** (Bruner 1990:9), society's values are reflected in the individual; "by virtue of participation in culture, meaning is rendered public and shared" (Bruner 1990:9). As Ayan Ahmed notes in her article, "The Complexity of Naïve Acceptance of Socially Manipulated Beliefs," it is society's "routines that define its realities" (2003:1). And nowhere is that more true than in our daily routine of walking by homeless and ignoring them.

As we saw in the film *Awakenings*, however, true shifts in perspectives can occur. We saw cold, unfeeling, almost robotic doctors break from their routines and eventually grasp that their patients, even the ones stricken with the most debilitating ailments, are real people, and deserve the best of what the doctors can offer. Rather than disregarding his patients with vague diagnoses, Dr. Sayer (the role for the real life author and physician, Oliver Sacks, played in the film by Robin Williams) put all his attention on curing his patients, and regardless of whether he was successful in the long run, legitimately tried to help a group of people that had long since been stigmatized at the hospital. The homeless, similar to the patients in the hospital, are real people with real feelings, regardless of the fact that few acknowledge these feelings, as it is easier to ignore them. The longer they are ignored, the more stigmatized they become, and the more they are viewed as mere inconveniences to society, "objects of contamination" (1993:128), as Snow and Anderson put it.

There are many reasons why the homeless are constantly overlooked, and I would argue that most of those reasons are not a result of the homeless person's appearance, but more about the intricate and almost immediate reaction within the "overlooker's" head. As Erving Goffman notes in his piece, "Face-Work and Interaction Rituals," routine social interaction primarily is focused around convincing others of one's *social worth* (1967:156). But when the average person off the street interacts with a homeless person, there is no doubt about who is of greater *"social worth,"* and thus there is no need for any interaction. On the flipside of this matter, it would be difficult for a homeless person to convince the average person that he is socially valuable, and thus, conversation is still not warranted.

Wheelchair users are subjected to *dehumanizing interaction* in much the same way the homeless are. In a public setting, people with visible disabilities note that people simply avoid looking at them, as if they do not exist (Cahill and Eggleston 1994). Aside from the possible discomfort that some may feel, it is important to question why people treat other people as "non-human" and not worthy of interaction. Candace Clark, in her essay "Sympathy Biography and Relationships," introduces the concept of *sympathy margin*, the amount of sympathy one has a right to claim (Clark 1987:218). Clark goes on to define the rules of the "economy of sympathy," the second of which is "do not claim too much sympathy" (1987:221). I would posit that when one sees a homeless person or a person with a physical disability, there is a certain amount of implied sympathy that the observer thinks is being asked of him or her. Walking by a homeless person, an observer feels as though his sympathy is being asked of him, regardless of whether or not it is. After some amount of time, most likely before adulthood, the observer has witnessed enough of this, and now determines that the homeless are claiming too much sympathy, thus violating rule number two of the sympathy economy, and in effect, excludes them from being granted any sympathy whatsoever. Another main point that Clark makes is of the *reciprocal nature of the sympathy economy* (1987). Sympathy is granted to those that the sympathizer believes could possibly sympathize with him in the future. Relating back to Goffman, the homeless are believed to have almost no *social worth*, thus their sympathy has very little value. Just as "gifts of sympathy given by superiors…are imbued with greater value than the same gift from an equal or an inferior" (Clark 1987:226), the sympathy gift from a homeless person would be viewed as having little or no value compared to the sympathy from an equal. Due to the fact that the sympathy economy is reciprocal in nature, and that sympathy from a homeless person carries little or no value, people feel as though the homeless have no right to claim sympathy from them.

The fact of the matter is that regardless of the reason for such dehumanizing interaction, it is a self-perpetuating cycle. As Bruner points out, "society exists in action and must be seen in terms of action" (1998:320). That is to say that the treatment of the homeless, the constant apathy and disregard, is only a trend because day in and day out, that treatment is continued. Even the fact that we have a term, "homeless," for these people is a good example. This term is a prime example of a *master status* (Anderson 1990) when we refer to their individuals. If someone is deemed "homeless," that sole attribute takes priority over all other descriptors, and immediately we start to subconsciously conceptualize what that person looks like, what their *social worth* is, etc. We can dismiss someone as homeless, which is a lot easier and more pleasant than thinking about how terrible his or her life actually is and thinking about how he or she got there and what can be done to help. As long as they are treated like "non-people," they will continue to be "non-people."

The perpetuation of this dehumanizing behavior is analogous to the German citizens during the Holocaust, although certainly to a lesser extent. This behavior characterizes the *"banality of evil,"* as Hannah Arendt put it. The theory of evil arising from "ordinary persons [acting] in ordinary contexts" (Berger 2002:399), I would argue, is also applicable in this situation. Just because something is ordinary, typical, or common does not make it inherently not evil, and the dehumanization and mistreatment of the homeless is a prime example.

In Joel Best and Frank Furedi's article "The Evolution of Road Rage," we see that people will jump on a bandwagon of media attention in order to attract more attention to their particular problem that they want to push into the spotlight. This piggybacking of interests onto a social problem with high visibility is not a new phenomenon. We rarely see, however, media attention on the homeless, much for the same reason that people avoid eye contact with the homeless; out of sight, out of mind. In the rare instances that the homeless do make it into the news, it is because of stories of horrific violence or unbearable weather conditions. A few days a year, when the temperature in Boston is around its lowest in the year, we sometimes see the homeless on the news getting blankets, or news anchors warning that people could die overnight if unprotected from the harsh cold. At that point, most people turn to the person they're watching the news with and say, "Boy, that would suck, huh?" But we never see stories without a hook, without some kind of reason that the homeless are on the news, aside from the fact that they live in continual uncertainty about where they will eat, get water, or sleep.

Just this past March a homeless man, who was sleeping in Langone Park in the North End, was doused with lighter fluid and set on fire. That story made the news, and people naturally were appalled, but very few people probably imagined that if he hadn't been set on fire, that man would have never been on the news, and he most likely would have continued to live anonymously, out of sight and out of mind of the public. In fact, "hunger and homelessness increasing in the US" has been the fourth most marginalized story of 2005-2006 (Klotzer 2006:27). The main point here is that homelessness is a horrific problem in and of itself, and yet people need some extra incentive to put it on the news. Like when we walk down the street and see a homeless person, we are fully aware of their terrible situation, but it's just shy of bad enough to actually do something.

Another reason that people may fear homeless interaction is the same reason that people fear getting old, dying, showing emotion. All of these fears revolve around dependence and/or vulnerability. One theme brought up in the film *Tuesdays with Morrie* is the "shame of dependence." Mitch tells Morrie that he "never cries," and Morrie deduces that Mitch is afraid to show emotion; he also tells Mitch that he is afraid of dying and of getting old. When Mitch first comes for his weekly visit, he is clearly uncomfortable with Morrie's dependence on his caretaker and his frail and vulnerable body. Here we see a duality inside Mitch, seeing his teacher in such a state makes him want to care for him, but at the same time, the sight of it makes him uneasy, and he wishes that he didn't have to see it. This is not surprising to Morrie, however, who writes in his book, "be prepared to deal with profound contradictory feelings" (Schwartz 1997:46). Morrie was aware that dualities are normal, and in some cases, those dualities may become apparent.

The homeless are ignored much in the way that people ignore those with physical ailments, or those who are dying. It is easier to ignore these people than to go through the process of psycho-sociologically analyzing oneself to understand why it is we ignore these people in the first place. Morrie understands this, and, in time, allows Mitch to cure his own *"dis-ease" about mortality* (Cahill and Eggleston[1] 1994). I believe that creating similar opportunities for meeting the homeless would also cure an observer's "dis-ease" around them. Such "Tuesdays with a Homeless Person" scenario would forcibly expose people to what they are uncomfortable with, and force them to deal with it.

So what can be done about the situation? How can people act in a less dehumanizing manner towards the homeless? Aside from giving money and/or volunteering at a drop-in center like Rosie's Place, there are other ways in which we can, through simple self-observation, analyze the way we treat people inhumanely, whether subtly or otherwise. One simple and powerful change people, and I for that

---

[1] The concept is adapted from Cahill and Eggleston's term regarding discomfort around wheelchair users.

matter, can make is to simply not avoid eye contact with the homeless out of discomfort. Just look at them exactly as you would another passer-by, say "how are you doing?" as you would to a friend, and if you are asked for change, just say yes or no, give money or don't, but at least you will have treated them as a person. As the sociologist Morrie Schwartz wrote, "[The] need to feel connected to other people is as vital to human survival as food, water, and shelter" (1997:73). Morrie Schwartz came to understand human nature very well in his last stretch of life, and I believe that his words are as profound as they are relevant to the homeless. Like food, water and shelter, the connection to other human beings is both something that most people take for granted, and something we do not usually give homeless people access to. These "homeless" are people first and homeless second, and they deserve to be acknowledged as such.

The research that this paper has led me to has introduced me to many innovative ideas that may help the plight of the homeless. In an article from *Media Asia*, the magazine's Big Issue has involved the homeless in their first advertising campaign in Japan. The magazine, whose circulation had recently been suffering, opted to employ the homeless to sell the magazine, "as a means of helping them get back on their feet…and raising awareness of the plight of homeless people" (Murphy 2005). Minoru Kawasaki, head of the advertising firm in charge of the campaign, said, "We would like to change the consciousness of the public from 'disregard' to 'understanding' towards the homeless issue" (Murphy 2005). It is revolutionary thinking like this, which incorporates the homeless in ways that are mutually beneficial, that will help our society to improve the situation of the homeless or at least raise awareness of the problem.

Simply writing about the subject of homelessness has led me to both reconsider my actions concerning the topic, and has given me specific ways that I can change my own actions in order to accomplish the societal shift in the treatment of the homeless. The story of Morrie Schwartz is another example of someone's inner questioning bringing clarity to many others. In fact, the entire spiritual and philosophical journey that Morrie embarked on late in his life was all due to his "writing for his own benefit" (1997:66). Morrie began the sequence of becoming a celebrity not intending to do so, but rather, he wanted to "distance [him]self from [his] illness and remind [him]self of what [he] needed to do to maintain [his] composure throughout [his] illness (1997:66). Morrie continues his explanation, in a very DeSalvo-esque manner, by saying that his goal was also to "objectify [his] experiences and be a witness to [his] own process" (1997:66).

In writing this paper, I have unknowingly accomplished Morrie's goal; I have become a witness to my actions and much of this paper has been possible because I have been able to do so. In being a witness to my own actions, my writing has followed the stages laid out in Chapter 7 of DeSalvo's book. That chapter, entitled "Stages of the Process, Stages of Growth I" (1999:108), has laid out the stages that I have unknowingly gone through while writing this paper. The stage described in this chapter that I identify with the most is the germination stage, in which "fragments of ideas, images, phrases, scenes, moments" (1999:110), mostly concerning my and others' reactions towards homeless people, were flying through my head, and this paper is a result of my trying to make sense of it all. The process has not only elucidated the changes that I can make pertaining to my actions, but the process of writing has also been a therapeutic one as well. I took DeSalvo's advice to "trust that in time something worthwhile will emerge … [and] trust, too, that engaging in the writing process, by itself, is valuable" (1999:85). This counsel has proven true for me, and I hope that something valuable has emerged from a process that has already been valuable to me.

Every member of our society is for the most part only in control of his or her own actions, but through this individual control, one may also realize that our society's nature and structure are also malleable and subject to change, and not static. We saw Billy Elliot have a profound effect on the smaller society in which he lived, changing people's notions about boys doing ballet and the stereotypes that accompany it. But achievements more significant than that may have happened years after Billy Elliot left his small mining town. Not only did Billy change his own people's views, he or the film about him made people rethink why they have the particular views that they do have. The result was a much more civilized, rational society. The "banality of evil" (Berger 2002:399) was evident; Billy's dad and brother disliked him doing ballet because that's not what boys do, but when confronted, their strong opinions proved to be just a façade of unstable and unneeded convictions.

Society must change; we must propose an *alternative to the social script* (Berkowitz and Padavic 1999) that currently dominates people's attitudes towards the homeless.

BIBLIOGRAPHY

Ahmed, Ayan. "The Complexity of Naïve Acceptance of Socially Manipulated Beliefs," Human Architecture: Volume II, Issue 2, Fall 2003/Spring 2004

Anderson, Elijah. 1990. "The Black Male in Public." Pp. 334-344 in *Inside Social Life: Readings in Sociological Psychology and Microsociology*, Fourth Edition, edited by Spencer E. Cahill. Los Angeles: Roxbury Publishing Company, 2004.

Berger, Ronald J. 2002. "The Historical Construction of the Holocaust." Pp. 398-409 in *Inside Social Life: Readings in Sociological Psychology and Microsociology*, Fourth Edition, edited by Spencer E. Cahill. Los Angeles: Roxbury Publishing Company, 2004.

Berkowitz, Alexandra and Irene Padavic. 1999. "The Contrasting Agendas of Black and White Sororities." Pp. 279-292 in *Inside Social Life: Readings in Sociological Psychology and Microsociology*, Fourth Edition, edited by Spencer E. Cahill. Los Angeles: Roxbury Publishing Company, 2004.

Best, Joel and Frank Furedi. 2001. "The Evolution of Road Rage." Pp. 386-397 in *Inside Social Life: Readings in Sociological Psychology and Microsociology*, Fourth Edition, edited by Spencer E. Cahill. Los Angeles: Roxbury Publishing Company, 2004.

Blumer, Herbert. 1998. "Society in Action." Pp. 320-324 in *Inside Social Life: Readings in Sociological Psychology and Microsociology*, Fourth Edition, edited by Spencer E. Cahill. Los Angeles: Roxbury Publishing Company, 2004.

Bruner, Jerome. 1990. "Culture and Psychology." Pp. 7-15 in *Inside Social Life: Readings in Sociological Psychology and Microsociology*, Fourth Edition, edited by Spencer E. Cahill. Los Angeles: Roxbury Publishing Company, 2004.

Cahill, Spencer E. and Robin Eggleston. 1994. "The Presentation of Self." Pp. 178-189 in *Inside Social Life: Readings in Sociological Psychology and Microsociology*, Fourth Edition, edited by Spencer E. Cahill. Los Angeles: Roxbury Publishing Company, 2004.

Clark, Candace. 1987. "Sympathy Biography and Relationships." Pp. 216-229 in *Inside Social Life: Readings in Sociological Psychology and Microsociology*, Fourth Edition, edited by Spencer E. Cahill. Los Angeles: Roxbury Publishing Company, 2004.

Cooley, Charles Horton. 1983. "The Self as Sentiment and Reflection." Pp. 24-29 in *Inside Social Life: Readings in Sociological Psychology and Microsociology*, Fourth Edition, edited by Spencer E. Cahill. Los Angeles: Roxbury Publishing Company, 2004.

DeSalvo, Louise. 1999. *Writing as a Way of Healing: How Telling Our Stories Transforms Our Lives*. Boston: Beacon Press.

Goffman, Erving. 1959. "The Presentation of Self." Pp. 108-116 in *Inside Social Life: Readings in Sociological Psychology and Microsociology*, Fourth Edition, edited by Spencer E. Cahill. Los Angeles: Roxbury Publishing Company, 2004.

Goffman, Erving. 1967. "Face-Work and Interaction Rituals." Pp. 156-166 in *Inside Social Life: Readings in Sociological Psychol-

ogy and Microsociology, Fourth Edition, edited by Spencer E. Cahill. Los Angeles: Roxbury Publishing Company, 2004.

Klotzer, Charles L. 2006. "Media Silence will Haunt Our Society for Decades to Come." *St. Louis Journalism Review*, Vol. 36 Issue 289. Retrieved December 8, 2006. Available through the database: Communication & Mass Media Complete.

Mead, George Herbert. 1962. "Neurology and the Soul." Pp. 30-35 in *Inside Social Life: Readings in Sociological Psychology and Microsociology*, Fourth Edition, edited by Spencer E. Cahill. Los Angeles: Roxbury Publishing Company, 2004.

Milkie, Melissa. 1999. "Media Images' Influence on Adolescent Girls' Self-Concepts." Pp. 46-61 in *Inside Social Life: Readings in Sociological Psychology and Microsociology*, Fourth Edition, edited by Spencer E. Cahill. Los Angeles: Roxbury Publishing Company, 2004.

Murphy, James. 2005. "Circulation Drop Sparks Outdoor Ads for Big Issue." *Media Asia*, December 2, 2005. Retrieved December 8, 2006. Available through the database: Communication & Mass Media Complete.

Sacks, Oliver. 1990. "Neurology and the Soul." Pp. 2-6 in *Inside Social Life: Readings in Sociological Psychology and Microsociology*, Fourth Edition, edited by Spencer E. Cahill. Los Angeles: Roxbury Publishing Company, 2004.

Schwartz, Morrie. 1997. *Morrie: In His Own Words*. New York: Dell Publishing Group.

Snow, David and Leon Anderson. 1993. "Salvaging the Self From Homelessness." Pp. 127-138 in *Inside Social Life: Readings in Sociological Psychology and Microsociology*, Fourth Edition, edited by Spencer E. Cahill. Los Angeles: Roxbury Publishing Company, 2004.

Washington Profile. 2006. "Homeless in America." Washington, DC, Retrieved December 9, 2006. Available on-line: http://www.washprofile.org/en/node/2295

Wikipedia. 2006. "Demographics of the United States." Wikipedia.org. Retrieved December 8, 2006. Available on-line: http://en.wikipedia.org/wiki/Demographics_of_the_United_States#Religious_affiliation

Films:

"Affluenza. 1997." Written by John de Graaf.
"Awakenings. 1990." Directed by Penny Marshall. Based on the book by Oliver Sacks. Screenplay by Steven Zaillian.
"Billy Elliot. 2000." Directed by Stephen Daldry. Written by Lee Hall.
"Tuesdays With Morrie." 1999. Directed by Mick Jackson. Based on the book by Mitch Albom. Teleplay by Thomas Rickman

Love and Marriage
Through the Lens of Sociological Theories

Ana Carolina Fowler

Tufts University

carofowler@gmail.com

Abstract: This paper seeks to apply sociological theories to the concepts of love and marriage in order to better understand their construction and how they function in modern Western society. Illustrated by examples from my own life, the paper attempts to examine love using sociological micro-theories such as phenomenology, symbolic interaction, rational choice theory and the dramaturgical perspective. Macro-theories such as conflict theory, functionalism, and post modernism are used in order to analyze love as it relates to marriage and the ways in which the meanings of these concepts and their positions in society have changed.

Since I was very young I have believed that you grow up looking for that one special person with whom you are entirely compatible, the person that will be your partner in life through the good and the bad---someone you can depend on and who can depend on you, a person whom you have fallen in love with, and without whom you cannot imagine living the rest of your life. When you find that person, you marry them and then you have children.

This may be quite an idealistic perception, but it is the gist of what I had learned, from observation, from stories, from the media and from my parents; in short, I have been socialized to believe that this is the way things are generally supposed to go. However, my upbringing was also quite liberal and although this is what I understood to be the norm and what was generally desired, I also knew, understood and respected others' ideas of what was desired and that not everyone would marry the person they loved, or want to get married to or have children with at all. I knew that these variants were common and acceptable in my own culture, but I also knew about other cultures and other time periods and the different family forms that exist other than this one. Even though I was aware of all of this, part of my own stock of knowledge and something I considered to be mutual knowledge, was that the typical marriage in our current Western society was based on love. Or, in the words of Sammy Cahn, immortalized by the voice of Frank Sinatra, "Love and marriage, go together like a horse and carriage."

However, in the face of the same-sex marriage debates that have been going on in

---

Ana Carolina Fowler is an undergraduate student at Tufts University, majoring in International Relations and Sociology. She wrote this paper while enrolled in the course Soc. 341, "Elements of Sociological Theory," instructed by Anna Beckwith (Lecturer of Sociology at UMass Boston) during the Summer Session I, 2007.

the United States for the past few years, a variety of definitions for marriage have been put forth. Much to my surprise, however, few of these definitions have anything to do with love. In fact, Republican Senator Sam Brownback from Kansas has said in his criticism of legalization of same-sex marriage that, "If marriage begins to be viewed as the way two adults make known their love for each other, there is no reason to marry before children are born rather than after. And if it is immaterial whether a couple should be married before the birth of a child, then why should they marry at all?"[1]

Naturally, I found this statement quite shocking, given my understanding that marriage was "the way two adults make known their love for each other." In the past it may have been the case that most marriages were entered into as a political or economic arrangement in order to secure a more favorable position for one's self or one's family. It was also seen as the only acceptable beginning of a new family, since sex was something that couples engaged in only after marriage and—at least in the Catholic religion—only for procreation. But it has been my understanding that our modern times have allowed these concepts to change. Women no longer have to depend on their husbands for financial, social or political security; sex before marriage and not solely for procreation also seems to be generally accepted by society, and many couples who do get married cannot or choose not to have children at all. Thus, it would appear that marriages in Western societies today are by and large entered into as a public manifestation of love, a notion that is also confirmed by Beigel: "By the end of the nineteenth century love had won its battle along the whole line in the upper sections of the middle class. It has since been regarded as the most important prerequisite to marriage. The American concept that considers individual happiness the chief purpose of marriage is based entirely on this ideology" (Beigel 330).

Given that a national debate over who one can marry has become such a centerpiece of political discussion, as evident in the same-sex marriage debate, perhaps it is wise to explore love and marriage again. It is interesting that for a topic as popular as love has been in literature, films, music, media and popular culture for centuries, only recently have social scientists really paid much attention to it. Philosophical, poetic and scholarly explorations of the nature and definition of love abound, but only as of the twentieth century have methodical and scientific studies been performed by social scientists with the hopes of better understanding love and relationships.

This paper will present an analysis of love and marriage using my won personal experiences considered through the lens of a variety of sociological theories, supplemented by several studies and views put forth by other social scientists on the subject. It will be an effort to reach a better understanding of these illusive and seemingly controversial concepts. I will begin with an exploration of love with the use of concepts from sociological micro-theories, since love is experienced in the personal social interactions of everyday life. I will then proceed to an examination of love as it relates to marriage, where I will attempt to apply various concepts of macro-theories in hopes of clarifying the place of love and marriage in our society as a whole.

The concept of "chemistry" as it applies to relationships is one that is widely recognized in reference to romance, such that people who get along very well with each other and seem to have some sort of "spark" between them are described as having "good chemistry." In his 1809 novel, "Elective Affinities," Goethe further developed the idea of interpersonal chemistry, where he metaphorically compared the process of

---

[1] http://www.nationalreview.com/comment/brownback200407090921.asp

attraction between two people to a chemical reaction. In addition, recent neurological studies, such as Michael Liebowitz's "The Chemistry of Love" (1983), have been able to describe the actual chemical processes that occur in the human body when a person is experiencing love. However, the understanding of the biological mechanisms that allow men and women to live are merely the starting point for understanding the human experience. As Peter Berger and Thomas Luckmann explain, human beings have the unique distinction of being born "**unfinished**" and as such they must continue to develop in order to become a fully formed and functioning human being in relationship with society. If human beings are necessarily social and cannot exist outside of society (Farganis 300-301), although love can be described, to a certain extent, as a biological and chemical process, its significance can never be fully understood without an analysis of its social aspects. In Berger and Luckmann's view, human beings are not born into a world that is prefabricated and their choices limited by biology, instincts and drives. Human beings must engage in world-building activities and thus create things such as culture and social organization to live their existence (Farganis 301). Love, as a cultural and social phenomenon, can be perceived in this light as one of the mechanisms human beings use in order to organize their world. Love is one of the processes through which human beings become attracted to one another, and in one of the way we have become accustomed to doing it in modern times, we seek a single partner with whom to fall in love with. For the purpose of forming a family, therefore, love may be one of the ways we use to select someone to have children with.

Historically, however, mates have not often been chosen on the basis of love but rather—as previously noted—on the basis of convenience; at times mates are selected by the parents or families of the individuals to be married. Berger and Luckmann believe that in the process of **world-building**, humans **search for a balance** with the world and within themselves (Farganis 301). In this light—and perhaps in a more romanticized perspective—finding the person that one wants to spend their lives with may be only one way in which humans are able to find that inner balance.

As uniquely social creatures, humans need the presence of others in order to survive. Friendships are one way in which humans surround themselves with a microcosm of society which functions as a network of emotional support when it is needed. Love can be regarded as an even deeper level of this social behavior. Love may be regarded as combination of friendship and sex, and although it may not actually be that simple, this definition clarifies the idea that the physical attraction that is a part of romantic love may take the friendship aspect into a deeper level and thus fulfill a deeper need for emotional support and companionship that may not necessarily be fulfilled by friendship alone.[2]

But how do we know what to look for in a mate? Why should we look for only one that will be our life-long partner, and not try to have multiple, short-term relationships instead? How do we know when we're in love? Berger and Luckmann observe that although humans are world-building creatures, they are born into a world that predates them and as such, those who have lived in it before must teach the newcomers how to interact with it (Farganis 301). This is the process of **socialization**, and it remains the same no matter how much society changes and develops. Berger and Luckmann's proposed process of world-build-

---

[2] I should again note here that what is being explored here is a social phenomenon observable in modern Western society: the nature and definitions of love as a framework for selecting a life partner and how this relates to definitions of marriage. It is not my intention to assert that this is the only framework available or that those who deviate from this framework are right or wrong.

ing, or what they famously call, the **social construction of reality**, consists of three phases or aspects that they call **externalization**, which is when individuals construct new realities and structures in culture and society; **objectivation**, which is when those constructions become sedimented, legitimated, and perceived as "objectively" given for human actors newly entering the process; and **internalization**, which is when human actors not only have to learn and understand the meanings of the existing and previously "objectivated" cultural and social constructions, but are trained and socialized to take them for granted and to enact them as part of their subjective realities, identities, and lives.

It is in this last process that socialization becomes crucial, for it is what will turn the objectified world into an internalized framework of action. Using my own life as an example, I can perhaps begin to understand the feelings that I have for my fiancé in terms of how I have been socialized. Socializing institutions such as my family and the media have transmitted to me an idea of what love is supposed to feel like so that when I detect those feelings in me, I know that love is the emotion that I am experiencing. These ideas have become part of what Alfred Schutz calls my **stock of knowledge** (Farganis 285), which includes the "commonsense" facts that I have of the world. I rely on what has become understood to be **mutual knowledge,** and because of the possibility of **reciprocity of perspectives** (Farganis 287) made possible in social interaction, I assume that my fiancé, when experiencing similar feelings, will also identify them as love and we can come to the conclusion that we are in love with each other. In the same way, I can assume that he will understand as such the expressions that I show him of my love and that he will express his love either in the same way or in a similar way that I can also understand.

In line with Berger and Luckmann's discussion of socialization, Schutz notes that the stock of knowledge of an individual is mostly **social in origin**, so that although some of the ideas that I have about love come from my own personal experience, most of it was given to me by my family, my friends, my school and other **significant others** and socializing agents (Farganis 288). However, due to what he calls the **biographically determined situation** of a human being, at any given time, a person's **definition of a situation** is determined not only by the physical space which they occupy but also by their status and role in society; likewise, an individual's moral and ideological positions are determined by his or her own history and the biographical experiences he or she has had (Farganis 285). This means that the definitions that I have of love, or the interpretation that I would have of a certain situation—such as a conversation with my fiancé about marriage—are not mine alone but also shaped by my own unique personal biography; hence, although I can assume that other's definitions might be similar to mine based on observation and **typification**, they can never fully understand my, and I their, biographically determined situation and can only hope to grasp a fraction of it (Farganis 290).

For instance, in conversations that I have had with my fiancé about our wedding, I have expressed my desire to have my whole family there and to invite my closest friends. But since I am quite a social person, as are my parents, we have lots of people whom we love and consider important enough in our lives to invite them to the wedding. I cannot assume, however, that my fiancé feels the same way. As a matter of fact, he does not, and while I have a long list of people I would really like to have at the wedding, he only wants to invite his parents and his two brothers. Although I can use the knowledge I have of his personality and of the events in his life and through **role taking** attempt to understand the reasons for which he does not feel close enough to his friends to invite them to his wedding or what his ideas of closeness are, I can never fully grasp the way that he feels, how he perceives the world and how he defines certain situations.

The idea of role taking is present in George Herbert Mead's theories, where the **self** is the process of a constant inner conversation, or **self-interaction** between its two phases that are both object (**me**) and subject (**I**). The object of the "me" is in relation to others and only through this relationship can one become aware of the subjective "I." In Mead's words, "[t]he 'I' reacts to the self which arises through taking the attitudes of others. Through taking those attitudes we have introduced the 'me' and we react to it as an 'I'" (Cahill 33). Thus, only through processes such as figuratively placing myself in my fiancé's shoes (an exercise which in this process is done automatically and not consciously) am I able to be aware of my own self and can react to his words and actions with the added information and perception I gain from taking his role and applying them to the inner conversation between the two phases of my self.

Being aware of another's ideas and perceptions is a concept that is also very important to Charles Horton Cooley's concept of the "**looking-glass self**." In Cooley's view, the feeling we have for ourselves is constructed in three stages that occur almost simultaneously: imagining our appearance to others, imagining how others are judging that appearance, and the feeling we get in regards to that judgment (Cahill 28). Love can be analyzed through this perspective if one thinks of love as an imagination of how we appear to the person we love, imagining that they judge us favorably and love us and thus feeling satisfaction, security, happiness, etc. However, it is important to clarify that this will be the case when one is speaking of requited love, such that the imagination of how we look to our lover and the imagination of his or her favorable judgment are likely triggered by some emotional or physical indications of their affection. When I observed the way in which my fiancé acted towards me when we were a few months into our relationship, the things he said to me and how he treated me, I appealed to the stock of knowledge I had acquired through the socialization process of my childhood and adolescence in order to interpret them as indications of his attraction and deepening affection towards me. These ideas allowed me to (subconsciously) take his place and imagine how he must see me, imagine that he judges me favorably and in fact loves me, and feel happiness, satisfaction and security with regards to that judgment.

In the sense that one must constantly be taking the roles of others in order to properly react to situations, Mead asserts that **multiple personalities** are in fact quite normal (Cahill 35). In my opinion, this concept is akin to the **dramaturgical** theories that the sociologist Erving Goffman proposes as well. For Goffman, there is no such thing as a genuine or "core" self, but rather our selves are made up of all of the different roles or "characters" we perform in our daily lives (Cahill 349). Our performances rely on the reaction of our audiences in order for them to be legitimized, and the better we perform, the more acceptance and validation we will receive. Therefore, in my role as fiancée there are certain expectations that I have to fulfill in order to be accepted as such by my fiancé. If I don't fulfill some aspect of that role, he will become upset with me in the same way that I would become upset with him if I felt that he wasn't fulfilling his role. This act of being upset is what Goffman would qualify as a **disruption of a performance**, where the audience is not convinced by a performer's portrayal of a role, and it is something that we as performers try to avoid as much as possible. The dramaturgical metaphor that Goffman uses to describe how he sees social interactions may seem off-putting and be difficult to accept because it sounds like he is claiming that all of our social interactions are inherently fake, and that we are always trying to hide something. In my opinion, his metaphor should not be taken so literally and I feel that he is only trying to illustrate the idea that we all have a multitude of roles we play in our lives—for instance, I am a fiancée but I am also a student, a sister, a daughter, a woman, an intern, etc.—and that we try to perform our roles as well as possible in order to be perceived by others as "good" at whatever it is we're supposed to be.

Elements of the **Social Exchange Theory** may also be enlightening when analyzing love. In exchange theory, human behavior is seen as a rational choice where one seeks to maximize pleasure or benefit and minimize pain or cost. According to the sociologist George C. Homans, when someone enters into a social interaction they will gauge the reaction of others to what they are saying or doing and will continue behavior that is enforced by the behavior of others. This, in a sense, seems similar to what Goffman meant by needing the approval of the audience for one's role to be validated. Thus, the **cohesiveness** or strength of a social bond is determined by the degree of reinforcement that members of the group receive (Farganis 245). In this way, if the loving behavior I am expressing toward my fiancé is reciprocated through his loving behavior towards me, our social bond is stronger and we have more cohesiveness than if one's behavior is not reciprocated and thus enforced by the other's. According to another sociologist and social exchange theorist, Peter Blau, "Social attraction is the force that induces human beings to establish social associations in their own initiative and to expand the scope of those associations once they have been formed" (Farganis 258). For him, a person is attracted to another if they perceive a reward from the relationship that they establish, and when there is mutual attraction based on intrinsic benefits, such as the pleasure of the other's company. Then, a relationship between lovers is likely to develop.

The relationship between lovers that has been termed romantic love, which had historically been relegated to relationships outside of the marriage, has in fact developed into the very basis for marriage in present day Western (and especially American) society. This is what Andrew J. Cherlin has observed in the changes of the meaning of marriage that have occurred in the United States (and some European countries) over the last century. In his article, "The Deinstitutionalization of American Marriage" (2007), Cherlin suggests that especially after the 1960s marriage came to be regarded as a means for self-development and emotional expression, rather than a vehicle for satisfaction in performing traditional roles of spouse and parent. He notes that modernist (Giddens, for example) and postmodernist sociological theorists have also suggested the increasing individualization of marriage. Thus it seems that this shift in the meaning of marriage from "institution to companionship" is correlated with shifting perceptions about the nature of society as a whole, as evidenced by the transition from classical theories of social interaction to modernist and postmodernist theories of the same. Below, I will attempt to describe the differing meanings of marriage from the perspectives of each of the major macro theories of sociology in order to simultaneously illustrate both the theoretical and the socio-cultural developments pertaining to the issues under consideration.

As the capitalist economic model took over Europe and then underwent its cyclical and deepening crises, Karl Marx and Frederick Engels developed theories to explain social relations on the basis of what has been termed **conflict theory**. In their view, the history of society is a history of **class struggles**, involving power struggles among groups with irreconcilable interests for scarce resources. They were particularly concerned with the power of the bourgeois capitalists over the working proletariats in the modern period, and predicted that the inevitable progress of history would see the rise of the proletariat against its oppressor leading to the rise of workers to power. Marx's **materialist conception of history** was developed as a way to analyze the way in which human societies are based upon and change in response to their **mode of production of material life**. Thus for Marx, "it is not the consciousness of men that determines their existence, but, on the contrary, their social existence that determines their consciousness" (Marx, in the Preface to *A Contribution to the Critique of Political Economy*). The **relations of production** in a particular society are centered on a division of labor, where, under capitalism, the owners of capital (the **bourgeoisie**) live by exploiting the labor of others (the **proletariat**). Both Marx and Engels appear to regard marriage as being an expression of such a class struggle: "The first class antagonism which appears in history coincides with the development of the antagonism between man and woman in monogamian marriage, and the first class oppression with that of the female sex by the male" (Engels 17).

Crucial to this conflict theory of marriage is the idea that the interests of the different groups (or classes) are perpetually irreconcilable so that the success of one group is inevitably linked with the exploitation of another. Engels argues that as the structure of the family developed into a monogamous, patriarchal unit in which the man was the breadwinner and the woman the homemaker, the administration of the household historically entrusted to women as both a public and a private activity lost its public dimension. This means that the exploitation of the proletariat that can be observed in industry is echoed by the unpaid domestic labor of the woman in the household so that, "The modern individual family is based on the open or disguised domestic enslavement of the woman; and modern society is a mass composed solely of individual families as its molecules" (Engels 21). In the industrial age where women have the opportunity to work outside the home, they are faced with another dichotomy: If they have to participate in public production by joining the labor force they cannot fulfill their duties at home; but if they remain at home, they are deprived of the possibility of earning their own living independent of men (Engels 21).

While the Marxist conflict theory sees marriage as a result of the human relationships that develop as a result of economic structures, functionalists perceive marriage and the family as institutions whose preservation is vital for the maintenance and reproduction of society. The **functionalist** perspective views society as interrelated structures, such as **social institutions**, that have specific functions that work together by means of consensus to allow society to operate properly and to reproduce itself successfully. If one of the parts is not working correctly, the organism will find a way to fix it so that the whole is able to return to **equilibrium**. Thus, if there are behaviors that are perceived as upsetting to the balance of the social structure, the society will find a way, based on shared norms and values, to discourage or eliminate it.

The main difference between the conflict theories and the functionalist perspective is that conflict theories base their understanding of society on the assumption that change is constant and inevitable and based on the struggle between different interests, and that control is often achieved by means of coercion, while functionalist focus their explanations on the assumption that society naturally seeks to maintain its equilibrium and that control is derived from consensus regarding a specific set of values.

Talcott Parsons, a leading functional theorist, is known for developing what he called the **theory of human action**, based on his ideas of works by classical theorists such as Emile Durkheim applied to modern society. For Parsons, human action is predictable and patterned, and is determined by the structure of the society that the individual inhabits. Parsons identified four types of action systems, each tied to a specific function, that work together to maintain the total societal structure. The **behavioral system** is tied to the function of **adaptation** so that the systems can adapt to the particular environmental conditions in which they are embedded. The **personality system** is **goal-oriented** so that the actor or actress internalizes the goals, values and beliefs of the society as their own and strives to achieve them. The **social system** functions to **integrate** human action with the various **normative standards** that serve to maintain the whole. Finally, the **cultural system** is tied to the **latency** function, which establishes values and norms that motivate individuals to perform their roles according to the expectations of society (Farganis 162).

In this view, if one were to consider typical marriage at the beginning of the twentieth century, one would be able to identify a culturally defined goal, such as economic stability, that a person might be motivated (latency) to achieve. One of the most prevalent ways to achieve such a goal was through marriage. Therefore, the (goal-oriented) actress in the middle or upper class, for instance, is motivated to perform the role that is expected of her by society, namely, becoming a good wife and mother. She would therefore decide to enter into a marriage with a man that has a good job with a steady income (so as to adapt to the socially organized environmental conditions at the time for the woman's survival and for bearing/raising children) and would dedicate herself to complying with the normative standards associated with her roles (integration).

In the Parsonian model of human action, when people exhibit behaviors, or when institutions pursue activities, that are not in line with the functions that the society perceives as necessary for its survival and perpetuation, that behavior or activity is classified as a dysfunction and a remedy is sought in order to return the society to its healthy, functioning equilibrium. Even thought this theory maintains that all the functions of prevalent social behavior are good and necessary for the survival of the society, Robert Merton, another functionalist theorist, has a slightly different interpretation of the functions of social behavior and institutions.

In his theory, Merton suggests that social institutions and human behaviors while serving a visible and expected function in society, i.e., a **manifest function**, they may also serve another, less obvious and often imperceptible function that he calls a **latent function**. Some of the functions may in fact even be **dysfunctional** for society or for a specific group while still being functional for another (which alludes to the idea in conflict, and especially Marxist, theory that the success of one group is inevitably linked to its exploitation of another). Therefore, Merton emphasizes the importance of recognizing all of these functions in order to be in a better position to explain the emergence of **functional alternatives**.

Keeping with the theme of marriage, I would suggest that for Merton the manifest function of marriage in the first half of the twentieth century, for instance, was to secure the economic stability of a woman, to supply a man with a counterpart to provide domestic services while he earned his income outside the home and to raise a family that would be able to inherit his wealth. The latent functions of this arrangement *for the man* could have included personal satisfaction and a sense of fulfillment in participating and succeeding in roles that were highly regarded in society: that of being a male spouse and a parent. For the woman, however, Merton may argue, the latent function of this arrangement was women's continued subordination to and dependence on the man, and the perpetuation of male dominance in marriage and by extension in society as a whole.

In the hundred years between mid

nineteenth and mid twentieth centuries, the liberalization of society resulted in the change of many of the values, goals, and norms of accepted behavior. The meaning of marriage was one of the many things that changed a great deal in the twentieth century. Cherlin notes that from a cultural perspective, an increased emphasis on emotional satisfaction and on the importance of romantic love in relation to marriage, as well as en ethic of "expressive individualism," were significant developments. From a materialist perspective, the transition from agricultural subsistence to wage labor, rising standards of living, and the eventual joining of married women to the work force, were also instrumental in changing the meanings that were associated with marriage (Cherlin 187).

The first major transition is "from an institution to a companionship," according to Ernest Burgess, as quoted in Cherlin. This was a shift observed mostly in the 1950s; although, then, the traditional divisions of labor were still highly persistent, married couples were supposed to be each others' partners, friends and lovers. A greater importance was placed on the emotional bonds of the family, increasing its individualization, even though spouses still derived much of their satisfaction from participation in the nuclear family (Cherlin 188). In the 1960's however, the rise in the number of young adults that remained single as they went through college and started their careers, as well as the rise in childbearing outside marriage, divorce rates, same-sex unions and a greater acceptance of cohabitation before marriage, led to the second great change in the meaning of marriage for society. Marriage transitioned from the companionate model to what Cherlin calls "individualized marriage" (189), quoting F. M. Cancian (1987) who characterizes the nature of this transition as a shift from concern with playing a role to concern with self-development and emotional fulfillment.

In terms of Merton's concepts, one might express this transition as a transformation of latent functions into manifest ones, where for instance, if marriage was once a means for economic stability and the reproduction of society that had the latent function of providing personal fulfillment for the individuals involved, the personal fulfillment is now seen as the main purpose of marriage and economic stability and raising a family may be seen as latent functions. I can observe this in my own life as well. The reason I have decided to marry my fiancé is that I love him and am loved by him and being his wife will contribute to my personal development and emotional satisfaction. In terms of economic stability, I am perfectly capable of providing for myself, so the stability that I might gain from being married to him is a secondary consequence. We do want to have children, but there are many families that do not intent to have children or cannot have children, but nonetheless are, or want to be, married. These changes have also led to the acceptance of a variety of structures that can be termed a family—including single parent families, stepfamilies, cohabitation and same-sex unions—which have been argued to be able to provide social functions parallel to those provided by traditional, heterosexual, monogamous marriages and nuclear families and are thus prime examples of Merton's functional alternatives.

However, as marriage seems to be receding from its central importance in social life and becoming simply another lifestyle to be selected from a variety of alternatives, the majority of people in the United States today still see getting married and raising a family as goal. Cherlin suggests that this may be due to the symbolic significance of marriage as a status symbol, a public expression of the quality of the relationship, and a capstone achievement of adult life, rather than its foundation (Cherlin 193). In this sense perhaps the notions of the conflict sociologist Max Weber on **status** might be applied.

Weber, unlike Marx, believed that power could be derived not only from one's class (economic status and degree of material wealth) but also from other social positions such as status groups (determined by degrees of honor and esteem) and political parties. The symbolic meaning that marriage retains despite the decline of its traditional practical significance, speaks to its powerful role as a status symbol. Since today it appears that a greater emphasis is placed on individualized satisfaction of emotional needs and on the perception of marriage as an avenue for such satisfaction, when a couple gets married it is a public declaration of their ability to maintain a loyal, stable and emotionally fulfilling relationship, thus elevating them to a privileged status. At the same time, however, the increasing lack of faith in the ability of marriage to provide this satisfaction, or in the durability of such a union and the negative connotations that it evokes among today's youth (female repression, lack of professional freedom, etc.) contributes to a degree of negative attitude towards couples who decide to get married. In my own life, most of my friends seem to be happy that I have been able to find a person with whom I can have a relationship that is loving and rewarding enough to give me the confidence in its long run durability, allowing me to decide to get married. Many of them are seeking similar relationships themselves. Other friends, however, are less enthusiastic and even quite skeptical of the situation, especially because they consider me too young to be making this commitment.

Cherlin suggests that for postmodern theorists modernity, which is associated with the power of social norms and laws that regulate family structures, has declined and that traditional sources of identity such as class and religion have begun to lose their influence, and instead personal relationships have become the main source of identity (Cherlin 189). The changing focus of society—from community based action dedicated to the maintenance of its successful operation to action based on the individual and aimed at maximizing individual satisfaction and development—has affected the meanings attached to traditional institutions such as marriage. While for postmodernists the change underway is a linear trend, however, for sociologists such as Immanuel Wallerstein, this transition could be partly explained as a recurring shift between a **phase A** (economic growth with corresponding optimism and expansion) to a **phase B** (economic contraction with corresponding frustration and rebellion against the system) of the world-system which leads to a period of transition plaguing the population with feelings of vulnerability and unpredictability. Wallerstein believes that the calls for the resolution of crises usually lead to a falling back into ritualized and familiar practices, which could also be a reason for the continued symbolic importance of marriage. At the same time, relaxation of norms and laws regarding marriage and the family and the declining practical importance of traditional forms of marriage in society can be seen as the continuation of the rebellion against the traditional, community-based, conservative society.

Even though Wallerstein is not a postmodernist, the ambiguity and uncertainty that he observes in the current transition may correlate with the postmodernist idea that the unpredictability of social development is derived from the increasing social and cultural fragmentation and heterogeneousness of modern society. Relativism thus replaces the objective assumptions of the **metanarratives** inspiring previous social theories, based on the belief that there is a single coherent reality or truth about society and that it is knowable, and that its development is progressive and determined by specific laws. The nature of the changes in the meaning of marriage, the increased emphasis on romantic love and emotional fulfillment as the principles upon which to base a marriage and the increasing acceptance of various forms of families and conjugal unions all represent this individualization, this transition from collectivity to self, from ascription to achievement, and from particularism to universalism---if we use Parsons's **pattern variables**. However, postmodernists will add that although these pattern variables are indeed the main themes of modern society, individual and collective behaviors are not entirely determined by the structure of society. Whatever the pattern variables prevalent at the time, people and groups have the ability to choose whether or not to act according to them.

The ideas that Marx and Engels put forth on the nature of the monogamous marriage relationship can be observed in real life. In my own considerations of marriage I have often struggled with myself on the issue of whether or not I would like to stop working when I have children. I would like both my husband and me to be the main participants in the upbringing of our children, but my fiancé is already established in a career that requires the majority of his time but that is also the major source of income for our family. Therefore, I know that in reality I will most likely be the one responsible for most aspects of our children's upbringing. I am in fact quite eager to take on that responsibility, as I believe that being a mother will give me great pleasure. At the same time, I would very much like to have my own job and develop a career, mostly because I feel like I would be unfulfilled if I don't participate successfully in activities outside domestic work and child-rearing and feel like I am using my abilities to contribute to society in other ways as well. This is a notion that I have also been socialized into by having been brought up in a society where a woman's options are much more diverse than they used to be, and where having a career has become expected. Since my mother is such an important role model for me, I also believe that it is important to take her advice into consideration, and even though she tells me that she has had a gratifying life so far, she also expresses some regret for having had to give up her own career a few years after getting married. But the circumstances of my parents' lives at the time were such that she feels that her choice was the right one. Given the great education that I have received in college, my mother's experiences, and my own desire for personal achievement in my career, I am faced with a difficult and perhaps irreconcilable decision that no doubt cause inner conflict in most women of my generation.

Meanwhile, considering the prevalence of increasingly acceptable alternatives to marriage, as well as the decreasing faith in its durability, I must consider why it is that I am deciding to participate in it. I believe that part of this desire comes from the way in which I was socialized, being taught to treat marriage and forming a family as natural stages in my life. But after considering marriage in many of its sociological interpretations and understanding the different meanings that it has taken throughout history, I believe that a larger part of my decision is based on the belief that this relationship will bring me emotional gratification and will help me on my path of self-development. It will provide me with support in difficult times and encouragement in happy ones, and the reciprocation of those attitudes towards someone I love will bring me gratification as well. Getting married, as opposed to cohabitation, is for me a symbolic occasion, meant to celebrate our love and dedication and make public our commitment to each other---something that I believe could be akin to Cherlin's suggestion that marriage can be thought of as a sort of status symbol, but also as what he terms "enforceable trust," or the freedom to invest in a relationship without fear of abandonment. Additionally, there is a sense of security that comes from knowing that if, for any reason, I decide not to pursue a career, my husband will be able to provide for our family. And finally, being married also provides for me a sense of balance and constancy, something that has been lacking in my life for a very long time—due to my family's constant relocation and my consequent lack of identification with a permanent home. In an ever changing and unpredictable world that may very well be in what Wallerstein considers to be the transitional phase B, O'Neill expresses in her book *The Marriage Premise* that, "Today, as never before, our marriages are assuming more responsibility for fulfilling the need to be known, for providing the continuity in our lives" (Ross 114).

Romantic love, once something that occurred outside of marriage, has replaced other social benefits such as economic stability and the formation of a nuclear family as the basis of marriage. This change is just one example of the transitions in the meaning of love and marriage as well as of the individualization and fragmentation apparent in society today. But this is a development that has prompted much criticism. Senator Brownback's conservative denouncement of same-sex marriage, for instance, and his refusal to accept functional alternatives to the traditional nuclear family structure has the manifest function of attempting to protect the institution of marriage and family as being critically functional for society. However, in reality it could be a latent attempt to return to what Wallerstein considered to be the ritualized and familiar practices of the past, or even to preserve a status quo that is favorable for Brownback's agenda, which is not in line with accepting changes that may be a step in the direction of reversing the dysfunctions that traditional marriage and the nuclear family present to society in general and to women in particular. In fact, it has been argued that the emphasis on romantic love as a basic premise for marriage has affected this institution in a way that is quite contrary to what Brownback accused it of doing. As Beigel puts it,

> Love aims at and assists in the adjustment to frustrating experiences. To measure its effect on marriage it must be judged in its true form and not in poor falsifications. Seen in proper perspective, it has not only done no harm as a prerequisite to marriage, but it has mitigated the impact that a too- fast-moving and unorganized conversion to new socio-economic constellations has had upon our whole culture and it has saved monogamous marriage from complete disorganization. (Beigel 333)

BIBLIOGRAPHY

Beigel, Hugo G., Romantic Love. *American Sociological Review*, Vol. 16, No. 3. (Jun., 1951), pp. 326-334.

Brownback, Sam. Defining Marriage Down. National Review, July 2004.

Cahill, Spencer E. *Inside Social Life*. Fifth Ed. Roxbury Publishing Co., 2007.

Cancian, F. M. *Love in America: Gender and Self-Development*. Cambridge, England: Cambridge University Press.

Cherlin, Andrew J., The Deinstitutionalization of American Marriage, in Susan Ferguson (ed.), *Shifting the Center: Understanding Contemporary Families*, Third edition (McGraw Hill, 2007), pp 183-201.

Engels, Frederick, Engels on the Origin and Evolution of the Family. *Population and Development Review*, Vol. 14, No. 4. (Dec., 1988), pp. 705-729.

Farganis, James. *Readings in Social Theory*. Fifth Ed. (McGraw Hill, 2008).

Ross, Ellen. The Love Crisis: Couples Advice Books of the Late 1970s. *Signs*, Vol. 6, No. 1, Women: Sex and Sexuality, Part 2. (Autumn, 1980), pp. 109-122.

Lifting the Fog
Finding Freedom in Light of the Sociological Imagination

Keyon Smith

University of Massachusetts Boston

keyon.smith001@umb.edu

Abstract: I have noticed that as time goes by, my inner urge to go against what society deems correct grows. It is almost as if I sense that there is something wrong with the way things are. How did I come to this conclusion of things not being quite right? I was not always like this; nor did I wake up one morning a changed person. This change occurred over a period of time and I do not believe that it is yet complete. The most dramatic of that change occurred after I achieved a degree of clarity. Prior to that, other issues in my life served as a fog clouding my perceptions. Though I could not clearly "see" it, I knew there was something not right. I could hear it, taste it, and feel it. Drawing on various readings selected from the anthology by Spencer E. Cahill (2004) as well as the ideas of the late sociologist Morrie Schwartz, among others, this essay explores the causes of the blinding fog and how I came to lift it. It also explores how I was able to better understand what I find wrong with our society as a result of achieving this clarity.

I have noticed that as time goes by, my inner urge to go against what society deems correct grows. It is almost as if I sense that there is something wrong with the way things are. It would be selfish for me to say that they seem wrong for just me; I think that they are wrong for the majority of us.

How did I come to this conclusion? I was not always like this; nor did I wake up one morning a changed person. This change occurred over a period of time and I do not believe that it is yet complete. The most dramatic of that change occurred after I achieved a degree of clarity. Prior to that, other issues in my life served as a fog clouding my perceptions. Though I could not clearly "see" it, I knew there was something not right. I could hear it, taste it, and feel it. I guess it relates to what Oliver Sacks said in his article on "Neurology and the Soul" (Cahill 2-6), when he introduced Heraclitus' concept of the stream. "I do not feel alive, psychologically alive, except insofar as a stream of feeling—perceiving, imagining, remembering reflecting, revising, recategorizing—runs through me. I am that stream—that stream is me" (Sacks 5). Somewhere along the same lines, I sensed that there was something wrong with the "stream's" flow. As if something was causing it to not be what it could have, or perhaps what it should have, been. There was once a time where I was oblivious to the im-

---

Keyon Smith is an undergraduate student at UMass Boston, majoring in Biology and Medical Technology. He wrote this paper while enrolled in the First Year Seminar Soc. 110G-3: "Insiders/Outsiders," instructed by Mohammad H. Tamdgidi (Assistant Professor of Sociology at UMass Boston) during the Spring 2007 semester.

pediment in the flow of the "stream," and the "stream" itself for that matter. A time where I wanted very much to conform to the guidelines set by society.

During that time I was very much concerned with my **looking-glass self**. In the article, "The Self as Sentiment and Reflection," Charles Horton Cooley defines the looking-glass self as being a social self in the sense that "the social reference takes the form of a somewhat definite imagination of how one's self—that is, any idea he appropriates—appears in a particular mind; and the kind of self-feeling one has determined by the attitude toward this attributed to that other mind" (Cooley 25). The looking-glass self has three aspects: 1. How we imagine others view us; 2. How we imagine they judge us as a result of how we imagine they view us; and 3. How we feel about that judgment. It is also possible that as time and experience shape and change us, our looking-glass selves can change as well.

It mattered to me a great deal what I thought others thought of me. The fact that this was so important to me played a key role in providing the conditions that allowed the blinding fog to form and maintain itself. I wanted to do what was expected of me or what I perceived to be expected of me by my family, teachers and friends. Everyone feels that way at some point in his or her life. Whether the looking glass self is particular to the society we live in today, or a part of what Jerome Bruner (Cahill 71-5) calls "**human universals**"---the concept pretty much captures my experience here.

I was exemplifying the looking glass self by wanting to do everything in the order which was deemed "proper" by society: Go through grade school, then college, then a career, then marriage and a family. I think everyone shares those feelings as well at some point or another in their life. It is another sentiment thought to be universal among humans. With the universality of this sequence of events, coupled with my humanity, I had my mind set on following that prescribed order, even if that meant not being myself, whoever myself was, whatever being myself meant.

I was not exactly sure why I wanted to do things that way until very recently, when I achieved the clarity I spoke of earlier. It not only allowed me to see more clearly that something is wrong with society, but it also helped me to see that something was wrong with me. I am still not exactly sure what all of the reasons for my wanting to conform to society were, even though I have a few ideas. One of these have to do with the realization that the course of my life was not merely a "natural" process, but one shaped and form by the culture I live in. And this realization does not apply to me, only, but to society at large. As Jerome Bruner put it, "The divide in human evolution was crossed when culture became the major factor in giving form to the minds of those living under its sway... culture (instead of nature) now became the world to which we had to adapt and the tool kit for doing so" (Bruner 8). It was after recently reading that particular passage in Bruner's article "Culture and Psychology" that gave me the idea that one of the reasons for how I was, was my childhood, especially my early childhood and my surrounding environment during that time period. "[H]uman beings do not terminate at their own skins; they are expressions of a culture" (Bruner 8-9).

I was not the product of the "socially defined" relationship. My parents were never married and they were separated not long after the completion of my first year in life. Despite my having half-siblings in far away Michigan, with whom I am today very close, my family in those early days included my mother, my grandmother, my two uncles, an aunt-in-law, and my cousin. That was my familial makeup for the first six years of my life. My father was in and out of it here and there---more often out than in. I was lacking and in need of my father's guidance or that of a father figure for that matter. To compensate for that absence I had to substitute him with something. I found my substitutes in fictional characters and places. While a good portion of my values came from my mother and grandmother, another good chunk of them came from these fictional characters. One of the most prominent of those characters was Superman.

He was and always will be my absolute hands down favorite. With Superman being the moral foundation that he is I suppose I came to emulate and idolize him. Because there was really no father figure in my life until I was seven or eight years old, there were some lessons that went unlearned or were learned the hard way. There were also some learning tools and techniques that are described as normal that I did not have at my disposal due to my father's absence. One of those was the role taking that is commonly found in young children's developmental stages. Although somewhat similar, my role taking play days weren't like exactly like those mentioned by George Herbert Mead in "The Self as Social Structure": "playing with an imaginary companion… is a **play at something**. … The roles which the children assume are made the basis for training. When a child does assume a role he has in himself the stimuli which call out that particular response or group of responses" (Mead 32). I never played the role of father or father-like figure. Instead, I would play the role of Superman. It even reached to the point that when faced with certain situations I would ask myself: "What would Superman do?" And I would do just what I thought my hero would, well within my limitations of course. I knew perfectly well that Superman has his powers due to the radiation from our yellow sun, which is different than that of his native red sun. I also clearly knew that I could never have those powers because I am a native of this planet. However, superpowers aside, my moral standpoints nearly mirrored those of the man of steel. I think it is because of that that as a child I never really got myself into too much trouble, and I always tried to help people if I could. This "training" I think actually later proved to be somewhat harmful to me as I moved forward in life.

I actively continued along this path for the most part until I was about eleven years old. Many facets of my early socialization started to change when I was between the ages of ten and eleven. My grandmother, whom I was very close to, was diagnosed with lymphoma (cancer of the lymphatic system). My mother who was the one primarily taking care of my grandmother had become engaged and I was due to gain a stepbrother and stepsister. At fifty-six years old, my grandmother succumbed to the cancer during the summer of 1990. Her death caused a major shockwave with very long lasting tremors to occur through my childhood. The tremors may not have been as lengthy had I not exhibited **responsibility exclusion**. Arthur W. Frank speaks of responsibility exclusion in his piece, "The Social Contexts of Illness" (Cahill 247-256). He writes, "Illness excuses people from their normal responsibilities, but the cost of being excused is greater than it appears at first" (Frank 253). My responsibilities of being "just a kid" with a sick grandmother were excused and a new responsibility was bestowed upon me. I had to be strong for my family because everyone else was falling apart. I had to be the rock that everyone could lean on. For that reason I did not cry at my grandmother's funeral, and I comforted those who did. Later, I realized that this was not the best approach to that situation. According to Morrie Schwartz:

> Grieving, mourning, crying are natural emotions. … Grieving is an important part of living because experiencing loss is inevitable for everyone. … Therefore, you need to work out a way of handling

grief. The best way is to let yourself grieve freely and mourn losses. … Without this kind of release you're apt to be left with an inner pain that can affect your life in many ways. (Schwartz 29-30)

Although I managed to keep my emotions in check I had no problems in letting go of my faith. It was during this time that my belief in God began to falter. I took a closer look at things and the fog thinned a little bit when it came to religion. From that point on I began believing less and less in God as I saw the world growing into a darker and more hate-filled place. I could no longer believe that a god, such as the one I was raised to believe in according to the Bible, could allow the world to fall into the state that it is in. Without a doubt, my grandmother's death left within me a great void and an immense pain that would not begin to be healed for years to come. And while the fog did thin at one part it grew even thicker in others.

Four months after my grandmother's death, per her wishes that they be married that year, my mother and stepfather got married. And while I did gain a father figure and siblings whom I could grow up with, I in some ways lost my mother. My stepsiblings had a lot of issues stemming from their drug addicted biological mother, and they needed a lot of attention. I did too. It just was not as obvious. I suppose I played the role of "normal" kid to a tee. I had perfected the "normal" role during my youth through my years of pretending to be Superman, which also included his mild-mannered secret identity, Clark Kent. The way I portrayed my "normality" to my family was a form of presenting a **purpose-serving self**. The purpose-serving self is introduced in the excerpt from Erving Goffman's book, similarly titled "The Presentation of Self." He says that we portray ourselves in certain ways depending on the situation and the desired result.

[W]hen an individual appears before others, his actions will influence the definition of the situation which they come to have. … Sometimes he will intentionally and consciously express himself in a particular way, but chiefly because the tradition of his group or social status require this kind of expression and not because of any particular response (other than vague acceptance or approval) that is likely to be evoked from those impressed by the expression. (Goffman 110)

I started my middle school years as a **social isolate**. Much of my first year in middle school was spent in isolation. This is not because I was an "individual with no real friends" as Peter and Patricia Adler (270) define it in their study, "Preadolescent Cliques, Friendships, and Identity." It was because I had chosen to be that way mostly as a result of my grandmother's illness and death from the previous year. I would never share my accomplishments with or seek help from my family. I became somewhat of an isolate on the home front as well as the issues with my stepsiblings grew worse and they became more attention needy. Their antics and the issues that they created within the family eventually resulted in our having to attend family therapy sessions, which I absolutely abhorred, but in which I did play my part. While I was at home I would go through the motions when necessary as well. I would **"do family"** as Nancy Naples said in her essay, "A Personal Story of Doing Family" (Cahill 204-215). I would assume the role expected of me while I was there. Naples states that her reason for "doing family" while with her biological family was because it acted as a "form of boundary maintenance—controlling who and what can enter for fear that the family constellation is so fragile any slight disruption will cause permanent damage" (Naples 212). This situation seemed to apply to me as well.

As my middle school career progressed I did manage to re-assimilate myself with the friends I had had in elementary school. Many of the issues that emerged during my middle school years continued on through high school. By the time I started high school family therapy was a thing of the past. The issues with my stepsiblings still existed, though, as did my isolation from my family. However my social isolate days were well behind me as I had graduated to the **middle-level friendship circle**. This group is defined as being "the people who were considered non-popular, who didn't try to be cool or to be accepted by the cool people" (Adler 267-268). It was also in my freshman year in high school that I met my two best friends. They essentially became my new family, and in a lot of ways my real family. If I wasn't with one of them, then I was with the other, if not with both of them. Despite the fact that we don't speak nearly as often as we once did, the bond is still there. My sophomore year added a new dynamic: relationships, or perhaps it is better to say the lack thereof. Continual rejection and heartache was the social theme for me during that year. However that theme led to the emergence of something else, writing. I started writing poetry that year. The poems that I composed were not for some school assignment, but they were for me. Writing them served as a way to get out the things I was feeling and to be able to look at them and work my way through them. I found that during that time, writing actually helped me to deal with the matters of the heart and maintain my sanity. "Through writing, we change our relationship to trauma, for we gain confidence in ourselves and in our ability to handle life's difficulties" (DeSalvo 45).

Towards the end of high school, I really started to change. I took up interests in other cultures and ideas. Not so much to convert to them, more so to expand my knowledge and to be able to compare and contrast the different workings of things. I even participated in an international exchange program between my school and one in Mexico during my junior year. It was that experience that led me to a new discovery: love. I was truly in love for the very first time and I had found someone who felt the same for me. Now I thought I had been in love before, but I discovered that true love was not involved in those prior situations. When you are seventeen and truly in love for the very first time and involved in a very serious relationship, that relationship tends to take control of your life. It creates a whole new thickness to the fog, which blocks out a completely different spectrum of light. That is exactly what happened in my case. I found myself involved in a very serious long distance relationship for almost four years. This relationship accompanied me out of high school and into college.

Because I was in my first serious relationship and because I was completely devoted to it, everything I did was for that relationship, or so I thought. The truth is that I let that relationship control my life and it subsequently led to the failure of my first attempt at college. Not only that, but it caused me to dismiss and miss out on quite a few once-in-a-lifetime opportunities. Instead of going to Northeastern University, I took the fall semester of 1997 off and decided to travel to Mexico to see my girlfriend. I then came back and started the spring semester at UMass Boston. That first semester was a full one with two science courses, a math course and good old English 101. I did poorly in all but one of those courses, which resulted in my being unable to renew the two scholarships I had been awarded from high school. All I could think about during the course of that semester was finishing so I could go back to Mexico, never mind the schoolwork! Somehow I failed to see that my doing well in school and earning a degree would provide security to a future that we had many times dreamt of. My then-girlfriend however had seen this, had even brought it to my attention, and after a while, after an empty assurance that I could and would focus on my studies, saw that the only way that she could help me was by ending the relationship. She wanted me to do things for myself and to achieve the goals that I had spoken of and I never would have done so while still in the relationship.

I of course did not see it this way. I had construed it as being the end of the world. I overreacted and on many levels I shut down; almost as if someone else had taken over, or perhaps another self---a **multiple personality** was set in motion, if you may call it that. Not to be confused with the extreme cases of multiple personality disorder, where one is unaware of the things he or she does while under the control of a different personality, such as the cases portrayed in the documentary film *Multiple Personality: The Search for Deadly Memories* (HBO). However, Mead has pointed out that "A multiple personality is in a certain sense normal. ... To a person who is somewhat unstable and in whom there is a line of cleavage, certain activities become impossible, and that set of activities may separate and evolve into another self" (Mead 34). This other self in me took five weeks off from work, and stayed inside the house the whole time. After the self-imposed exile I regained control and did something that in retrospect I realize I never should have done. I got involved in another relationship. It took me almost six years to discover why I did this, and one more year to discover its name.

That relationship lasted for a year. Shortly after that I got myself into another relationship, which lasted a month or so. Another relationship followed that, which ended up lasting almost five years. This is where the Superman "training" I mentioned earlier proved harmful. I fell back on helping others as a way to avoid dealing with the reality of the pain that I had yet to earnestly address. I entered all of those relationships with the impression that the friends needed help, that they needed me to help them. It was true that they needed help, but the "needed me" part was not entirely true. I was really in no position to be trying to solve someone else's problems. It was not too long ago actually that I realized this. I also recently realized that I didn't really value myself for who I was and that I defined my worth in terms of my value to others or my perceived value to them. Through that I became saturated with feelings of failure and the feeling that I was letting everyone down by not meeting their expectations. As a result, "I lost it" as Peter N. Sterns put it in his article "The Historical Struggle for Self-Control in America" (Cahill 78-91). He simply defines the phrase "I lost it" as follows: "The 'it' may refer to our temper, our mastery over grief, or another currently expected inhibition" (Sterns 78). My mastery over the grief caused by everything going on had surpassed its limitations.

There was another side affect that arose. I was **codependent** and I had been so since the breakup with my first girlfriend. "Codependency is [generally] described as a psychospiritual 'condition' that allegedly causes people to 'lose touch with' themselves through their preoccupation with others, sometimes depicted as an 'addiction'" (Irvine 2000:142). Leslie Irvine, in her study, *Narratives of Self in Codependents Anonymous*, writes that these people who become codependent often have a feeling of failure and they usually will seek help after a serious relationship gone sour. "They come in search of answers to the question 'What happened?' but lurking beneath this is a deeper question: 'What's wrong with me?'" (Irvine 142). Though I did not seek professional help, I did have those same questions burning within me especially after my first relationship ended.

In the midst of my codependency I also

became semi-suicidal. Maybe that is an exaggeration, but I definitely spent a lot of time depressed and thinking about what it would be like, were I not around. I was definitely in a lot of emotional and psychological pain. In retrospect I probably should have found professional help. DeSalvo is right when she writes that one should not substitute writing for seeking help when being in danger of self-harm" (DeSalvo 167). I have since leaned that the self-harm that I was committing was an effort "to alleviate [the] profound psychic pain" (DeSalvo 159) resulting from the termination of my first relationship. I think the only thing that kept me going was something that came out of that five-year relationship, the best things by far: my son and my daughter. Those are the two things that kept me going. They were my guiding light. They put a whole new perspective on life. And although I still did not really value myself and practiced "cutting" from time to time, the mere fact that my children were there kept me from going completely over the edge to the point of no return.

I would like to take a moment to reflect a little more on the end of that last relationship, mostly because it proved to be one of the major catalysts of my healing and self-realization process. Things had basically gone to hell. I think the only reason that it lasted as long as it did was because there were children involved. (That, by the way, is no reason to prolong a relationship. It only causes more problems, especially for the children.) After a month of being separated, my ex had become engaged and had informed me that she was taking my children to another state. For a Mr. Mom type father such as myself, that was a lot to handle. I did spend as much time as possible with my kids, before she left. And then one day she left and took them with her. My world had almost come to an end that day, but a very good friend helped to remind me that tomorrow was coming and that my kids still needed their father, even if I was 8 hours away.

Two weeks later my son was back with me and my daughter came the month following that. I spent the following six months as a single parent, while their mother seemingly dropped off the face of the earth. A lot changed for me from January to June of 2006 as the fog began to lift. I realized a few things and as a result made some changes. One of those changes was my relationship with my father. He had changed a few years back, but I was not very receptive to those changes. I suppose I still had a lot of anger within me. Morrie Schwartz advised, "'Forgive yourself before you die. Then forgive others.' ... 'There is no point in keeping vengeance or stubbornness. These things ... I so regret in my life. Pride. Vanity'" (quoted in Albom 164). Everything that happened or did not happen with my father was in the past. What really mattered was the present, so I called him one day last July and I have seen him at least once a week since then, usually on tuesdays.

I also began to understand my codependency and was able to overcome it. One of the people in Irvine's study said "All this time, because of codependency, I haven't been able to be myself. ... I've learned who I really am, for the first time in my life" (Irvine 144). I related to that immediately when I recently read it, it nearly brought tears to my eyes. It brought me back to the previous year when I had all those revelations, the day that I began to clearly see through the fog that life's circumstances had put in place. And I came to an understanding very similar to this:

> We can sometimes experience a long-lived journey into despair and an intense inner psychic struggle. Our old ways of thinking and behaving seem empty and self-defeating. We move, perhaps, to the brink of self-extinction. But, because of some sudden and pro-

found insight, we turn back and reclaim the potential and possibilities of life. We are, in a sense, reborn into a new life. (DeSalvo 155-156)

The day of my "rebirth" was Valentine's Day, 2006. In retrospect it strikes me as being a bit ironic that on the day of love, I finally began to love myself. And once that happened the fog dissipated enough for me to see myself as an active member of society instead of someone just caught in the current. In a way this was very similar to the type of awakening that Dr. Sayer experienced towards the end of the film *Awakenings*. Because of the wake-up call that he received from Leonard, Dr. Sayer was able to open up and do what he felt was right as opposed to being oblivious to everything outside of his own bubble. From my awakening I was able to begin to truly embrace my thoughts and feelings of how I thought things should be, and what I saw as "wrong" with the way things are.

Two things helped me to see this. One of them was the concept, **special mental lenses**. Eviatar Zerubavel mentions this concept in his article "Islands of Meanings" (Cahill 16-21) when he writes, "Being a member of society entails 'seeing' the world through special mental lenses. It is these lenses, which we acquire only through socialization, that allow us to 'perceive things'" (Zerubavel 20). When I found myself socializing and participating in society I was able to acquire the special mental lenses, implant them, and use them to see even more clearly through the fog. It was from my perceptions that I was able to change the prescription of the special mental lenses previously acquired and see things in a different light and from different angles.

Oliver Sacks named the second concept that helped me to see the glitches in society. In his piece "Neurology and the Soul," Sacks quotes Goethe and introduces something that one may call "organ knowledge exchange." His quote of Goethe states: " 'The Ancients said that the animals are taught through their organs; let me add to this, so are men, but they have the advantage of teaching their organs in return.' Through experience, education, art, and life, we teach our brains" (Sacks 5-6). When I was finally able to see through the fog of my depression and codependency I was able to exchange knowledge with my organs. I was able to reflect upon life experiences to determine what I felt was wrong with our society.

I see things such as greed and overstimulation. We saw first-hand in the documentary PBS film *Affluenza*, how this determination to own the "latest and greatest" ruins people. It causes things like chronic stress, bankruptcies, and fractured families. We are overstimulated by technology. We are in the postmodern era afflicted with what Kenneth J. Gergen calls "**social saturation**":

> Social saturation furnishes us with a multiplicity of incoherent and unrelated languages of the self. For everything we "know to be true" about ourselves, other voices within respond with doubt and even derision. This fragmentation of self-conceptions corresponds to a multiplicity of incoherent and disconnected relationships. These relationships pull us in myriad directions, inviting us to play such a variety of roles that the very concept of an "authentic self" … recedes from view. The fully saturated self becomes no self at all. (Gergen 413)

As I read that article by Gergen titled "The Dissolution of the Self," I kept saying to myself "This is exactly what I have been sensing!" Another problem I have noticed is impatience. Morrie Schwartz similarly comments on our current cultural gravitation towards immediate gratification. We expect things right then and there. When we are not able to have that desire fulfilled we become frustrated. "When I don't get it, I'm frustrated. But if I don't demand that it be there at this very moment, the frustration is reduced and the objective will still be achieved, though it takes a while" (Schwartz 18). After realizing some of these faults in society, I have been able to strive against them and fashion my life into something that is more functional for me.

Even though I have managed to fashion my life in such a way that I am on track to obtaining the type of life I want for myself, the fog is always there. It may not be of a zero visibility thickness, but it is still there. The molecules are still present and waiting for the right conditions in which to form themselves in such a way that blocks vision. Very recently, the fog made a very strong attempt to return. This time it once again was hidden behind the topic of my children. Their mother once again decided to move out of state with them. This time, however, I decided to fight against it and I lost. Now had this been pre-Valentine's day 2006, I very well could have relapsed. I think that it is safe to say that I may very well have gone over the edge and ceased to exist. I am here though because I was "reborn." I am stronger because of it and I will be ok. My determination to succeed is akin to that of Billy Elliot. In the film, *Billy Elliot*, Billy was determined to be a ballet dancer. Despite all of the resistance he encountered, he didn't let anything stop him. It is with that same style of determination that I absolutely refuse to allow that fog to settle again.

One way of keeping the fog at bay is expressing our feelings, especially the negative ones, such as frustration, complaints, or anger. They are very powerful and can consume us. They also all lead to stress, which serves as a distraction and invites that blinding fog. "If a lot of frustrations have been building up, you need to talk about them. … Have confidence in yourself and realize that eventually you will be better off because you have expressed your feelings" (Schwartz 24-25). What I, and all of us for that matter, have to do is continually adjust the mental lenses. By saying that I mean that we have to be observant of the environment which surrounds us and remain vigilant against those stimuli that cause the fog to set.

In another class I saw a film called *The Motorcycle Diaries*. In the film, Alberto Granado and his cousin Ernesto Guevara set out on a motorcycle, to see Latin America. Throughout the journey they see many of the injustices that have been perpetrated against the native and poor populations. Ernesto, especially, is deeply affected by what he perceives and wonders how it can be fixed. By the end of the journey Ernesto realizes that he has been changed by the experience and must take time to think about who he has become. He resurfaced a few years later as Ché Guevara, one of the leaders of the Cuban revolution. Though his methods may have been questionable, he had the best of intentions at heart. We must perceive the changes and adapt to or change them. To ignore our surroundings is to remove the lenses and let ourselves become enshrouded by the fog. To do that is to surrender our true freedom and allow ourselves to be mere parts of the machine that is society, parts which have no function other than to promote and advance the wills and desires of others. at the expense of our own willful action.

References

Adler, Patricia and Peter Adler. "Preadolescent Cliques, Friendships, and Identity." Pp. 258-278 in Spencer E. Cahill, *Inside Social Life: Readings in Sociological Psychology and Microsociology*. 4th edition. Los Angeles:

Roxbury Publishing Company.

Albom, Mitch. 1997. *Tuesdays With Morrie: An Old Man, A Young man, And Life's Greatest Lesson.* New York, NY: Random House, Inc.

Bruner, Jerome. 2004. "Culture and Psychology." Pp. 7-15 in Spencer E. Cahill, *Inside Social Life: Readings in Sociological Psychology and Microsociology.* 4th edition. Los Angeles: Roxbury Publishing Company.

Cahill, Spencer E. 2004. *Inside Social Life: Readings in Sociology Psychology and Microsociology. 4th ed.* Los Angeles, CA: Roxbury Publishing Company.

Cooley, Charles. 2004. "The Self as a Sentiment and Reflection." Pp. 24-29 in Spencer E. Cahill, *Inside Social Life: Readings in Sociological Psychology and Microsociology.* 4th edition. Los Angeles: Roxbury Publishing Company.

DeSalvo, Louise. 2000. *Writing as a Way of Healing: How Telling Our Stories Transforms Our Lives.* Boston, MA: Beacon Press.

Frank, Arthur. 2004. "The Social Contexts of Illness." Pp. 247-256 in Spencer E. Cahill, *Inside Social Life: Readings in Sociological Psychology and Microsociology.* 4th edition. Los Angeles: Roxbury Publishing Company.

Goffman, Erving. 2004. "The Presentation of Self." Pp. 107-116 in Spencer E. Cahill, *Inside Social Life: Readings in Sociological Psychology and Microsociology.* 4th edition. Los Angeles: Roxbury Publishing Company.

Irvine, Leslie. 2004. "Narratives of Self in Codependents Anonymous." Pp. 204-215 in Spencer E. Cahill, *Inside Social Life: Readings in Sociological Psychology and Microsociology.* 4th edition. Los Angeles: Roxbury Publishing Company.

Kenneth J. Gergen. 2004. 2004. "The Dissolution of the Self." Pp. 411-419 in Spencer E. Cahill, *Inside Social Life: Readings in Sociological Psychology and Microsociology.* 4th edition. Los Angeles: Roxbury Publishing Company.

Mead, George Herbert. 2004. "The Self as Social Structure." Pp. 30-35 in Spencer E. Cahill, *Inside Social Life: Readings in Sociological Psychology and Microsociology.* 4th edition. Los Angeles: Roxbury Publishing Company.

Naples, Nancy. "A Personal Story of Doing Family." Pp. 204-215 in Spencer E. Cahill, *Inside Social Life: Readings in Sociological Psychology and Microsociology.* 4th edition. Los Angeles: Roxbury Publishing Company.

Sacks, Oliver. 2004. "Neurology and the Soul." Pp. 2-6 in Spencer E. Cahill, *Inside Social Life: Readings in Sociological Psychology and Microsociology.* 4th edition. Los Angeles: Roxbury Publishing Company.

Sterns, Peter. 2004. "The Historical Struggle for Self-Control in America." Pp. 78-91 in Spencer E. Cahill, *Inside Social Life: Readings in Sociological Psychology and Microsociology.* 4th edition. Los Angeles: Roxbury Publishing Company.

Schwartz, Morrie. 1996. *Morrie: In His Own Words.* New York, NY: Bantam Doubleday Dell Publishing Group, Inc.

Zerubavel, Eviatar. "Islands of Meaning." Pp. 16-21 in Spencer E. Cahill, *Inside Social Life: Readings in Sociological Psychology and Microsociology.* 4th edition. Los Angeles: Roxbury Publishing Company.

Films:

"Affluenza." (1997). Bullfrog Films.

"Awakenings." (1990). Columbia/Tristar Studios.

"Billy Elliot." (2000). Universal Pictures.

"Multiple Personalities: The Search for Deadly Memories." (1994). Home Box Office.

"Superman" is the property of DC Comics.

"Tuesdays With Morrie." (1999). Touchstone.

The Quinceñera Rising
Self-Discoveries on the Heels of City and Rural Town

Krystle Santana

University of Massachusetts Boston

ricankrystle1437@yahoo.com

Abstract: When a Hispanic young lady turns fifteen, there is usually a huge celebration in her honor to welcome her into adulthood. This ceremony is called the Quinceñera. After the dedication portion of the ceremony, the father of the quinceñera makes his own speech. At this time, the father switches the little girl's white flat shoes into her white high heels. When I became a teenager, I was living in Revere, Massachusetts. With much of my family in Boston, I was mainly raised in the heart of the state. However, in the middle of my adolescence, at the age of fifteen, I was moved out of Massachusetts, to Franklin, New Hampshire, where my whole life changed. Everything I once knew and understood didn't matter anymore because the country lifestyle in New Hampshire was completely different from the city. Once I had the opportunity to leave New Hampshire, I took it. I am a city girl to the core, and the rural atmosphere was never adequate. However, after reflecting on how different my life in Massachusetts and New Hampshire was, I see that there were many benefits to living in New Hampshire. In this article, using various sociological concepts, theories, and literature in the sociology of youth, I explore how I grew, and continue to grow, on the heels of my experiences of living in both the city and the rural town.

Adolescence is one of the most important phases one goes through during their lifetime. The period of **adolescence** is when the individual establishes a new **ego identity**—"a feeling for who one is and one's place in the larger social order" (Crain, 281). Location, culture, nationality, and upbringing can all shape how everyone experiences their youth.

When I became a teenager, I was living in Revere, Massachusetts. With much of my family in Boston, I was mainly raised in the heart of the state. However, in the middle of my adolescence, at the age of fifteen, I was moved out of Massachusetts, to Franklin, New Hampshire, where my whole life changed. Everything I once knew and understood didn't matter anymore because the country lifestyle in New Hampshire was completely different from the city. Once I had the opportunity to leave New Hampshire, I took it. I am a city girl to the core, and the rural atmosphere was never adequate. However, after reflecting on how different my life in Massachusetts and New Hampshire was, I see that there were many benefits to living in New Hampshire.

According to William Crain, in "Erik-

Krystle Santana is an undergraduate student at UMass Boston, majoring in Criminal Justice. She wrote this paper while enrolled in the summer course Soc. 201: "Youth and Society," instructed by Anna Beckwith (Lecturer of Sociology at UMass Boston) during the Spring 2007 semester.

son and the Eight Stages of Life," Erik Erikson considered youth as a moratorium. **Moratorium** is defined as "a period during which young people take time out to try to find themselves" (Crain, 272). The whole point of moratorium is to set the adolescent on "a life course that is rich and rewarding" (Cote and Allahar, 74). Cote and Allahar said it best, in *Generation on Hold*, that "if the environment nurtures the individual's capacity and encourage self-discovery instead of stifling these things, it can enrich one's life" (77). Although my parents did not intend to stifle my self-discovery, they definitely deterred me from discovering myself because I focused too much of my time adjusting to my new environment. My moratorium became very complex because of this.

When I lived in the city, I would take the train or the bus to anywhere I liked with my best friend Craig.[1] We ventured off to different parts of the city with no adult supervision. My main goal during my early adolescence was to go to places that I have never been to. I wanted to discover new hangout spots, new stores to shop in, or even new places to eat. This may not seem like I was trying to discover myself, but I was. The whole purpose was to discover what I enjoyed, what location I felt comfortable in, and where I could see myself living in in the future. However, when I moved to New Hampshire, my interest in different locations had to diminish because there was no public transportation. I had no way of getting around unless one of my parents drove me. Therefore, I focused on a different aspect of myself. My self-discovery efforts became focused on concerns with my outward appearance and discovering my true identity. By "true identity," I mean what makes me the way I am, rather than what makes me comfortable. Cote and Allahar would say that this would be my "identity moratorium" (74). Crain stated that "even though identity-formation is a lifelong process, the problem of identity reaches its crisis at adolescence" (282). By **crisis**, I think Crain meant that it can be both an opportunity and an emergency where the future is dependant on how the crisis is resolved. Moving to New Hampshire forced me to figure out my true identity.

Erikson mentioned that during the adolescence phase, youth tend to focus on their identity. In my new school, much of the students didn't accept me because I didn't grow up with them. Many of the students in this school had known each other since they were in elementary school. I was the new girl from the city who dressed differently, spoke differently, and had seen things in a different light. When some of the students learned that I was Puerto Rican, they really saw me as an outsider even though I thought that I would be able to blend in because of my fair complexion. These students were part of such a small town and didn't have much direct experience with minorities.

I was always proud about being Puerto Rican. Even though my skin complexion is fairly light, it never stopped me from claiming my nationality. If anyone mistook me as a different ethnicity, I always made sure that they understood what I really was. At Revere High School, I never had a problem with being Puerto Rican because that school was very integrated. We had such diversity in my class that everyone understood and embraced everyone else's heritage. However, I believe that the students at Franklin High School were not very accustomed to Hispanic people or minorities in general. Therefore, they felt as though it was fine to treat me like an outsider. I heard everything from discriminatory slurs to petty name-calling. It was clear to me and everyone else that I wasn't accepted.

In her book *Jocks and Burnouts*, Penelope Eckert discussed two major categories

---

[1] All personal names in this article have been changed to respect privacy.

in a particular high school, Belten High. The two categories were the Jocks and the Burnouts; she also mentioned that there existed a small minority of In-Betweeners. In this context, the classificatory terms are words that reflect the structure of the school. According to Eckert, the development of "the differentiation between Jocks and Burnouts arose 'overnight' upon entrance into junior high" (76). Junior high was a starting point for much of development of the students' senses of self. The **Burnouts** were known as troublemakers and the **Jocks** were more popular because they were participants in the school's activities and teachers rewarded them for their behavior. Eckert also described how "clothing and other forms of adornment, ways of speaking, territory" distinguished them (49). At Franklin High, I think most of my classmates considered me to be a burnout because I dressed differently, spoke differently, and acted differently from all of the popular students. In Revere, I would be considered a jock because to them I dressed, spoke, and acted mostly like everyone else; I was a favorite to many of the teachers at the school, and I also focused on doing well academically. Unfortunately, my first couple of months at my new school did not quite reflect the status I had at the previous high school.

At first I thought that I should focus on trying to fit in, but I soon realized that there is no point in working to fit in. I started to discover myself away from what everyone was saying about me. Erikson mentioned that "it is the thought that one might not look good to others or meet others' expectations" (Crain, 281) that concerned the youth the most during this moratorium phase. During my first few months of school there, I was concerned with that, but there is only so much work one can do. Therefore I made sure that I fit the exact profile they thought of me. I continued to dress the way I dressed; continued to speak the way I spoke; continued to publicize my nationality; and most of my classmates refused to try to become my friend because I made sure they knew that I wasn't like them. Although I was just expressing who I am, in a sense I was rebelling against the norm at that school. Then again, even though I couldn't fit in with the students, I still tried to find my own **clique**—small group that is derived form the school setting (Bensman and Rosenberg, 80).

It is hard to survive high school without a few friends that one can trust. I wanted to find my own peer group in this school. **Peer group** is defined as "such a group [that] is an association of self-selected equals who coalesce around common interests, tastes, preferences, and beliefs" (Bensman and Rosenberg, 80). I grew up with many of the people in my peer group at Revere High. Nevertheless, we always welcomed newcomers of different backgrounds. Many of the people within my group had the same interests as I, so making friends was never a problem. However, it was so much harder to make friends in New Hampshire. Everyone had his or her peer groups already fully developed.

A little after I started school at Franklin High, another girl from Massachusetts moved up. Her name was Tiffany and she was half Puerto Rican and half Italian. Naturally with everything we had in common, we became best friends. It happened within a matter of days, but it changed our lives forever. We found a new member that also recently moved to the area. She was African American and she was from the South. Her name was Abby. We all became good friends because we shared the same interests such as hip-hop music, dancehall music, step dancing, and going to nightclubs. We even dressed very similar and had the same speech patterns (used the same slang) aside from our individual accents. Because none of us originated from New Hampshire, it created a stronger bond between us and a weaker bond with any of our other classmates. Although we all had different upbringings and cultures, I felt more compatible with them than the other predominantly white students at the school. They also felt that same way.

In the film *Ghost World*, the two best friends, Enid and Rebecca, were very similar to my very small group at Franklin High. Enid and Rebecca were very different in personality. The other two girls and I were very different in personality also. However, similar to Enid's and Rebecca's relationship, we were able to understand each other's differences. In *Ghost World*, Rebecca was focused more on leaving home and working on getting an apartment. She wanted something better for herself. Enid, on the other hand, was comfortable where she was. She took life as a joke and rarely did anything to better herself. She was less of a conformist and instead used sarcasm to knock down society. Tiffany and I were very goal-oriented. Our main goal was to do well in school and hopefully find a way out of New Hampshire. Abby was a different story. She was more like Enid. Life was one big joke to her. When she started acting differently and spent time with those who primarily disliked us, she started to develop interests that Tiffany and I couldn't relate to.

During our senior year together, Abby spent so much time with our male classmates and other girls' boyfriends. Then there were numerous rumors about her promiscuity. However, as many times as we told her to be careful what she does and who she spends time with, she thought we were trying to tell her what to do. We just cared and wanted the best for her, but she couldn't see that. Everyone else saw her as a slut, though. She was very sexually active, but she didn't sleep with every guy she spent time with. However, the other girls and even some of the other guys at our school did not believe that. They believed that she was sleeping with every guy. What I found interesting was that according to Cecile Wright, in "Black Femininities Go To School," most black girls are thrown into a category which is perceived as "loud, naughty, confident, and overtly sexual and how this means that they are, inevitably, negatively stereotyped" (105). It may be possible that my classmates viewed her this way because she is African American and they probably placed her within this category. However, what was really upsetting was that the white guy that she spent the most time with was very sexually active himself for several years. However, she developed the bad reputation and he was known as a popular guy. It is possible that being a white male gave him the leeway to do whatever he pleased, with no negative judgment coming from his peers. She was ultimately a victim of a double standard.

Abby didn't see anything wrong with being very sexually active at her age. In *SLUT!*, Leora Tanenbaum stated that the double-standard is "the idea that women are disgraced by sex outside of marriage, that sex transforms them into 'sluts'" (76). I never considered Abby a slut because I knew the person behind the reputation, but she never attempted to change the way people viewed her. I think that much of it had to do with the fact that it was our last year in high school, and she didn't care what people thought of her. She took herself out of our peer group because she had newly developed interests and some male friends who shared them. In the end, I managed to find at least one friend to trust. After I adapted to my new environment and found someone to relate to, I still didn't feel like I could truly find my identity until I left Franklin. That was still my main preoccupation.

After I became comfortable with myself in Franklin High School, I felt more comfortable to do well academically similar to how I was in my pervious school. The impressions of the other students didn't bother me anymore. I was more focused on making a good impression on the teachers and staff, so I joined many clubs and also joined the volleyball team. I engaged myself in many extracurricular activities. Basically, I did anything that would look good on my college application. In my experience, there was definitely an "emphasis on future thinking during this time, where adolescents begin to envision life possibilities…" (Herr 50). I thought that everyone considered me to be a burnout because I didn't quite fit in, but I worked my way to jock status. Tiffany and I even started a club of our own which was called the Hip Hop Dance Club.

The Hip Hop Dance Club was our way of finding some common ground with our peers. We were worried that we wouldn't get a good number of females to join, but we did. To our surprise, many of the females (all white) thought that this would be a good experience for them. Tiffany and I were just expressing our passion for dance; we never thought that our peers would actually give it a chance. After five months of practice, the girls in the club managed to master a dance routine. Tiffany and I slipped in a little bit of salsa, to introduce our culture, into the routine also. All the girls agreed that the salsa was the best part of the routine. Similar to the double-dutch discussed in "Dancin' in the Street to a Black Girl's Beat," our main interest when teaching the other girls was "keeping the rhythm, [and] not interrupting the meter and the flow of the musical experience" (Gaunt, 273). The club performed during the last couple of months of my senior year and we received unbelievably great feedback. This was such a great experience for Tiffany and me because we finally made a connection with our peers. What was even better was that the school board agreed to continue the Hip Hop Dance Club every year.

What I really didn't like was that when I was participating in the clubs and sports, it seemed as though everything was monitored. Even the Hip Hop Dance Club had to have adult supervision in order for us to practice after school. How can a student strive to be a leader and start something on their own, if it wouldn't pass the school boards unless there is an adult present? This might be what Nancy Lesko called "youth as probation." "**Youth as a probation**" is the trial period of youth where everything they do is monitored through adult supervision. In her "Time Matters in Adolescence," Lesko stated that "**youth were defined as always 'becoming,'** a situation that provoked endless watching, monitoring, and evaluating…slow, careful development-in-time was identified as the safest path" (111). The moratorium phase is where youth is supposed to free themselves from adult responsibilities, but school monitors youth because they have the power to do so. They also tend to encourage youth to become more productive citizens by their definition.

This monitoring and adult advising contradicted the idea of moratorium. All I wanted to do was to express my hobby of dance to the rest of the school, but I had to delay my idea until an adult agreed to sign on. Cote and Allahar believe it to be "unreasonable to expect individuals to learn the requirements of maturity and responsibility without allowing them to perform roles in which maturity and responsibilities are exercised" (108). One of the ways I learned maturity and responsibilities was by getting a part-time job. During the time I was focusing on being a productive student, I was also earning an income.

I started working during my junior year in high school. Some of the reasons why I picked up a job were to help out my parents by taking some of my financial burdens off of them. I wanted to earn money in order to purchase the latest sneakers, the latest clothes, and anything that would set me apart from my classmates. I held a temporary part-time job at a local supermarket. I worked in one of those low paying, no benefit, and very little upward mobility jobs. This job I held was very boring and simple. The scanner did much of the work, which proves Cote and Allahar's idea in *Generation on Hold* that "a major consequence of modern technology is the deskilling of segments of the labor force" (36). There was no need for me to calculate the prices of each object because the scanner calculated the total, therefore deskilling the job into something monotonous. The mentality that I had in high school is much like what Susan Willis mentioned in "Teens at Work: Negotiating the Jobless Future" about how teens only strive for immediate compensation (353). The only benefit I saw in working there was to earn the income to become a "good consumer." Teachers, parents, and most other adults teach youth how to become productive citizens which entails being consumers, employed, and not dependent on the government. I guess they taught me well. However, as I transitioned from high school to college, my view on everything including work changed.

Because I didn't let the negativity from the other students bring me down, I accomplished everything I wanted to in high school. I accepted the fact that school was a benefit for me. I envisioned being a child advocate lawyer in Boston, Massachusetts, and succeeding academically in high school would take me one step further to my dream. Therefore, I had to make the best out of the situation I was dealt with. Penelope Eckert said it best in *Jocks and Burnouts* that the "high school career…is essential to entrance into a good college" (103). With everything I achieved and the high grades I earned, I was accepted to the University of Massachusetts Boston. My main goal of high school was to get out of Franklin and back to the city. As I mentioned previously, once I got the chance, I took it.

My latest self-discovery was back in Boston; where I felt I belonged. Although I was happy to move out of my monotonous life, my parents did not seem as excited. In actuality, my family was very close as a result of the move. Jessica Sawyer, in her article "Confessions of a Maine-iac: The Family, Academia, and Modernity," mentioned that the media usually depicts family as an embarrassment and the friends are the one that truly understand adolescents (193). In my case, my family was the ones that truly understood me the most. However, I couldn't let them be the reason why I stayed. Even though family emotions bind children and parents together (Bensman and Rosenberg, 80), I had dreams to fulfill on my own. Ultimately, the move helped me appreciate my family more, but as Sawyer stated "young adults are encouraged to and expected to reach their full potential, even if this goes against the interests of the family" (194). I was no longer some adolescent that needed to be monitored all the time. It was the time for me to excel on my own.

I went to college to find myself on a whole different level. In high school, I discovered how to distinguish between friends and foes. I discovered that if anyone tried to stop me from doing anything, they would never be able to stop me. I discovered myself to be full of determination, dreams, and strength. I took these faculties with me to college. On the other hand, there is still so much to discover. As Crain mentioned, "identity-formation is a lifelong process," so it was clearly going to take me quite some time until I discover my true identity. Going to college meant that I would be able to allow my individuality to prevail. Sawyer defined **individualism** to be "encouragement to be yourself, to develop your own talent, to try your best, and to build up your own career" (196). Those were much of the goals I had as I went into college, but I still had the doubt in my mind of whether this was a good move for me.

One of the biggest concerns about college was how I was going to pay for it. In high school, I worked just to buy materialistic things, but since I have a lot more responsibilities, I have established different work ethics. To fulfill my dream, I would have to do years of undergraduate and law school. Cote and Allahar stated it well in *Generation on Hold* that "those coming of age now face the prospect of remaining in school for a prolonged period primarily in order to attain high levels of educational credentials" (35). Because I am going to be in school for a long period of time, I had to find a way to pay for it.

Throughout high school, all I wanted to do was get out of New Hampshire and college was my ticket out. Ironically, leaving New Hampshire caused more problems for me. Although I returned back to the city, I missed my family, Tiffany, and the lack of responsibilities. As for college being my ticket out, I probably should have gone to a New Hampshire college. Being an out-of-state student meant that I have double the tuition of in-state residents. Once again, tuition was my biggest burden.

With the minimal availability of permanent jobs and the lack of time to keep a permanent job, I was forced to pay for tuition with credit and the little money I earned. I paid for school through loans, which are useful, but I pay back more for borrowing than the original amount I needed. The types of jobs I am able to hold do not provide benefits; healthcare would have been a problem if my mother's insurance didn't still cover me as a student. Ryan Moore mentioned in his article, "Downward Mobility, Affect, and Postmodern Narrativity," that most white-collar job are being downsized and that professional occupations in fields like law (which is where I want to be) are being proletarianized with the introduction of technology (259). As I search for an occupation that matches my "educational credentials," the opportunities may not be available. My future quality of life is in jeopardy.

My journey even up into the present was based on self-discovery. Although I have accomplished much in my life, I would not consider myself an adult. Then again, I wouldn't necessarily consider myself an adolescent either. I am at an in-between stage in my life right now. In the article "Adolescent Rites of Passage," Lynn Hoffman discussed how all adolescents eventually "navigate their passage from late childhood to adulthood" (58). **Rites of passage** are basically the path that adolescents take that transitions them into adults. Some adolescents would consider themselves adults when they learn how to drive or get a part-time job (58). However, Hoffman mentioned that "our culture lacks a systematic way of transitioning adolescents into adulthood, and we do not identify a set of achievements that would mark that status" (58). In my case, I don't consider myself an adult until I graduate from law school and get my first full-time job with salary and benefits. My family on the other hand considered me an adult at the age of fifteen.

When a Hispanic young lady turns fifteen, there is usually a huge celebration in her honor to welcome her into adulthood. This ceremony is called the Quinceñera. The whole ceremony is very long and meaningful. One of the first things the quinceñera (the young girl who is turning fifteen) does is walks into the hall or church with a very delicate, but plain white dress. Along with the dress, the young lady must be wearing white flat shoes. The white in the dress and shoes symbolizes the pureness of the young lady because it is suggested that the young lady is still a virgin. The flat shoes symbolize a young girl. There is a small flower presentation where the grandmother or the eldest woman of the family gives a bouquet of flowers to the young lady as a gift. Soon after, everyone has a chance to say something to the quinceñera including the mother, friends, or other family members. After the dedication portion of the ceremony, the father of the quinceñera makes his own speech. At this time, the father switches the little girl's white flat shoes into her white high heels. The switching of the shoes is the quinceñera's passage into adulthood. The father then presents the once little girl to everyone as a young lady: an adult. The father has the first dance with the quinceñera as a lady. However, every Hispanic family had their own way of doing the celebration. This is what my family considered my rite of passage into adulthood. To everyone else in my family and in my culture, I am already an adult. However, in my eyes, I am not done growing.

I have not become an adult yet. The moratorium phase of adolescence is supposed to be a time when you spend time without adult responsibilities and discover who you are. I did a lot of self-discovery, but I don't think it ends when one becomes an adult, which for some means at the age of eighteen. I am twenty and I have already gone through my rite of passage into adulthood according to my culture. But I am still figuring out who I really am. I agree with William Crain that identity-formation is a life-long process. I've lived two completely different lifestyles during my youth, and I have grown from both to become the person I am now. There are, or should certainly be, many different theories about youth and adolescence because this period of time is different for everyone. Therefore, it is seen differently by everyone. I see my adolescence as the undergraduate level of my self-discovery and the years to come is the law school of my self-discovery. There is still so much to understand about myself; I know that I am not ready to be an adult yet.

Work Cited

Bensman, Joseph and Bernard Rosenberg. "The Peer Group." *Socialization and the Life Cycle*. Ed. Peter I. Rose. St. Martins Press, 1979. 79-96.

Cote, James E. and Anton L. Allahar. *Generation on Hold: Coming of Age in the Late Twentieth Century.* New York: New York University Press, 1995.

Crain, William. "Erikson and the Eight Stages of Life." *Theories of Development: Concepts and Applications*. 4th Ed. Prentice Hall, 2005. 271-290.

Eckert, Penelope. *Jocks and Burnouts: Social Categories and Identity in the High School*. New York, NY: Teachers College Press, 1989.

Gaunt, Kyra D. "Dancin' in the Street to a Black Girl's Beat: Music, Gender, and the Ins and Outs of Double-Dutch." *Generations of Youth*. Ed. Joes Austin and Michael Willard. New York University Press, 1998. 272-292.

Ghost World. Dir. *Terry Zwigoff*. Perf. Thora Birch, Scarlett Johansson, Steve Buscemi. MGM, 2001.

Herr, Katherine. "Problematizing the 'Problem' Teen: Reconceptualizing Adolescent Development." *Contemporary Youth Culture*. An International Encyclopedia. Edited by Shirley Steinberg, Priya Parmar, and Birgit Richard. Volume One. pages 47-56. Westport, CT: Greenwood Press.

Hoffman, Lynn M. "Adolescent Rites of Passage." *Studying Youth Culture*. 58-62.

Lesko, Nancy. "Time Matters in Adolescence." *Act Your Age! The Cultural Construction of Adolescence*. Routledge Falmer, 2001. 107-134.

Moore, Ryan. "Downward Mobility, Affect, and Postmodern Narrativity." *Generations of Youth*. Ed. Joe Austin and Michael Willard. New York University Press, 1998. 259-270.

Sawyer, Jessica. "Confessions of a Maine-iac: The Family, Academia, and Modernity." *Human Architecture: Journal of the Sociology of Self.Knowledge*. Vol. III, No. 172, Fall 04/Spring 05. 193-203.

Tanenbaum, Leora. *Slut! Growing Up Female with a Bad Reputation*. Perreneal, 2000. 157-201.

Willis, Susan. "Teens at Work: Negotiating the Jobless Future." *Generations of Youth*. Ed. Joe Austin and Michael Willard. New York University Press, 1998. 347-357.

Wright, Cecile. "Black Femininities Go To School: How Young Black Females Navigate Race and Gender." *"Problem" Girls*. Ed. Gwynedd Lloyd. 103-112.

The Broken Path
Juvenile Violence and Delinquency in Light of Sociological Theories

Sylvia Khromina

University of Massachusetts Boston

sylvia.khromina001@umb.edu

Abstract: An examination of the causes and effects of juvenile violence and delinquency through an exploration of the retributive Juvenile Justice System, the struggles of the urban poor and the effects of juvenile crime on the success of all of society. Drawing on the six key sociological theories, this paper will investigate the possible reasons behind current policies and crime itself.

I have always been interested in the study of people's everyday struggles and it had been made very clear to me from early on that education was the "key to success" in the United States; my parents made certain that this idea was etched in my mind. We emigrated from Russia when I was eight years old, and my parents knew that paying for me to go to college was beyond their financial means. Throughout my childhood, I saw my parents work long hours (at jobs that did not satisfy them mentally or financially) in order to give my sister and I a better future. My personal struggle has always been to put aside all of my vices in order to achieve the so-called 'American Dream' for me and to make my parents proud and justify all of the effort that they have put forth on my behalf.

I attended a very diverse (and very affordable) Catholic high school in Cambridge, Massachusetts, and it was there that I first came to an understanding of just how fortunate I am. I only battle my own internal limitations in order to excel in life, but there are people all around me that have to struggle with their surroundings in order to 'make it' in this world. During my high school years I also spent much of my free time working as a mentor with underprivileged teen girls in a program run by a non profit magazine called *Teen Voices*. The girls that partook in this program were from impoverished inner city families and the program worked to focus the girls' attention on education as way out of their grim reality and into a better future.

Both in my high school and at *Teen Voices,* I saw how crime and violence impacts individuals' lives and hinders their opportunities for success. I developed many close friendships in these two areas of my life and had the opportunity to take a closer look into the lives of the people that

---

Sylvia Khromina is an undergraduate student at UMass Boston, double-majoring in Psychology and Sociology. She wrote this paper while enrolled in the course Soc. 341-4: "Elements of Sociological Theories," instructed by Mohammad H. Tamdgidi (Assistant Professor of Sociology at UMass Boston) during the Spring 2007 semester.

seem to me to have been forgotten or discarded by the mainstream society. For the first time, I began to venture into the 'unsafe' neighborhoods of the city, and get to know the 'unconventional' families that had to struggle with what seemed to be all the problems of the world. These problems included a lack of economic opportunities, a lack of educational opportunities and (as a result of these) a high risk of violence and crime in their day to day lives.

I developed a close friendship with a group of girls who resided in the Mission Hill projects in Roxbury. Among these girls, Alexis became my close friend and my makeshift guide through the reality of life for the urban poor. Alexis has all of the internal qualities for success; she is intelligent, dedicated when she puts her mind to her work, confident despite her situation, attractive and in full control of her self image. Alexis would often tell me stories of her friends who had been killed in one way or another mostly by their own peers. With an almost matter-of-fact attitude, Alexis attended roughly six funerals of boys her age who were killed as a result of juvenile violence. When I asked about her cold attitude toward the death of her neighbors and childhood friends, Alexis replied that "when you see death, drugs and violence all around you throughout life, your heart turns from grief to anger and retribution." She said that if she allowed herself to ponder on the horrors of her surroundings, she would become depressed and 'crazy.' I began to take her approach to violence and crime, and found myself paying less and less attention to the newspaper stories and television news stories of people killed due to youth violence in the poor neighborhoods of Boston. I felt that although this violence was all too real, it was invisible for as long as I avoided it. I thought, "as long as I have my friends, classmates and neighbors, I don't need to focus on the rest."

All of that changed one night in the summer of 2006. Alexis and I were spending some time with a few former classmates and catching up on life after high school. It was a hot July night and many people were outside of their homes in a little courtyard in the middle of the Mission Hill projects. As we enjoyed each others' company along with the beautiful summer weather, time passed unnoticed. Finally, Alexis, I and one other girl realized that it was getting late and decided to head over to the local pizza shop before it closed for the night. The streets were beginning less and less lively as people went inside for the night and we hastily headed over toward Boston House of Pizza to eat some late dinner. We left behind a small group of girls, one of whom was Anna, a former classmate who was that day mourning the one year anniversary of the death of her brother.

Once inside the pizza shop, Alexis received a frantic phone call from a friend who told her that Anna had been shot while we were gone. We rushed back to the little courtyard that we had abandoned just minutes earlier. There were people everywhere, and police were arriving on the scene to seal off the area where Anna had been attacked. She was being wheeled into an ambulance, as numerous people screamed and cried at the sight of this young woman covered in blood. Alexis decided to go to the hospital, but I chose to go home, feeling that the hospital is a place for family members and close friends. Later on that night, I received a phone call from Alexis, who coldly informed me that Anna had passed away.

It turned out that Anna who had managed to overcome numerous obstacles in her short lifetime was killed by her ex-boyfriend in an irrational display of rage. Anna was a good student, who managed to go to school while raising her daughter (one she gave birth to at the age of sixteen). I still remember the sight of Anna carrying her daughter up to the podium with her during our high school graduation ceremony. She then attended college, worked, and raised her then four-year-old child. Anna was even able to overcome the grief that comes along with losing a brother (who was killed on the same day one year prior to her death). However, despite her internal strength of character and will to succeed, external circumstances ended her life and left her daughter to struggle in this cruel world without a mother.

This situation affected me more than I would like to admit; it became a moment of epiphany for me. It made me realize many things about life and it made me appreciate every minute of it. I was removed from the crime scene for just a few minutes, but it was those minutes that turned out to be crucial in determining Anna's fate as well as mine. Anna was an example of a 'success story' in the projects, but despite all of her inner success---being able to raise a child, she motivate herself to finish school and attend college and had the capacity to not allow the sorrow in her life to bring her down---she paid the ultimate price due to youth violence. My inner success had always been enough to get me through because I did not have to deal with other variables such as crime, drugs, violence and gangs in my everyday life. It became clear to me then that 'education is the key' was not enough to achieve success in this life for the unfortunate bunch that ended up at the socioeconomic bottom. Violent crime, which arises from many external and internal causes (often during one's youth), can be a lethal stopper in the flow of success even for the most determined individuals.

Anna's emotionally disturbed and trigger happy assailant had many excuses for his behavior. He is the child of a poor urban family; he grew up with many psychological problems and had disrupted any educational and economic opportunities that he might have had by becoming a juvenile offender at a young age. The state did not treat his psychological and social problems and helped to send him on his way into a lifelong criminal career by placing him in an institutionalized correctional facility for minor crimes he committed while still a child (under the age of 17). Anna's killer's case makes one wonder: What could have been expected of this psychologically disturbed person whose emotional state was hindered, rather than being helped, by the Massachusetts Juvenile Justice System?

The Juvenile Justice System in this state, as well as most others, still highly favors the retributive justice model, which has proven to be ineffective for many reasons. Incarceration has many long lasting negative effects on the offender, the public and social trends in general. These effects are especially visible in the Juvenile Justice System because juvenile offenders are basically children from the ages of seven to seventeen.

The most visible impact of incarceration is a dramatically higher rate of recidivism when compared to community based programs for juvenile offenders. A youth who is sentenced to serve time in jail is much more likely to be a repeat offender and even to develop a criminal career. This high recidivism rate is primarily due to a lack of behind-the-wall programs which prepare youth for reentry (Jenson, 1998). There is also a large amount of brutality in correctional facilities on the part of offenders and staff members. This leads youth to become affiliated with behind-the-wall gangs for protection, to develop violent and antisocial tendencies and to foster high rates of distrust and anger toward people in general (Patchin, 2006). The disconnection with the community also leads to high recidivism rates because prior offenders have little concern for the community and the community gives them little support when they are released (Christian, 2003).

The costs associated with incarceration are also drastically higher than costs of community correctional programs. The cost of juvenile incarceration is estimated at

$43,000 per person annually; however there are programs which cost as much as $64,000 per person annually. A large percentage of the yearly cost of incarceration for juveniles goes toward operation costs, medical care, and supervision (Einstein Law, 2007). Contrary to public opinion, youth correctional facility costs are driven down when educational programs are implemented in these facilities. Aside from actual operational costs of incarceration, it is important to consider the costs that are associated with re-offending; which include victim damages, court costs and community costs (Knoester, 2005).

Despite the high costs of incarceration, many studies suggest that the threat of incarceration is not a good deterrent for youth (and for adults) (Pettit, 2004). The model of retributive justice (under which incarceration falls) has the negative effect of separating 'criminals' from the rest of society and leads to a stratification of society. This makes it difficult for 'ex-criminals' to reintegrate into society and become positive contributing members of their communities (Christian, 2003).

The problem of juvenile delinquency is ever present in the society of the United States. Although much has been done to reduce juvenile delinquency and to throw out the retributive justice approach to crime in general, youth crime and especially violence is still very real in our society. There are six major theoretical approaches which can be utilized to answer two key questions regarding juvenile delinquency. The first question is the possible causes of and justifications for juvenile delinquency and especially violence, on a micro or internal level. The second question is the possible causes and justifications for juvenile delinquency and especially violence, on a macro or societal level.

The theory of **Functionalism** in sociology, although coined and developed after WWII by Talcott Parsons, may be said to have originated in the works of early sociologist Émile Durkheim, who examined the division of labor in our society and stated that this division of labor creates *social solidarity*. The idea of *organic solidarity* also arose from this theory because Durkheim insisted that the division of labor into specific functions performed by individuals causes interdependence among individuals and leads to organic solidarity. Functionalism examines the many functions that occur within society and establishes the benefits and consequences of these functions for specific groups and individuals. Functionalism, especially in its later varieties such as that found in the works of Robert Merton, holds that while some functions are positive in their effects for one group or set of individuals, the same functions could produce negative effects for other groups or individuals.

There are many varieties of functionalist theory, which were developed after the creation of Durkheim's original model. Later sociologists created the theory of *structural functionalism* which examined how social order is maintained and created through the maintenance and promotion of societal structure. Structural functionalism also devoted much attention to the phenomenon of *social change* which is a process of 'evolution' in which *social institutions* become highly functional through their differentiation as well as their adaptation of common norms. *Neofunctionalism* is a later development of the functionalist social theories, holding on to the core of functionalism but going into a deeper exploration of social change and social conflict and the incorporation of various micro perspectives. Functionalist theorists examine social practices and their impact on society and the individual and define these social practices as any social occurrences that have a pattern and are repetitive in their nature. These social practices include *social roles, social structures, social norms* and social institutions. The later version of functionalist was synthesized with conflict theory by Lewis Coser in order to come to a better understanding of the function that conflict plays in modern society (Wallace and Wolf, 2005; Farganis, 2004).

According to Functionalism, juvenile delinquency serves a function both for the offender and for society as a whole. There are many cited studies that prove that politicians use the perception of high crime rates as a platform for their elections. These false uses of important issues are visible in poll data through participants' higher interpretation of crime rates during election years. Taking attention away from the real issues at hand, and concentrating instead on crime and violence which is usually 'battled' with the increase of incarceration rates (Bureau of Justice Statistics, 1999).

Juveniles use violence and therefore crime to serve many functions; in order to belong to a group, to defend themselves against their environment, in order to get monetary benefits that they are unable to attain through other means and as a way to express and filter out their internal rage (Tetlack, 1984).

The **Conflict Theory** in sociology is comprised of four major propositions. First, that social life is predominantly shaped by social *conflict* among individuals and/or groups. The conflict arises from the presumed fact that individuals and/or groups are in competition for limited resources. The second major proposition of this theory is in regard to what constitutes the essence of the conflict; the assumption is that the fight is essentially over power and economic resources. The third proposition holds that the conflict over resources results in the formation of dominating or controlling groups in society, and this pattern continues over long periods of time. The fourth major proposition of conflict theory is the disproportionate influence that the *dominant societal groups* have in society. The dominant groups shift the structure of society through the control of major resources and their allocations.

There are two major branches of the conflict theory in sociology; the first is the Marxian view of conflict theory which holds that the division of social classes based on economic interests causes the majority of conflicts in society. The second view held by sociologists such as Max Weber and (later) Randall Collins, proposes that not just, or primarily, the economic, but as well political, ethnic and religious *ideologies* (or sets of beliefs) can cause social conflict and the creation of social classes, status groups, and parties in society. These later sociologists hold that conflicts arise due to major societal factors, but are not limited to the economically based social class divisions. They also believe that conflict is a permanent part of society and can not be eliminated with the removal of social classes in society. Weber along with his counterpart theorists strongly believed that bureaucracy and its' desire for order often increases and produces conflicts, while Marxist theorists subject the behavior of *bureaucratic organizations* to the nature of economic forces (Wallace and Wolf, 2005; Farganis, 2004).

One of the best explanations for high incarceration rates is provided by the Conflict Theory because it holds that human groups are in constant competition, and therefore the dominant societal groups work to oppress the underclasses. In this case, dominant classes work to further oppress the poor classes that tend to have the highest instance of youth violence and delinquency. By incarcerating youth, we are limiting their chances at future success. We are therefore further oppressing the under classes and ensuring that they remain in their current underprivileged states.

Juveniles are also in competition, but they are on the losing end of the battle with underqualified schools, lack of legitimate economic opportunities and struggles to keep themselves physically safe. Therefore, they turn to violence as a way to improve their situation and to release inner psychological and emotional problems (Knoester, 2005).

Theories of Rational Choice state that humans are rational creatures that function by making calculated, rational choices based on the set of *norms, beliefs* and *values* prevalent in society. Values are developed through a person's participation in a particular group, as well as natural selection of traits that are instilled in each individual. Value factors are at the core of rational choice theoretical explanations because they are a major guide in the human decision-making process. Rational choices are those that are carefully calculated based on the above mentioned factors, and are used to maximize *utility*. Utility is defined as that which creates the most positive outcome or effect for an individual or group. Rational choice theories assume that humans always have the capacity to calculate their choices based on their desired utility and the consequences that may come with specific choices, and therefore this set of theories are labeled *means-end-theories*. In other words, rational choice theories describe the means (rationalized calculations and choices) by which humans work to obtain their desired ends (which are within their sets of values, beliefs and norms).

This set of theories can be applied to *social dilemmas* or situations which create a conflict between individual interests and those that are collective (interests of groups). In such situations, rational choice theories make it easier to distinguish between individual utility and the utility as determined by larger societal structures. However, rational choice theories are best used when they are applied to *face to face interactions* and *small group interactions*. Many sociologists criticize these theories because there is much research which supports decision making based on formulated *schemas* or sets of beliefs which are developed throughout life and used for categorization purposes. These critics claim that choices are made mostly based on our schemas and for the most part, lack rational calculations of utility. Rational choice theories go outside the science of sociology into economics and political science because schemas are not likely to impact decision making in these fields, and choices become more black and white (those that increase utility and those that hinder it) (Wallace and Wolf, 2005; Farganis, 2004).

Rational Choice Theories are often used in Criminology to identify and understand the motives behind crime. However, they do little to help us understand why society continues to incarcerate youth. Incarceration of youth does not lead to positive utility, and therefore is not a rational choice (Deschenes, 1998). However, in the case of juvenile delinquency; crime is often the rational choice. When youth are faced with external factors that prevent social success (such as lack of education, dangerous living environments and no hope of attaining economic success through legal means) and internal factors (such as mental illness, childhood trauma and a lack of sufficient motivation), crime seems to be an easy means by which to attain desired utility (Knoester, 2005).

Symbolic interactionism is a theoretical perspective which explores how humans through the use language and *symbols* develop their senses of self, ability to think, and to communicate with others. Herbert Blumer coined the term symbolic interaction after George Herbert Mead's work in theorizing the self and how it develops. There are three parts to Blumer's theory; first, humans act based on the meanings that they assign to things; second, these meanings are formed through interpersonal interactions; and, finally, the definition and meaning of things is in a constant process of modification because human interpretations of events are constantly changing and evolving. This is a *social-psychological perspective* because symbolic interactions deal with an individual's internal thoughts and feelings in the context of his or her interactions with others. Opinion formation is an important part of symbolic interactionist theory because it holds that we form our interpretation of events based on the meanings that we have assigned to things. Symbolic interaction theorists believe that we live in an active environment, where change is constant; therefore the individual as well as society is in a constant process of change and development. In my interpretation of the theory, there are four key terms in symbolic interactionist theory; *process, agency, conditionality*, and *collective action*. Process refers to the ever changing and developing nature of symbolic interactions. Agency is the idea that humans have the potential to control their own actions, thoughts and feelings as well as their surrounding environment and those around them. Conditionality is the idea that humans are part of a society that has conditions to which they have to adjust, respond and get accustomed to. Collective action is any action that is taken by multiple participants; whether a few individuals or large groups. This type of action requires supervision, planning and good timing in order to be effective. On an individual level, symbolic interaction theories are some of the first to include emotions as an important aspect of human dealings with one another (Wallace and Wolf, 2005; Farganis, 2004).

Symbolic interaction theories are very applicable to criminology and are often used to explain why individuals commit crime. Youth in underprivileged life circumstances look to their relationships as a guide for behavior. Since many are surrounded by criminal activity, gang participation and drug use; they too partake in these behaviors (Patchin, 2006).

The retributive model of justice can also be attributed to symbolic interactionist theories because society as a whole is primed to fear crime, seek retribution and believe that underprivileged youth are more likely to commit and re-commit crimes. This process of priming occurs largely through the media due to its disproportionate coverage of minority crime. There is a high salience of crime in our society, but very little attention is given to the community based approach to solving the problem of crime and violence. Therefore we are only 'interacting' based on the negative ideas and trends in society rather than expanding our knowledge of the positive possibilities (Ditton, 2004; Goidel, 2006).

Phenomenology is the sociological theory that is based on the idea that human reality is comprised of events, objects and feelings which are perceived just as they are understood by an individual's *consciousness*. Therefore, this theory gives special attention to the internal consciousness and subjective nature of an individual. The main technique in phenomenology is to explain the process of how one's consciousness of everyday life develops. Edmund Husserl is the founder of phenomenology and known mostly for taking the concept of *intentionality* as the independent variable in his studies. Husserl believed that humans often experience the world in a spontaneous way with little reflection and calculation, therefore opinions of reality and an understanding of the world is formed through the process of *natural attitudes*. Alfred Schutz took Husserl's approach further by making human experiences concrete and open to empirical investigation. Schutz claimed that although human *subjects* were given free will to interpret and partake in the world, their actions and views can also be *objects* of scientific investigation. This social actor experiences the world from his/her natural attitudes and often does not interpret it in a questioning way (Wallace and Wolf, 2005; Farganis, 2004). Harold Garfinkel has developed the phenomenological approach further by seeking to understand everyday human behavior by problematizing and intentionally disrupting, for the purpose of study, what we usually take for granted as our commonsense social reality. This way, the nature of social reality as what Berger and Luckmann refer to as having been, and being continually, *constructed* and reconstructed becomes evident.

Phenomenology makes it possible for us to see how the everyday lives of violent youth, as well as the institutional frameworks and processes of the Juvenile Justice System, are not natural orders of things but ones that are socially constructed, and thereby can be further reconstructed and transformed. Narrowly interpreted and practiced, however, phenomenology may make the ideas of justice and crime fully subjective and malleable to different interpretations. If not careful, we may condemn youthful offenders to a life of crime by interpreting their behaviors as emanating from a subjective thought process (Zimring, 2006). As such, we take what we have narrowly learned about crime, about youth and about justice and formulate large scale opinions which influence policy.

When we attempt to examine the reason behind youth crime through phenomenology, we may notice that there is little rationality present in these criminal activities and they are largely spontaneous events shaped by internal forces and ideas. However, such criminal ideas and behaviors are a product of many years of seeing 'the negative side of life,' and learning to live in a way to accept the world around them as a subjective reality (Patchin, 2006).

All of the above theories provide some insight into the causes of crime and violence as well as the reasons for our perception of the need for incarceration and for the lack of focus on community-based programs for our underprivileged youth.

The death of my classmate Anna has made me realize the many external factors that hinder the success of the urban poor. Among these problems is the crucial issue of juvenile delinquency and violence. This problem makes it almost impossible to be sure of a positive future for those that are forced to live in unsafe communities. In the United States, little is being done to combat the problem of juvenile delinquency and violence for the urban poor. Instead, this population is deprived of successful and positive educational environments, economic opportunities and the possibility to have strong, supportive communities. All of these problems help increase juvenile delinquency and violence because youth begin to see violence as their only way out of economic struggles and emotional and psychological issues.

A possible way to help in the reduction of juvenile delinquency and violence is to reduce the current trend of incarceration and to begin implementing community based intervention and residential and reintegration programs. These programs will allow youth to gain the skills and knowledge that they need in order to gain economic success. They will address the psychological problems that plague many children growing up in the stress of problematic family lives, poverty, and lack of self esteem. And finally, they will create a community network and greater awareness of the problems that face this nation and the world.

REFERENCES AND FURTHER RESOURCES

Juvenile Justice System:

1) Patchin, J.W., Huebner B.M., McCluskey J.D., Varano, S.P., & Bynum, T.S. (2006). Exposure to Community Violence and Childhood Delinquency. *Crime & Delinquency*. 52 (2), 307-322.
2) Foster, M., & Rehner, T. (2003). Delinquency Prevention as Empowerment Practice: A Community-Based Social Work Approach. *Race, Gender & Class*. April 30, 2003. 10 (2), 109.
3) Christian, Steve. (2003) Out of lock-up: now what? A large number of youthful

offenders released from confinement end up back in the system. Helping kids re-enter the community can help them stay out of trouble and save states money. *State Legislatures.* 29, 21-24.

4) Knoester, C., & Haynie D.L. (2005) Community Context, Social Integration into Family, and Youth Violence. *Journal of Marriage and Family.* 67, 767-780.

5) Jenson J.M., & Howard M.O. (1998) Youth crime, public policy, and practice in the juvenile justice system: recent trends and needed reforms. *Social Work.* 434, 324-335.

6) Felson R.B., & Staff, J. (2006) Explaining the Academic Performance-Delinquency Relationship. *Criminology.* 44 (2), 299-315.

7) Deschenes, E. P., & Greenwood P.W. (1998) "Alternative placements for juvenile offenders: results from the evaluation of the Nokomis challenge program." *Journal of Research in Crime and Delinquency.* 35 (3), 267.

Public Opinion about Corrections:

8) Zimring, F.E., & Johnson, D.T. (2006) Public Opinion and the Governance of Punishment in Democratic Political Systems. *Annals of the American Academy of Political and Science.* 605, 266-278.

9) Sigler, R.T., & Lamb, D. (1995) Community-based alternatives to prison: How the public and court personnel view them. *Federal Probation.* 59(2), 3-9.

10) Smith, K.B. (2004) The Politics of Punishment: Evaluating Political Explanations of Incarceration Rates. *The Journal of Politics.* 66 (3), 925-938.

11) Brocke, M. Goldenitz, C., Holling, H., & Bilsky, W. (2004) Attitudes Towards Severity of Punishment: A Conjoint Analytical Approach. *Psychology, Crime & Law.* 10 (2), 205-219.

12) Roberts, J.V., & Stalans, L.J. (2004) Restorative Sentencing: Exploring the Views of the Public. *Social Justice Research.* 17 (3), 315-331.

13) Zamble, E., & Kalm K.L. (1990) General and Specific Measures of Public Attitudes toward Sentencing. *Canadian Journal of Behavioral Science.* 22(3), 327-337.

Corrections Statistics:

14) Pettit, B., & Western, B. (2004) Mass Imprisonment and the Life Course; Race and Class Inequality in U.S. Incarceration. *America Sociological Review.* 69, 151-169.

15) Stucky, T.D., Heimer, K., & Lang, J.B. (2007) A Bigger Piece of the Pie? State Corrections Spending and the Politics of Social Order. *Journal of Research in Crime and Delinquency.* 44, 91-123.

16) Bureau of Justice Statistics (1998) Attitudes Toward The Most Important Goal Of Prison, By Demographic Characteristics, United States, 1996. *Sourcebook of Criminal Justice Statistics.* (1998), 131.

Crime and Media Statistics:

17) Ditton, J., Chadee, D., Farrall, S., Gilchrist, E., & Bannister, J. (2004) FROM IMITATION TO INTIMIDATION: A Note on the Curious and Changing Relationship between the Media, Crime and Fear of Crime. *British Journal of Criminology.* 44(4), 595-610.

18) Goidel, R.K., Freeman, C.M., and Procopio, S.T. (2006) The Impact of Television Viewing on Perceptions of Juvenile Crime. *Journal of Broadcasting & Electronic Media.* 50(1), 119-139.

19) Bureau of Justice Statistics (1999) Attitudes Toward Contributions To Violence In Society, By Demographic Characteristics, United States, 1999. *Sourcebook of Criminal Justice Statistics.* (1998), 122.

Class Materials:

20) Milburn, M.A., & McGrail, A.B. (1992) The Dramatic Presentation of News and Its Effects on Cognitive Complexity. *Political Psychology.* 13(4), 613-630.

21) Parenti, M. (1992) Inventing Reality: The Politics of News Media. New York, Wadsworth Publishing. 62-74.

22) Bennet, L. (1996) News Content: Messages for the Masses. *News: The Politics of Illusion* (3rd ed.), White Plains, NY, Longman. 37-73.

23) Edelman, M. (1971) Politics as Symbolic Action: Mass Arousal and Quiescence. *Information and Cognition.* New York. Academic Press. 329-335.

24) Tetlack, P.E. (1984) Cognitive Style and Political Belief System in the British House of Commons. *Journal of Personality and Social Psychology.* 46 (2), 365-375.

Statistics:

25) Bureau of Justice Statistics (2001) Attitudes Toward Level Of Crime In The United

States, 2001. *Sourcebook of Criminal Justice Statistics*, (2001) 122.
26) Bureau of Justice Statistics (1999) Attitudes Toward Level Of Crime In The United States, By Demographic Characteristics, 1998. *Sourcebook of Criminal Justice Statistics*, (1999) 116.
27) Bureau of Justice Statistics (1999) Respondents Indicating Too Little Is Spent On Selected Problems In This Country, United States, Selected Years 1973-98. *Sourcebook of Criminal Justice Statistics*, (1999) 123.
28) Bureau of Justice Statistics (1999) Attitudes Toward The Level Of Spending To Halt The Rising Crime Rate, By Demographic Characteristics, United States, Selected Years 1983-98. *Sourcebook of Criminal Justice Statistics*, (1999) 124-125.
29) Bureau of Justice Statistics (1999) Attitudes Toward The Most Important Problem Facing The Country, United States, 1982-99. *Sourcebook of Criminal Justice Statistics*, (1999) 96.
30) Bureau of Justice Statistics (1999) Attitudes Toward Important Issues For The Government To Address, United States, 1993-99. *Sourcebook of Criminal Justice Statistics*, (1999) 97.
31) U.S. Census Bureau (2000) DP-2. Profile of Selected Social Characteristics: 2000, *Census 2000 Summary*.
32) U.S. Census Bureau (2000) DP-3. Profile of Selected Social Characteristics: 2000, *Census 2000 Summary*.

Websites and other Electronic Sources:

33) Einstein Law (2007) Juvenile justices FAQs. *Juvenile Justice FYI*.
34) Johnson, L. (2007) State Juvenile Justice Profiles: Massachusetts. *www.ncjj.org*
35) Massachusetts Bar Association (2007) About Our Legal System: Juvenile Courts. *www.masslawhelp.org*
36) Commonwealth of Massachusetts (2007) Mass. Law About Juvenile Justice. *Massachusetts Trial Court Law Libraries on the Web*
37) OJJDP (2000) National Crime Victimization Survey, cited in Juvenile Offenders and Victims: 1999 National Report (OJJDP).

Additional Classroom Materials

38) Gest, T (2001) Crime & Politics: Big Government's Erratic Campaign for Law and Order. Chicago, Oxford University Press. 270.
39) Wallace, R. A., and Wolf, A. (2005) Contemporary Sociological Theory: Expanding the Classical Tradition. Sixth Edition. New Jersey: Prentice Hall.
40) Farganis, J. (Ed) (2004) Readings in Social Theory: The Classical Tradition to Post-Modernism. Fourth Edition. McGraw Hill College Division.

Why Do I Not Like Me?

Sociological Self-Reflections on Weight Issues and the American Culture

C. G.

University of Massachusetts Boston

Abstract: Back home in the Philippines I was very active and I was always playing outside with my friends. We would explore the seas and its inhabitants by jumping from corals to corals; the sea was practically my backyard back when I was a kid. We would swim in the sea every chance we got; and we would play whatever game there was to play outside. And because of these activities weight was never such a big issue to me. I loved being outside when I was young, but when I immigrated to the U.S. about 11 years ago I was confined to the house we were staying at. My parents would not let me out since it was such a different place for us. I also didn't want to go out because I had no reason to and because I didn't know any other kids that were willing to play with me. Therefore, I stayed at home watching TV and eating whatever there was I could find in the fridge. I turned to sweets such as ice cream, chocolate, cake, etc., as a form of comfort. I substituted my old friends in the Philippines for food here. In this essay I explore how the American culture, media, and consumerism influenced my self-perception and self-esteem surrounding weight issues, and how various micro- and macrosociological theories have helped me to understand and deal with the problem.

Back home in the Philippines I was very active and I was always playing outside with my friends. We would explore the seas and its inhabitants by jumping from corals to corals; the sea was practically my backyard back when I was a kid. We would swim in the sea every chance we got; and we would play whatever game there was to play outside. I could list over a hundred things that I did when I was a kid; but I am not going to. And because of these activities weight was never such a big issue to me.

I loved being outside when I was young, but when I immigrated to the U.S. about 11 years ago I was confined to the house we were staying at. My parents would not let me out since it was such a different place for us. I also didn't want to go out because I had no reason to and because I didn't know any other kids that were willing to play with me. Therefore, I stayed at home watching TV and eating whatever there was I could find in the fridge. I turned to sweets such as ice cream, chocolate, cake, etc., as a form of comfort. I substituted my old friends in the Philippines for food here.

C. G. is an undergraduate student at UMass Boston, majoring in Criminal Justice. She wrote this paper while enrolled in the course Soc. 341-3: "Elements of Sociological Theories," instructed by Mohammad H. Tamdgidi (Assistant Professor of Sociology at UMass Boston) during the Spring 2007 semester.

It was very hard adjusting to this place for me when I was young. So, after the years since I arrived in the U.S. I started packing on quite a lot of pounds. I never realized this, however, until one of my relatives called me a pig in my dialect. My whole childlike innocence was shattered when I got here. I never knew what a big deal physical appearance was until I was constantly insulted and made fun of most of the time in my family gatherings.

The insults and cruel jokes that I received led me into a state of depression for more than four years. I would always ask myself what was wrong with how I look? Am I really that ugly? Am I really that fat? Am I being punished for looking the way I do? Do I deserve to get hurt like this because I am ugly and fat? These questions and many more were always haunting me throughout the depressed stage of my life. Through the years I grew to believe what everyone else was telling me about myself and I grew to believe that I was deserving of all the pain and agony that was being inflicted upon my soul and my being. Even now the emotional abuse and trauma that I have encountered still lingers within me. I still don't believe that I am attractive enough. I still don't believe that being me is good enough for anyone and for me. I still have a hard time not disliking myself.

I have been like this for so long now that I have taken this part of myself for granted and have perceived it to be a normal part of my life. Now, however, I will question this part of my self. **Phenomenology** encourages us to problematize what we hold to be normal. Phenomenologists would ask us to be strangers to ourselves and our environment so we can better analyze and questions our norms. Phenomenologists believe that we take things for granted in our everyday lives and that we are not aware that these things were socially constructed and thus can be changed. In their book, *Contemporary Sociological Theory* (2006), Ruth Wallace and Alison Wolf state that the "basic proposition [of phenomenology is] that everyday reality is a socially constructed system of ideas that has accumulated over time and is taken for granted by group members" (262). Berger and Luckmann also state that "people continuously create, through their actions and interactions, a shared reality" (Wallace & Wolf 285). This encourages us to question our reality and implies hope by suggesting that we can change it. **Ethnomethodology,** according to Harold Garfinkel who coined the term, studies people's methods of making sense of their everyday activities (Wallace & Wolf, 269). Phenomenology and ethnomethodology are **microsociological** traditions in sociology, exploring one-on-one interactions individual have with one another. Symbolic interaction is another microsociological tradition to which I turn while exploring my issue.

According to Herbert Mead, human beings have a self and that "**the self**" is an active organism that behaves in his or her own way depending on how he or she interprets the behaviors of others towards him or her. The self is the central subject matter studied in **symbolic interactionism,** focusing "on the interaction between a person's internal thoughts and emotions and his or her social behavior" (Wallace & Wolf 205) in the context of the broader interactions he or she has with others. When I gained weight and my relatives' insults started occurring the self that I had when I used to live in the Philippines changed. The issue of my weight and the insults that came with it was so new to me that I interpreted it as something that was wrong with me. I interpreted this problem as my fault and since I interpreted it this way I became depressed.

One of the basic premises of symbolic interactionism is that **the meaning of things arises out of the social interaction one has with one's fellows**. This suggests that the meaning of objects are socially constructed and that the only way one can knows what the real meaning of something is through interaction with other human beings. I learned through my interactions with my relatives that being fat or overweight means being hideous. The meaning that I learned that was associated with being fat led me to interpret to myself that I was ugly and that it was all my fault. Therefore, I do agree with Sheerin Hosseini's statement that a child's "environment and life experiences… has the power to shape her perception of herself, or her self-esteem" (30). Hosseini was always trying hard to be noticed by her friends and family. She would compare her abilities with her other peers and see that she wasn't better than them. These comparisons, however, led to low self-esteem because she thought that she wasn't good at anything like the other people around her.

Another concept that is part of symbolic interactionism is "**the looking-glass self**," coined by the sociologist Charles Horton Cooley. Cooley identifies the three elements of the looking-glass self as "the imagination of our appearance to the other person; the imagination of his judgment of that appearance; and some sort of self-feeling, such as pride or mortification" (Wallace & Wolf 203). This is when an individual imagines how he or she appears to others and imagines how others are judging him or her. The feeling that the individual gets is the result of this process. As I continued to gain weight I became very aware of my physical unattractiveness and I started being paranoid and insecure. I worried all the time about how I looked. I would start imagining how other people see me and base on that assumption I would imagine how they would judge me. I imagined that they saw a really fat girl and that they judged me to be unattractive, so I started to feel mortified about how I looked. I realized through media and entertainment that being super skinny was to be attractive and because of these implicit and explicit messages I wanted to be skinny so badly and hoped that maybe if I became skinny I would be happy too. I agree with Anna Schlosser's point in her article, "My Image Struggles in Capitalist Society," that "our culture has created this unattainable ideal which the majority of women do not resemble at all" (34). Schlosser wrote about the struggle she had to face in society as a woman. She mentioned that as women in a capitalist society we try to live up to an ideal image and when we don't live up to it we suffer consequences such as being ostracized.

Erving Goffman, another important contributor to symbolic interactionism, compared people in society to actors in a theater. This approach to understanding everyday human behavior came to be known as **dramaturgical sociology**. Goffman states that individuals seek to guide and control the impressions that others form about them. He called this **impression management**. Goffman believed that the way an individual manipulates their impression given to others is by distinguishing two regions in their everyday interactions. The **front region** is "that part of the individual's performance which regularly functions in a general and fixed fashion to define the situation for those who observe the performance;" this region is usually conducted in front of an audience. The **back region**, however, "is the place closed to and hidden from the audience where techniques of impression management are practiced" (Wallace & Wolf 239). As I was constantly being picked on I realized that I had to give an impression to my relatives that I was not bothered by their insults. I was afraid to be seen as being unattractive as well as being weak. Before family gatherings I would constantly prepare myself in my bedroom to expect cruel jokes about my weight and I would tell myself to just laugh along with them as well even if I was emotionally in pain due to their comments. By doing this I controlled how my relatives saw me. I made them believed that I had some strength and was not bothered by their jokes.

However, upon deciding to mask my pain with smiles and laughter I was hurting myself even more internally. I became anxious when it came to losing a lot of weight that I began to inhibit a minor event of eating disorder. It wasn't as extreme as stated in M.D.'s article "Body Image: A Clouded Reality" where she talked about her illness, anorexia nervosa; however I can still relate to it because she struggle with her image. M.D. wanted to be accepted in our society, and she thought that being skinny was a big factor in that societal acceptance. Because everyone complimented how she looked all the time she continued to suppress her hunger in order to keep her image in society so that she can be adored all the time. One year in my high school life I also decided not to eat except once a day. I was doing this for a year and I lost about 30 pounds. I felt sort of better about how I looked but it still wasn't enough for me. I wasn't happy still. As M.D. stated she felt as though she was in control when she wasn't eating and that's how I felt too. This feeling was probably one of the main factors that make anorexics go on with their disorders. I didn't continue with this method because I felt as if it wasn't working faster for me so I turned to diet pills and other dietary methods and products for a few years.

It is amazing to me how our society implicitly and explicitly gives us the message that physical attractiveness is the basis for being human and one of the big factors that many of us base our physical appearance on is our weight. Our media tells us that being skinny is the ideal and coveted weight by constantly showing us through music videos, movies, games, magazines, etc., women who are really skinny. The models depicted on these media outlets are symbols of what is attractive in our society. This technique that our media chooses reminded me of a point brought up by Marnia Lazreg on March 27th during the fourth annual Social Theory Forum held at UMass Boston. Lazreg stated that colonialism was a system that was based on violence. She stated that the techniques for obedience to colonialism are symbols, sounds, music and pain. These techniques are clearly apparent in our culture especially throughout the media manipulating our generation. She also states that colonialism has different effects on different individuals. This also goes to explain why some in our society accept the idea of skinny being part of an ideal beauty and why some are fighting against this idea stating that there shouldn't be a particular ideal body type that women should be held up to. Part of America's colonialism was to define masculinity and femininity and its definitions are conveyed constantly on our televisions screens. Even though it is seen to be accepted for women to be part of the workforce in our economy, we are still held to be "nuclear objects and desires, you know, 'dishes' and 'bombshells'" (Gordon 12). We would like to believe that we all are equal in our society, but how can we even believe this if the media constantly favors "patriarchal paternalism" (Gordon 12). Author and sociologist Avery Gordon sees the world to be hard for women because they live in a society that favors men. Even though women have fought to be seen as beings equal to men they cannot escape the perspective that many hold against them such as being attractive.

Obsessing about how attractive I look and about my weight is an evidence of my participation in our patriarchal society. It is therefore important that I study the issues I have with my self image on a **macrosociological** level as well, which concerns the larger picture of social roles and social structures shaping our everyday lives. C. Wright Mills, in his book about the **sociological imagination** (1959), suggested that there is a connection between the macro and micro social processes, and therefore our sociologies should take their interrelation into account. Exploring the causes of my distorted image through both macro and micro lenses is important. In the film *Matrix*, Neo chose the red pill to uncover the truth of his problems. Neo felt that there was something wrong with his world and he wanted answers to questions he had about this realization. He knew that his life was being affected by the world around him. Just like Neo I realize that my personal problems are affected by society at large. I want to know why most of us, including me, have this distorted self-image, one that makes us live in a fake, yet real, world of unattainable beauty ideals.

It seems that I have **internalized**, that is, accepted as **objectively factual** others' social values and ideals in society as part of my own personality. I have come to believe that being overweight is very unattractive, a notion which is socially constructed by others in society. Using Berger and Luckmann's concept of **objectivation**, it seems such values and norms had already become objectivated and established long before I arrived on the scene. Ever since I came to the U.S., in particular, I started to realize that reaching the ideal physical body was a big part of American life; therefore, watching your weight has become a common behavioral pattern and getting to that ideal is wrongly thought to be attainable by all Americans. Our **subjective realities** have thus become part of the larger socially constructed realities pertaining to unattainable beauty standards. The concept of "subjective realities" is one that helps point to why I became obsessed with the ideal body type. It had come to mean a lot for me to become skinny in order for me to be happy. This reality also offered me the hope that if I became skinny my relatives would stop picking on me. I believed that if I became skinny I would become socially attractive and therefore become socially accepted by everyone. People would want to interact and become friends with me more. According to **Social Exchange Theory** social interaction is an exchange for tangible or intangible goods and services, which mean that being skinny, a tangible good to society, can bring in more social acceptance and friendships during my interaction with others. To attain such intangible good as social acceptance, then, it would be necessary to **assimilate** into the American way of life. I tried to assimilate as fast as I could during my high school years by not eating for a whole year and by taking diet pills to lose weight.

Studying the micro and macro perspectives empowers me to act like the man in *Twelve Angry Men* who was the only one who said not guilty in the beginning. He was questioning the evidence that was presented to the jurors and questioning the held beliefs of the witnesses. He was courageous enough to problematize the reality that was given to him by the prosecutor and witnesses. And here I am problematizing an internalized view of myself which I have come to believe to be part of me. I am now even more aware that I can escape from the negative reality that I have made for myself and that society has encouraged.

I find that a way for me to escape these self-destructive thoughts of myself is to look at the society that I live in and question it. A macrosociological perspective that could help explain why I obsess about my weight and self-image is **conflict theory**. Conflict theorists see the world as an arena where people in different groups or category fight for power (Wallace & Wolf 68). According to Randall Collins, a conflict theorist, "there are certain goods…that people will pursue in all societies… [He also assumes] that people have certain basic interests wherever they live and that they will act accordingly [in order to achieve those interests]" (Wallace & Wolf 139). The **goods** that Collins was talking about were wealth, power, and prestige. Being a woman in a patriarchal, capitalist society I come to realize that in order for women to have power they would have to be not only smart and successful but more importantly attractive. I saw that being smart and successful were factors that one could attain through hard work and effort. So those elements of power didn't really concern me as much as the one about being attractive. As a woman who does not believe in cosmetic surgery, I had no option to achieve attractiveness. I saw that my weight was one of the major things that was holding me back from looking attractive and therefore also holding me back from attaining power. Like many other women in our society, being skinny was a basic interest that I had to achieve so I could attain some power in society. Therefore, I acted according to this perceived necessity by dieting through the methods of pills and disordered eating habits. According to a recent study, "over half the females between the ages of 18-25 would prefer to be run over by a truck than be fat" (Gaesser 1996). Just from that statement it is apparent that in our society women realize that being fat is not valued in our society. They fear being fat so much that they would rather die than live in a fat body.

Randall Collins argued that the more "**mutual surveillance**---[that is,] the more people are in the physical presence of others---the more they accept the culture of the group and expect precise conformity in others;" this is where "automatic, mutual reinforcing nonverbal sequences will develop" (Wallace & Wolf 151). When I first came to America I lived with my family and with my relatives in a small house. There were many of us so I was constantly in the presence of others who were already exposed to the American culture. I tended to accept the culture of the group that I was living in because I was always in contact with them. Through the culture that I was exposed to in the house I lived in I saw that being overweight or fat was unacceptable and a target for insults. Attacking me with insults was almost automatic to them. Eventually, they did not even need to try to say anything to hurt my feelings. All it took was my imagining them doing so. As I continued to gain weight during my adolescent years I came to internalize the nonverbal insults that my relatives were always giving me. It was hard to ignore so I always battled with myself and my weight. Being laughed at was one of the "nonverbal sequence" that I always faced continuously. It traumatized me so much that even now when I hear people laugh behind me or in front of me, even though I do not know what they are talking about, I cringe because I fear that they are laughing at me because I am still not as skinny as they hope for me to be. Collins adds that **"the stronger the emotional arousal, the more real and unquestioned the meanings of the symbols people think about"** (Wallace & Wolf 151). Since I was constantly being laughed at by my relatives I became emotionally aroused by it and concluded that laughter is a nonverbal action that people make when they make fun of me or other fat people. This is the reason why I become paranoid even now when people laugh. This symbol of laughter became so real to me that I do not even consider that people might be laughing because of something else other than me and what I look like.

The **Frankfurt School** is another sociological tradition in conflict theory. Theorists in this tradition analyzed society with two propositions. They proposed that **"people's ideas are a product of the society in which they live"** and that "**intellectuals should maintain a critical attitude toward their own work"** (Wallace & Wolf 102). Adorno, a conflict theorist, and his colleagues criticized popular culture. They believed that popular culture manipulates the people who live in it. They attacked **"popular music for its standardization, for distracting people and making them passive, and therefore strengthening the current social order"** (Wallace & Wolf 105). The idea that being skinny is an attainable beauty ideal has always been promoted by our popular culture. When the word supermodel is mentioned everyone automatically thinks of pretty, very skinny models. The reason why this is automatic is because we are always bombarded with images of skinny models in magazines and other forms of media. Weight is such a growing concern for women and girls nowadays that "42% of 1st-3rd grade girls want to be thinner" (Collins 1991) and that "46% of 9-11 year olds are 'sometimes' or 'very often' on diets" (Gustafson-Larson & Terry 1992). The media is affecting younger women even more now because they look to popular media for what is acceptable in our society. Major influences on them are music video, popular music artists, and celebrities. Most of the women musicians and celebrities they look up to are skinny and since the media always portray them to be beautiful, little girls just wants to be like them. My battle with my weight became hard due to our popular media. Like many girls I saw that skinny women were praised by the media outlets, such as television, magazines and radios. It seemed to me that our society prefers women this way and that if you are not as skinny as your idol then you are not one of the women that society admires and therefore it seems that you're worth nothing to society. Being fat is such a fear in our society that almost all popular media advertise diet pills and other diet methods. A recent study showed that "the diet and diet related industry is 50 billion dollar a year enterprise" (Garner & Wooley 1991).

The diet industry has been feeding off of other people's misery by promising consumers that their products would make them happy because they could make them thin enough for our society to accept them. After watching the movie *Affluenza* I have come to realize why the diet industry makes billions of dollars. The film portrayed how Americans are consumer addicts and that because of it many Americans are in debt. This necessity to consume all the time comes from a few factors such as the need to have new things constantly; the need to look good; and the need to be happy. What many American consumers don't know is that their massive consumption does not truly make them happy. The rush that they feel after buying certain goods is only temporary and their debt will only continue to go up. And for those who feel the need to be thin in order to be happy goes to the diet pills or other diet methods that they see on TV or other media outlets so that they could be socially accepted. Since many Americans desire to lose weight they compete in buying the latest diet pill or weight loss video that are advertised to them. They would try hard to lose weight fast so that they can feel happier. They believe so strongly that these industries are trying to help them when in fact what they are trying to do is get their money. And many people fall into this superficial need. I was one of them.

Like many American consumers I thought that certain material goods would make me happy and that looking good is an important attribute to have if you want to be part of the American life. For many years I struggled to be happy in this society. I have looked for many ways to win the battle with my weight. I tried diet pills and not eating. These methods worked but only temporarily and therefore the happiness that I was trying to achieve was never accomplished. Through these failed trials I also found that I wasn't truly happy when I lost some weight. I was still beating myself up. And I was still crying myself to sleep at night. It took me a while to figure out that what I wanted the most was to be happy with what I look but to be happy with myself. Throughout my emotional trauma during childhood, I learned not to love myself for who I truly am and to no see myself as a human being.

It was hard for me to learn to love myself. I have trained myself for so long to hate who I was that loving me became so difficult. However, I did not stop trying because I knew that the first step for me to become truly happy in the life is to learn to love and accept myself. Through **role-taking** and putting myself in others' shoes, I am coming to understand why people who are happy are happy, and I realize that they are happy not because they are slim. They are happy because deep within themselves they love who they are. And most importantly they accept their flaws.

I had some difficulty accepting my flaws and I wasn't surprised that this was so. I finally decided that I need to seek help from a therapist to learn to forgive myself and to learn to accept who I am and be content in the body that I live in. Even now, sometimes it is difficult for me to accept a few flaws that I see about myself but I have come to realize that loving me is an ongoing process. Ever since I started therapy my self-esteem has gone up and I hold my head up high more often than a few years ago.

Tuesdays with Morrie, both the film and the book, confirmed what I believed to be true about life. I especially could relate to one of Morrie Schwartz's sayings. He said, "Money is not a substitute for tenderness, and power is not a substitute for tenderness. I can tell you, as I'm sitting here dying, when you most need it, neither money nor power will give you the feelings you are looking for, no matter how much of them you have." I saw thinness as a source of power so I thought that by achieving it I would substitute my self-hatred with happiness and tenderness. It dawned on me, after meeting people who are better looking than I or had more goods than I, that these people are not always happy. They just look like they are. I saw that even though they have the things that many people want they still are looking for something and I concluded that what they are looking for is love, not just love for themselves but love from other people that surrounds them. I have devoted myself in love, particularly the love for who I am because I know that in the end I will not measure my life with wealth that I acquired or the methods I chose to lose weight. I know that I will only prosper when I give love to me and to others around me.

REFERENCES

Garner, D., & Wooley, S. (1991). "Confronting the failure of behavioral and dietary treatments for obesity." *Clinical Psychology Review*, (11). 729-80.

Gaesser, G. A. (1996). *Big Fat Lies: The truth About Your Weight and Your Health*. New York: Fawcett Columbine.

Gordon, Avery F. *Keeping Good Time: Reflections On Knowledge, Power And People*. Boulder, Colorado: Paradigm Publishers, 2004

Gustafson-Larson, A. M., and Terry, R. D. (1992). "Weight-related behaviors and concerns of fourth-grade children." *Journal of the American Dietetic Association*, 92 (7), 818-822.

Hosseini, Sheerin. (2005/6) "Accepting Myself: Negotiating Self-esteem and Conformity in Light of Sociological Theories." *Human Architecture: Journal of the Sociology of Self-Knowledge*. Vol. IV, Issue 1&2, Fall/Spring

M.D. (2003/4) "Body Image: A Clouded Reality." *Human Architecture: Journal of the Sociology of Self-Knowledge*. Vol. III, Issues 1 & 2, Fall 2004/ Spring 2005

Mills, C. Wright. 1959. *The Sociological Imagination*. New York: Oxford University Press.

Schlosser, Anna. (2003) "My Image Struggles in Capitalist Society." *Human Architecture: Journal of the Sociology of Self-Knowledge*. Vol. II, Issue 2, Fall/Spring.

Wallace, Ruth and Alison Wolf. 2006. *Contemporary Sociological Theory: Expanding the Classical Tradition*. 6th Ed. New Jersey: Prentice Hall.

Films:

"Tuesday with Morrie" (1999). Touchstone.
"Affluenza" (1997). KCTS-Seattle and Oregon Public Broadcasting.
"Twelve Angry Men" (1957) MGM.

Longing to Be Thin
Why I Wait Until Tomorrow to Change My Habits

Caitlin Boyle

University of Massachusetts Boston

caitlin.boyle001@umb.edu

Abstract: In this paper I write about my struggles with my poor body image and my weight. Through various sociological perspectives I try my best to gain insight into my poor body image and why I procrastinate to achieve something that I have always dreamed of being…thin. Why am I so wrapped up in becoming thin? The media definitely plays a role in the way I glorify thinness because of the way they correlate being thin with being beautiful, successful and happy. I want that, too, but at the same time why am I putting off making those better choices and exercising regularly? Is it because I am afraid of something that is unknown? My weight, as uncomfortable as it makes me, has become a sort of comfort shield and I am having a hard time getting rid of the final piece of that shield. Writing this paper has really been an eye-opener for me to realize that the longer I put off the healthier choices that I need to make, the more precious time I waste. That time I am never to get back, ever! I have to take the responsibility into my own hands, quit procrastinating, and stop listening to the media telling me how I should look and focus more on how I want to look.

Growing up I have been known for being two things, overweight and a procrastinator. One of my friends even jokes on numerous occasions that the only thing I have ever been early for was my birth (I was born five weeks premature). My weight was never a huge issue for me until eighth grade when one of my friends, whom I had a crush on at the time, called me fat. Up until then I had always known I was overweight, but I was still a child and so it did not really bother me. His comment was a rude awakening.

I started to look at myself as this disgusting blob of a human being. My confidence, which was never high to begin with, plummeted. I told my mom that I wanted to go on a diet the next day, but something came up and I decided to start Weight Watchers that Monday. Monday came and something came up again and well, needless to say, I did not start that Monday, nor the Monday after that, etc., etc.

Being overweight is something that I have grown accustomed to and, in a way, have become comfortable with. I look at my weight as being a shield that has kept the "real me" hidden. During the recent fourth annual Social Theory Forum held at UMass Boston on March 27-28, 2007 ("The Violence's of Colonialism and Racism, Inner and Global: Conversations with Frantz Fanon on the Meaning of Human Emancipation"), keynote speaker Lewis R. Gordon of Temple University spoke about how, according to Fanon, "people can be hidden in plain

---

Caitlin Boyle is an undergraduate student at UMass Boston, majoring in Criminal Justice. She wrote this paper while enrolled in the course Soc. 341-3: "Elements of Sociological Theories," instructed by Mohammad H. Tamdgidi (Assistant Professor of Sociology at UMass Boston) during the Spring 2007 semester.

sight." I have always felt that my weight has hindered me from portraying who I really am and how I feel on the inside. I believe that if I am thin I will feel better about myself, people will treat me differently, and perceive me differently. Why don't I do something about it, you may ask? Well, I have done some things about it, just not everything to my fullest potential. I have the tendency to say to myself, more often than not, "Oh, I'll start eating healthy tomorrow," or "I'll start making better decisions on Monday." I know I cannot be the only person who has this problem of procrastination, but why am I letting it get in the way of something I have dreamed of, being thin. Is being thin simply a personal idea I have, or is it part of a larger *ideology,* "a belief that reflects the interests of dominant classes and groups in society" (Kosmas, 79)?

In this paper I am going to try and explore the root of my problem. I am going to first analyze my problem at the **microsociological** level. The microsociological perspectives I will use basically focus on individuals in a social setting. Later on in the paper I will focus on the *macrosociological* perspectives which focus more on society and how society affects individuals.

Just recently, I would say within the past year or so, I have struggled with feeling feminine. This is because I am unable to wear regular women's sizes. Don't get me wrong though; some clothing for plus-sized women is great, but what I really want to do is go into any store and have free reign over all the clothes. I believe that if I had a thin body, I would look good no matter what I wore. In her essay, "Why am I so fat? A study of the Interrelationship between poor body image and social anxiety" (2006), UMass Boston student Jessica Haley writes, "Thinness is a symbol. I feel that it symbolizes the elite (125)." I want to feel feminine, people to notice me, and to turn heads, too, but I feel that that can only be done if I am thin. In my mind, I truly believe that if I am thin, I will receive way more **benefits** than **costs** and more **rewards** than **punishments**.

The **Social Exchange Theory,** studies exchanges of "tangible or intangible goods and services, ranging from food and shelter to social approval or sympathy" (Wallace & Wolf, 304). It "focuses on the assessments that individuals make and the costs, benefits, punishments and rewards of their participation in a certain action before it is taken" (Haley, 125).

The media plays a crucial factor in the way I glorify thinness and also how society and our culture view obesity. "Many studies have shown that idealization of slim bodies and motivation to achieve them is associated with low self-esteem and distorted perceptions of individuals' own body images. The conventional wisdom is that these body-image distortions are encouraged or perpetuated by thinness-depicting and thinness-promoting (and fat stigmatizing) media" (Brewis 549). Through the media, being thin is seen as a **social norm** and a culturally learned idea. These *norms* are established and maintained by power...and their substance may well be explained in terms of the powerful (Wallace and Wolf, 123). Ralf Dahrendorf argues that *stratification,* which is the separation of a society into levels or classes based on wealth or power (Wallace and Wolf, 123) is caused by "norms that categorize some things as desirable and others as not" (Wallace and Wolf, 123). In American culture having a nice body is desired and I would bet anything that if there was an experiment where you had two girls, one thin and one obese and asked people to judge which one was from the higher class, people would most likely pick the thin girl because our culture seems to base everything on appearance.

The media certainly has a lot of *power!* The media gives power to those in society who normally might not have much at all. For example, I give power to the girls who have the perfect look along with the perfect body by assuming that they are better than I. The media also "enables those who possess power to give orders and obtain what they want from the powerless" (Wallace and

Wolf, 122). The media portrays people who have that perfect look along with the perfect body as being part of a high *class* in society. That portrayal now reflects in everyday society. I have fallen victim to this false *class consciousness.* I look at girls who have that perfect look and the perfect body and I automatically assume that they are of a higher class than I, but it could very well be that they are not. The media outlets such as teen magazines *contradict* themselves through the information they print. For example, there will be an article in a magazine that will tell you the fast and easy steps to increasing your self-confidence is by exercising your way to the perfect body. Then, perhaps on the next page, there will be another article about how girls should be confident in themselves no matter what size they are. This is giving girls mixed messages on how they should feel about themselves.

I feel that I need to gain control over my own environment as well as my position in society. This means that I must supposedly partake in what the sociologist Talcott Parsons calls evolutionary process, *adaptive upgrading,* which "involves the idea of control or dominance of the environment" (Wallace and Wolf, 170) and for me this would involve losing a lot of weight and becoming thin. If I were thin then I would have a sense of *authority* or the sort of power that is connected to being that perfect girl with the perfect body in our society. If it were not for the media glorifying thin bodies, I probably would not be so preoccupied with my own negative body image. This preoccupation with my negative body image and the media's glorification of thin bodies lead to *alienation,* psychologically feeling separate from others, involving a loss of meaning. I cannot help but feel distant from others and depressed when I think about the negative views society has on those who are overweight. Last semester, I was in a class and a girl mentioned that her worst fear is being perceived or looked at as being fat (mind you this particular girl was as thin as a rail and would never, ever be considered overweight). It is rather depressing to know that I live as a person's worst fear. "The obese are subject to a particularly severe degree of ridicule, humiliation, and discrimination" (DeJong 75).

Because of these negative attitudes toward overweight people in the media, most of society now shares what Emile Durkheim refers to as a *collective conscience*, "the totality of beliefs and sentiments common to average citizens of the same society" (Wallace and Wolf, 20). Being thin is now seen as a social norm. However, **phenomenology** encourages us to question these "taken for granted assumptions and challenge these culturally learned ideas" (Haley, 123). Obesity in America is not only a *personal trouble,* "a trouble that occurs within the individual" (Wallace and Wolf, 107), but also a *public issue*, "matters that have to do with the institutions of an historical society as a whole with the overlapping of various milieus that interpenetrate to form the larger structures of social and historical life" (Wallace and Wolf, 107). It is estimated that nearly half of Americans are either overweight or obese (www.obeseinamerica.com).

We watched the film *Affluenza* in class which was a PBS program that explored the "high social and environmental costs of materialism and over consumption" (www.pbs.org). I now believe I have a serious case of affluenza! I see, through the media, advertisements for various products such as clothing, makeup, handbags and perfumes. The spokesmodels for these products are all thin and beautiful. I have set in my mind that if I am thin then I too will look like one of those girls and the products will make me feel like I am part of the elite. The media and advertisements, I feel, prey on people who are obese. Manufacturers come out with various products and advertisements to catch people's eyes and promise to bring instant results without the use of exercise. Or, they advertise foods that will magically drop pounds in minutes. They also promote other products that will make you look like you are 100 lbs less. Of course all, if not most, of these kinds of products are incorrect in their statements, but society buys into them anyway. I have bought into them myself, but thankfully have learned better because I tried them out and they never worked!

I feel that another movie we viewed in class *The Big One* directed by Michael Moore which---a film about the corporate downsizing of big companies and their relocation of factories overseas in order keep up and remain competitive---is similar to the film *Affluenza*. Through these films we see examples of how materialistic our culture is and how it affects us as a whole and as individuals. Most of us, me included, are spending way more than our budgets allow just so that we can be perceived as better off than we really are. Why am I even doing this? I should not even care what class people think I am part of, but yet I buy these handbags that cost me a month's worth of hard work. At the time, it's like "hey look at my new bag!" and then a week later it is more like "I really should not have bought this ..." I consume numerous brand-name products because those are what the beautiful people and the ***power elite*** or "those who hold dominate positions" (Wallace and Wolf, 107) have.

The media, advertisements, and the brand-name companies target people like me who have a poor image of themselves. They make us believe that a new Dior handbag or a new pair of Prada sunglasses will make us feel better about ourselves. Max Horkheimer, in his critique of mass culture, sees "popular culture as a means of manipulating the inhabitants of a totally administered society" (Wallace and Wolf, 105). I agree with Horkheimer's statement and critique because I have fallen to the pop culture manipulation by buying into the advertisements of products that will make you look better and supposedly feel better about yourself.

The media uses advertisements and the news to tell the world how to lose those extra few pounds, how to stay fit, or how to look better in a certain color. These are just a few of the headlines or leading stories you may come across on any given day. These kinds of headlines boost ratings because so many people want to know what color they look better in or how they can lose a quick 5 pounds. In *Keeping Good Time*, author and sociologist Avery F. Gordon tells of how a reporter named Beth Shuster in August of 1998 did a report for the *Los Angeles Times* about the fear people have of crime. The media instills in us a fear of crime as the crime rates around the nation drop. This is all because of the media focusing in on the fear people have of crimes. For example, Shuster writes "News organizations amplify fear by ratcheting up their crime coverage ... because it helps ratings" (Gordon, 58). This can also be said for the news media covering the latest diet trends. The fear of crime boosts ratings just as the fear of being fat boosts ratings.

Our culture and society seems to choose what is important to us. Morrie Schwartz, in *Tuesdays with Morrie* by Mitch Albom, describes how our culture and society determine for us what we value and how we think and what we should do about it: "The little things, I can obey. But the big things---how we think, what we value---those you must choose yourself. You can't let anyone---or any society---determine those for you" (Albom, 155). Another valid point Morrie has made about the culture we live in is that "the culture we have does not make people feel good about themselves. And you have to be strong enough to say if the culture doesn't work, don't buy it" (Albom, 42). Unfortunately, I am not strong enough to not buy into our culture of obsessing over how our bodies look. Talcott Parsons *functionalist theory* emphasizes the socialization process, "where societal values are internalized by a society's members" (Wallace and Wolf, 27). Again, I am going to have to be strong enough to not internalize the negativity placed on the obese by society. I am too good a person to let society's negative views rip me apart.

For years I joined Weight Watchers numerous times and lost a few pounds, but in the end I kept gaining weight. During my first year of college (2002-2003), my weight became an all time high, 260 pounds; 100 pounds heavier than I was in eighth grade. I took a look at myself in the mirror one day and started to cry. Why did I let myself get like this? Throughout my life food had been my comfort. It started when I was young. When I was 9 years old, something traumatic happened to me and ever since then I would turn to food as a way of comfort. So, because I was so upset, I turned to my usual *rituals*---"things we get emotionally attached to which shapes our reality" (Wallace & Wolf, 152)---to comfort me. The same food that hurts me is the food I seek refuge in.

I knew I needed something more than Weight Watchers to help me lose weight. I spoke to my doctor and she said that I should join the Mass. General Weight Center. In March of 2004, I was evaluated by a nutritionist, psychiatrist, and a medical doctor at the Weight Center. A few weeks later I got a call telling me that I had been accepted. I was set up with monthly appointments with a doctor who was going to monitor my weight, blood pressure, heart rate and overall progress. I was prescribed the appetite suppressant Phentermine and it immediately began working. When I began taking the medicine I cut out all fast food and soda from my diet and cut down on the portion sizes I consumed. Within the first 3 months I had already lost about 25 pounds. The weight was literally melting off of me. I was beginning to receive compliments I had never received before and I was beginning to get noticed by other people.

As I kept losing weight, I could sense my then boyfriend becoming uncomfortable with my weight loss (and his weight gain). One night he and two of my friends picked me up from work. We were standing around the car deciding on what to do and I suggested that we all go out to dinner. My two friends thought it was a good idea, but my boyfriend (now ex-boyfriend) said, in front of them, "Caitlin, all you ever want to do is eat." I never really **problematized** his actions or pointed out to him that what he had said was wrong in so many ways. At the time, I believed that he was right because all I did was eat, but I ate much healthier choices that were of benefit to me. Even though I was losing weight rapidly and my body was dramatically changing, I was still living with what W. E. B. Du Bois refers to as a **double consciousness,** "the sense of always looking at one's self through the eyes of other's, of measuring one's soul by the tape of a world that looks on in amused contempt and pity."[1] Though I had lost all this weight (close to 40 pounds at the time) I was still viewing and dressing my body as it was when I weighed 260 pounds.

Early in the semester we watched a clip from the film *The Matrix*. Neo, the main character, has to decide between taking a red pill or a blue pill. Will Neo choose to find out the truth about life or will he continue to go on with things the way they are? Before deciding on which pill to take Neo must have been contemplating his choices. He eventually chose to know the truth and because of this choice he had more to gain. I have the choice to continue to procrastinate or to find the root of my problem and change my reality. This using of the example of Neo's response brings to mind also how we interact in everyday life using symbolic language. Our very selves are shaped by this sort of interaction. This all pertains to the theory of **symbolic interactionism** which "focuses primarily on the individual, 'with a self' and on the interaction between a person's internal thoughts and emotions and his or her social behavior. Individuals are viewed as active constructors of their own conduct who interpret, evaluate, define, and map out their own action, rather than as passive beings who are impinged upon outside forces" (Wallace & Wolf, 199).

---

[1] Thanks to Crystal Zollarcoffer and her class presentation for this concept linkage.

It is through self knowledge that we can begin determining our own actions. I am setting myself up for failure every time I say "today is the day I start making better choices!" I know inside and consciously in my mind that, because of my patterns of behavior, I most likely will not follow through with those better choices and put them off for another day. According to Berger and Luckmann's theory of the **social construction of reality**, "whenever individuals engage in internalization, they are conforming to the expectations of existing social institutions" (Wallace & Wolf, 282). Because our actions and interactions with others make up our reality, in turn, if I can change my actions, I can also change my reality. In her essay, "The Roots of Procrastination: A sociological Inquiry into Why I Wait until Tomorrow," UMass Boston student Jennifer Kosmas writes, "if we can become aware of our own social constructions, then we can also break out of the self-destructive habits by knowing ourselves (74).

It is only through **self interaction** that I can reflect on what I have learned in the past and make my own interpretations and decisions in determining what course of action I am going to follow---in particular, paying attention to my past failures regarding healthy eating choices, exercise, and why I put them off for another day. During the recent Social Theory Forum conference at UMass Boston, keynote speaker Lewis R. Gordon also said that according to Fanon, "failure is productive" and we have to look at things that do not work out for us and learn from them. I have to take the time and reflect on my life and see where I failed, why I failed, and why I put things off. Am I afraid of something? Am I subconsciously afraid of being thin and not having the comfort of my weight to hide behind? Maybe it is all of the above, I just don't know ... yet.

When I am around my friends and family I engage in what Erving Goffman refers to as **dramaturgy**---the way in which we present ourselves in everyday life as if we were actors on a stage. On the **front stage** I do not show that my weight is a big issue for me, but **back stage** I am constantly thinking about my weight, body image, and how other people perceive me. The concepts of the front and back stage have to do with **impression management** and "the ways in which an individual guides and controls the impressions from others" (Wallace & Wolf, 230). My internal thoughts play a huge factor in my failing behavior. This is what George Horton Cooley calls the **looking-glass self**.

The looking-glass self is based on three elements: "the imagination of our appearance to the other person, the imagination of his judgment of that appearance, and some sort of self-feeling such as pride or mortification" (Wallace and Wolf, 203). I can really relate to this concept and also to SUNY-Oneonta student Kristy Canfield's essay, "Repairing the soul: Matching Inner with Outer Beauty," when she writes, "I have always had stress concerning my difference; how could I obtain a positive self-image despite the fact that external factors state that I was of an inadequate nature? The depressive state appeared because of constantly trying to acknowledge my identity. I felt as if society constructed a scale to measure humans' worth, and if I was viewed as an outsider by some, then it must have been true" (2002 22). I also see my weight as making me different from everyone else, which makes me stand out in a negative way. I have numerous friends, relatives and even doctors say to me "you're not even that overweight, it could be so much worse" or "but you have such a pretty face." These comments go in one ear and out the other not in a disrespectful way, but because I cannot see them for myself. As I said before, I still look in the mirror and see myself as I was when I weighed 260 pounds and that was over 60 pounds ago! When I look in the mirror I focus in on the unappealing parts of my body, sometimes it gets to the point where I do not even look at my body in the mirror just to save myself from becoming depressed and even more self conscious. A part of my personal *goal attainment* tasks is supposed to be, according to mainstream culture, that of focusing on my flaws and trying hard through rigorous exercise and a restricting diet to correct them. Instead, I should be more focused in on living a positive healthy lifestyle rather than having the perfect body.

We watched the film, *Twelve Angry Men*, early in the semester. This film was about twelve men who were serving on a jury and trying to decide whether or not a young boy is guilty or innocent of murdering his father. Eleven of the men are saying that he is guilty and only one man is questioning the young boy's guilt. So, why are these eleven men so quick to convict the boy? They did not take into consideration that people testifying might not always tell the truth, even under oath. The one man who boldly approached and questioned every so called truth from the case takes a phenomenological approach. He was able to see that not everyone tells or sees the truth (Haley, 124). You cannot assume that people are telling the truth, just as I cannot assume that what people notice first about me is my weight problem.

My "natural" attitude towards becoming thin has been that I would just want it to magically happen. I do not think I am alone in thinking that way, who wouldn't want something to just happen without putting any effort in it? But, I believe this sort of attitude is one of the main reasons why I procrastinate so often in terms of changing my eating and exercise habits. When I lost the first 50 lbs. in a matter of months I hardly exercised, but I did cut down drastically on what I ate and the portions sizes I consumed. My mentality now, unfortunately, is still that of when I was losing the 50lbs. I believe I have to change my attitude to incorporate regular exercise if I am to see anymore weight loss results because, now, eating less is just not cutting it anymore.

In conclusion, I believe that I have to start being conscious of how eating affects my life and my body and how that bag of chips is not worth eating. I need to realize I can have more control over what goes into my body, and that I am not going to live forever and by procrastinating I am only wasting precious moments of my life that I will never get back. Ever since I can remember I have turned to food in times of need, stress, and comfort and those acts have not helped me reach my goal of being thin and healthy. I can have more control over what goes into my body and now is the time to start and not wait until tomorrow to start watching what I eat.

In the book, *Keeping Good Time* author Avery F. Gordon speaks at an Alternative Graduation for non-traditional high school students and gives them this advice which can be related to the media negatively stigmatizing obesity and my longing to conform to the thin-body social norm. She writes, "I realize there are many pressures on you to not make trouble, but rather to conform. These pressures can feel close to the heart, as a long-standing and contradictory American tendency towards submission to authority affects our everyday lives" (Gordon, 71). I have to learn to not consume myself with the media and their portrayal of high class thin bodies and learn to love myself and my body no matter what. I realize that my body is the only one I have and to make the best of it and stop being my own worst enemy all the time.

In the movie *Tuesdays with Morrie*, Morrie says "you must love one another or die." This is one of the many aphorisms Morrie has shared with us. I believe this aphorism could also be interpreted as love *yourself* or perish. I relate to this because sometimes I am so caught up in my poor body image and comparing my body to those of others that I forget the real reasons why I am obsessing over becoming thin. The real reason why I should want to be thin is so that I can be healthy, not to look good or to be considered a member of a higher class. Those are superficial and materialistic rewards. Unfortunately, in my mind, becoming thin is a requirement for my social *integration* and *social mobility*, "the ability to move up on the social ladder" (Wallace and Wolf, 143).

Hopefully I can work on that once the semester is over and realize that looking good is not as rewarding as feeling good. As Minnie Ransom says, in *Keeping Good Time* by Avery F. Gordon, "There's nothing that stands between you and perfect health, sweetheart" (Gordon, 200).

Watching *Tuesdays with Morrie*, I have learned from Morrie that procrastination is a complete waste of time. I am going to take another one of his aphorisms to heart: "once you learn how to die, you learn how to live." If I learn that I am going to die at any moment, I will not procrastinate in regards to changing my eating habits and being healthy. If I continue this pattern of procrastination, then I may never reach my goal and it could end up being too late. I certainly do not want to live my life with regrets. I do not want to die without knowing how it feels to live as a healthy person.

I am going to end my paper with a final quote from Gordon's *Keeping Good Time*. This passage is one that I am going to keep with me until the end of time. This quoted passage is one by Toni Cade Bambara, a Black writer, filmmaker, community activist, and teacher who died from cancer in 1995. The words are quoted in the context of speaking about community, but I am going to take it out of the community context and put it directly into my own life and the context of dreaming to be thin one day. Bambara writes, "*The dream is real and the only unreality is the failure to make it real*" (Gordon, 201). It is all up to me whether I want to become thin. I have to take the responsibility into my own hands, quit procrastinating, and stop listening to the media and magazines telling me how I should look. I am going to change my eating habits and my exercise routines for me and no one else. No matter what I look like I will never change from the humble, quiet, fun loving, optimistic girl I have always been. Becoming healthier is the number one reason why I am going to change my bad habits. In the process of becoming healthier I will accomplish the goal that I have dreamed of reaching for a very, very long time. Becoming thin will not be the main reason, as I originally thought, for me to stop procrastinating and to start getting my act together and life a healthier life.

REFERENCES AND FURTHER READINGS

Albom, Mitch. 1997. *Tuesdays with Morrie*. New York: Broadway Books.

Brewis, Alexandra A. 1999. "The Accuracy of Attractive-Body-Size Judgment." *Current Anthropology*. Vol. 40 (4); 548-553.

Canfield, Kristy. 2002. "Repairing the Soul: Matching Inner with Outer Beauty." *Human Architecture: Journal of the Sociology of Self-Knowledge*, 1, 2. Fall 2002. 20-26.

DeJong, William. 1980. "The Stigma of Obesity: The Consequences of Naïve Assumptions Concerning the Causes of Physical Deviance." *Journal of Health and Social Behavior*. Vol. 21 (1); 75-87.

Evans, Caroline; Thornton, Minna. 1991. "Fashion, Representation, Femininity." *Feminist Review* (38); 48-66.

Farganis, James. 2004. *Readings in Social Theory: The Classic Tradition to Post-Modernism*. Fourth Edition. Boston: McGraw Hill Inc.

Gordon, Avery F. 2004. *Keeping Good Time: The Reflections on Knowledge, Power, and People*. Boulder, CO: Paradigm Publishers.

Haley, Jessica. 2006. ""Why Am I So Fat?" a Study of the Interrelationship Between Poor Body Image and Social Anxiety." *Human Architecture: Journal of the Sociology of Self-Knowledge*, IV, 1 &2, Fall 2005/ Spring 2006. 121-130.

Juffer, Jane. 1996. "A Pornographic Femininity? Telling and Selling Victoria's (Dirty) Secrets." *Social Text*. (48); 27-48.

Kosmas, Jennifer M. 2004. "The Roots of Procrastination: A Sociological Inquiry into Why I Wait Until Tomorrow." *Human Architecture: Journal of the Sociology of Self-Knowledge*. Volume II, Issue 2, Fall 2003/ Spring 2004; 74-81.

Milkie, Melissa A. 2002. "Contested Images of Femininity. An Analysis of Cultural Gatekeepers' Struggles with the "Real Girl" Critique." *Gender and Society*. Vol. 15 (6); 839-859.

Wallace, R and Wolf, A. 1999. *Contemporary Sociological Theory: Expanding the Classical Tradition*. Sixth Edition. New Jersey: Prentice Hall.

www.pbs.org

www.obeseinamerica.com

Films:

"The Matrix." 1999. Warner Brothers.
"Tuesday with Morrie." 1999. Touchstone.
"The Big One." 1997. Miramax Home Entertainment.
"Affluenza" 1997. KCTS-Seattle and Oregon Public Broadcasting. Bullfrog Films.
"Twelve Angry Men" 1957. MGM.

The Boston Irish Male: A Self Study

Anonymous

University of Massachusetts Boston

Abstract: This essay explores the personal struggles the author faces with regards to his career and educational choices. The author grew up in a predominately blue-collar Irish-American community. The community's opinions on work and career differ tremendously from those of the author. However, the community has also shown constant love and support towards the author; which creates conflict. This essay explains the author's reasoning with relation to key social theories and theorists.

A person's background can often dictate the type of life they will lead. The old coal mining towns are a good example of this. Generation upon generation worked in the mines. People were expected and encouraged to work the mine because it was part of the community ideology. Although most cities have a greater diversity in the work force, the type of work people do is greatly influenced by their **social structure**.

In the neighborhood I grew up in, I was always encouraged to work hard and get a good job. However, the types of jobs that most of the people in my neighborhood do are not ones that I really find intriguing. Yet, still to this day, my friends and family try to influence me into taking such jobs. I grew up in the working-class neighborhood of Dorchester, MA. My cohort of friends and peers shared many things in common. We all went to Catholic school, we are all first or second generation Americans whose parents or grandparents came from Ireland, many of us joined the military, and we all came from a middle-class background. The majority of my friends work in trades or city/state jobs. Although many of them make very good money, the majority of my friends are mostly blue collar/middle-class workers. By doing this work, they continue the working-class ethic that has been instilled in my neighborhood. Although my struggle is a personal one, it also has significance on the **macrosociological** level.

As noted before, I grew up in a working-class neighborhood. I always felt encouraged by my family while growing up. I bought into the whole "you can be anything you want to be" ideology. However, as I got older, that encouragement changed a bit. Instead of being whatever I wanted to be, I was encouraged to find a decent job. Some of these "decent" jobs were police officer, firefighter, trade/labor union, etc., positions. These jobs were encouraged for two

---

Anonymous was an undergraduate student at UMass Boston, majoring in Sociology. He wrote this paper while enrolled in the course Soc. 341-3: "Elements of Sociological Theories," instructed by Mohammad H. Tamdgidi (Assistant Professor of Sociology at UMass Boston) during the Fall 2005 semester.

main reasons. The first is because these were the types of jobs the people in my neighborhood did for a living. I had a lot of connections between family and friends, so it would be easy to slide into this type of work. Secondly, it was expected. Nobody I know discourages me from attending college, but rather discourages me from attending full-time instead of working full-time.

When thinking more critically, I wondered what has led my family to believe this way. In their work *The Manifesto of the Communist Party*, Karl Marx and Frederick Engels state that "society as a whole is more and more splitting up into two great hostile camps, into two great classes directly facing each other---**bourgeoisie** and **proletariat**" (Farganis 26). I am a first generation American. Both my mother and father were farmers back in Ireland. Farming was the family's work for as long as both my parents could remember. Ireland was under British rule until the early 20th century. This means that for years and years my ancestors essentially worked as slave laborers. The British profited off of their hard work. While Ireland gained its independence, it was difficult for my ancestors to lose their dependence on the British. Not knowing anything about business, they struggled to keep their farms up and running. This forced them into taking any type of work that would pay them a decent wage. This started the trend in my family of doing work that pays well, rather than work that satisfies oneself. This would also hold true for many of my peers, whose ancestors come from Ireland.

More times than I care to mention, I have been approached by friends and family to pursue certain areas of employment. I am a veteran and when I returned home from the Navy I was overwhelmed at how much I was being pushed to start a career. My friends encouraged me to take the firefighter and police tests, my brother and father encouraged me to join the pipefitters union to learn the trade, and my sister encouraged me to apply for a job with the security company she was working for. I use the word "encourage," but in reality it was not so encouraging. My friends said things like "you're an idiot if you don't get on the fire department." My brother told me "you need to start making some money." It seemed that everyone had a suggestion, but that no one wanted to hear what I had to say.

In many ways my friends and family made a lot of sense. Despite some of their criticism, they were sincerely looking out for my best interests. It is not mean or unusual to want someone you love to have security in life. I was very aware of this and often considered taking them up on their advice. However, while seeking **social approval** from friends and family, I was denying my own ambitions and aspirations. I had long dreamed of becoming a lawyer and was now ready to start working on achieving that dream. However, the pursuit of this dream created a **stigma** among my friends and family because to them, my ambition seemed illogical. In my **looking glass self**, I imagine my family and friends seeing and judging me as naïve, foolish, or as a dreamer.

In her essay, "Complexity of Naïve Acceptance of Socially Manipulated Beliefs," UMass Boston student Ayan Ahmed states "each generation… derives its principals and beliefs from the one that preceded it. It follows, then, that the influences the children in these societies obtain is social in nature." (2003/4). This is certainly the case in my neighborhood. This hard work ethic that my family and friends have comes from their Irish upbringing. My parents, as well as most of my friend's parents, were born and raised in Ireland. Most of them grew up on farms and had very little education. I always remember my mother telling me she had a day's work done before breakfast. When they came to the United States, our parents worked certain jobs because of their limited education. Most of the fathers worked as laborers, carpenters, and in other various trades. The mothers worked in various hospitality fields such as cleaning, waitressing, or elderly care. They in turn passed this work ethic along to their children. While I was growing up, my parents never put me down in any way, but they also never really made me feel as if I was great. In some ways, this was good because it taught me humility. However, in other ways I feel as if I was never encouraged to be the best. This is still the case in my life today as my family and friends still discourage me from prioritizing education before work.

Religion also played a big role in shaping the attitudes of my family. Everything I did as a child and teenager revolved around the Catholic Church. I went to catholic school, I played sports in catholic athletic organizations, I was an alter boy, I was a member of the Catholic Youth Organization, and I attended mass every Sunday. My parents encouraged me to do all of this. They deeply believed in the teachings of the Catholic Church. One of the main teachings of the Catholicism is that we are all God's children and no one is better than anyone else. Catholicism teaches that a person should be humble. This may be why my family and friends do the type of work they do, because they were taught to have humility in their lives. Perhaps it is more holy to work as a carpenter than as a banker.

The priests and nuns at my school stressed to me that God wanted us to be humble and I was told to never disagree with a priest or a nun. In her essay "From Alienation to Exploration: Breaking Free from the Iron Cages of My Life" (2003/4), UMass Boston student Annie Roper tells of her experience with catholic school; "we were made to study religious **dogma**; the catechism by rote, to not dare question any religious tenets or authority." This doctrine of humility was instilled in my parents from such a very young age, that it became part of their **objective culture**. However, for me this presents a **conflict** because I believe there is no shame in wanting to strive for success. If I am driven to pursue a different type of career path or to finish a certain level of higher education, then I do not feel as if I am any less humble for wanting such things. I concur that it would be more favorable in God's eyes to give up most of my ambitions to help others, but we are not all Mother Teresa. Most people want to be successful in their lives and they try to attain that success through work. In their textbook, *Contemporary Sociological* Theory, Ruth A. Wallace and Alison Wolf state that "theories of rational choice assume that people are rational and base their actions on what they perceive to be the most effective means to their goals" (p.303). When I use this definition of the **rational choice theory**, I see that work is an important part of my life and it makes sense to want to pursue a career that will make me happy even if it is in contrast to what others may think.

Religion was a big part of my life while growing up. Marx viewed religion critically. In his *Critique of Hegel's Philosophy of Right*, Marx famously stated "religion is the sigh of the oppressed creature, the heart of a heartless world, and the soul of soulless conditions. It is the opium of the people" (http://www.marxists.org/archivemarx/works/1843/critique-hpr/, 1). "For Marx, religion is something that the oppressed proletariat cling to and delude themselves with simply because they have nothing else in life in which to take comfort. When Marx wrote this text, opium was a very popular medicine and recreational drug. Marx says that religion is the only way the oppressed workers can convince themselves that their lives are worth living, though it is an illusion, simply a pretty fantasy, like an opium dream" (p. 1).

In the beginning of the movie *Twelve Angry Men*, the character played by Henry

Fonda stands alone as a juror who votes not guilty. None of the other jurors understand why he is doing so and only after quite a bit of convincing does he change their minds. Similarly, I often go through the same struggle when trying to explain my decision to devote myself to school. My family and friends are like the jurors, who are set on a certain philosophy and cannot understand why anyone would think differently. Like Henry Fonda's character in the film, I find myself having to defend my position. This continuing argument I have with family and friends does not sit well with how the Irish in Boston **construct their social reality** because in their reality, I am an Irish-American from Dorchester who comes from a hard working family and should get a job that will provide security. However, in my reality, I am a young college student who has an opportunity to be very successful in his career. **Georg Simmel** stated that "people sometimes become enslaved to the **objective culture**"; the objective culture being the things (money, property, work, etc.) that set the context for belonging to one or another class in society. The objective culture I seem to have belonged to is one of working middle class and it seems no matter how hard I try to escape this culture and class, there are forces holding me to it.

The objective culture that Simmel talks about seems to have been diagnosed with an illness in the United States these days. The film *Affluenza* showed how Americans are intrigued by materialistic things such as the ones Simmel described. These material goods become our way of showing our importance or status in life. I wish I could say I was above this, but unfortunately I can not. I have been influenced by America's obsession with wealth and power. I would like to say I believe everyone is human and no one person is better than the other, but if you asked me if I wanted to work as a janitor or a doctor, I will choose doctor. This choice has also been influenced by the media. Shows such as *ER* and infomercials such as the one for St. Jude's research hospital have portrayed doctors in a holier-then-thou way. We see this for other professions as well, such as for lawyers, businesspeople, judges, politicians, etc. We have been programmed to think that a suit and tie equals success. I am currently working as a security officer at a hotel in downtown Boston. I was recently promoted to supervisor. While I was an officer, I had to wear a security uniform. This uniform was not very flattering to say the least. I would often get ridiculed by the guests of the hotel because of this uniform. When I was promoted, I was allowed to wear my own personal suit to work. I saw an immediate change. If I were standing next to a uniformed officer, guests would ask me, rather than the officer, whatever questions they had. I was called "sir" by many guests, and I was treated with much more respect while responding to room complaints. Bronislow Malinowski's **social exchange theory perspective** explores "why and how people move from isolation to different forms of contact with one another" (Wallace & Wolf p.306), i.e., what costs and benefits accrue to taking one or another social role and what comes with the latter. This question held true when considering my transition from officer to supervisor. Because of my new position and new look, I was more comfortable around the guests. When addressing guest complaints, I was able to conduct myself with much more confidence. I experienced a personal change and growth in my personality, all because I was wearing a suit.

Maturity is determined by the degree to which you are able to put yourself in one's shoes. Wallace and Wolf write, "Mead explains that communication is 'a process by which each person takes the role of the other,' that is, each person 'assumes the attitude of the other individual as well as calling it out to the other." (208). What I want from my family and friends is to put themselves in my shoes and communicate with me with an understanding of the roles I have played and would like to play in society. By doing so, they will find out the **meaning** behind the decisions I make. It may not be easy to do so but, as it did with Neo, in the film *The Matrix*, the truth will be enlightening. In the movie, Neo has to accept a new reality which is completely different than the one he has always known. In order to do so, he has to give up everything he believed to be true in order to gain an understanding of the matrix. However, when Neo accepts his new reality he is enlightened by the truth.

In his book *Tuesdays with Morrie*, Mitch Albom discusses a similar awakening Morrie Schwartz had had in his life. In the book, Morrie makes a very emphatic statement; he says "once you learn how to die, you learn how to live" (34). Though this statement can be interpreted in many ways, to me it means that when we know our time left on earth is limited, we can truly start to appreciate and enjoy the most important things in life. This includes family, friends, children, nature's beauty, etc. This statement had a profound effect on how I view my own life, and with regards to this essay. I have discussed the forces that affect my educational goals, but those same forces are the friends, family, and community that helped shape me into the person I am today. When I stop and think of what I really care about in life, I realize that above all I want happiness for my loved ones. I have been blessed to be surrounded by wonderful, caring people. That is what really matters in life.

Although I wish the best for my loved ones, though, I also have to do what is best for me. I hope to give back to the community that has given me so much. However, I plan on doing this through a profession in politics. I feel the best way to get into politics is through education, particularly law school. I feel that education can only make me a better politician. Morrie Schwartz stated that "people haven't found the meaning of their lives, so they're running all the time looking for it. They think the next car, the next house, the next job. Then they find out that those things are empty too, and they keep running" (Albom 36). Right now, my pursuit of higher education is the central purpose of my life. I find it morally satisfying. I believe it is the meaning I have been looking for in life. I just hope that my loved ones will accept this as well.

My friends and family have a **blasé attitude** towards higher education. They feel that once you reach a certain age, it is time to start a career. This is one of the most interesting aspects of the Irish work ethic because even though our heritage traces back to Ireland, my entire community considers themselves Americans first and foremost. My friends and I joined the military after high school because we felt a patriotic duty to do so. Our parents created new lives for themselves in the United States because they believed in American equality. There is a true love for America spread throughout my community. What is interesting to me is that as much as my community believes in American values, they are indifferent towards one of its most precious values: education. Almost every organization stresses the need for education. It seems odd that my community, whom revel in being Americans, do not.

To add to this confusion is the fact that the most revered Irish-Americans from Boston are the ones who have gone on and been successful in higher education. Billy Bulger was a Boston College Law school graduate before he went into politics, former speaker of the house Tip O'Neill graduated from B.C. before entering politics, and Joe Moakley graduated from Suffolk Law School after his enlistment in the U.S. Navy. The reason I use these men as examples because they share two things in common with me: Boston-Irish roots and a love for politics. Looking at this, I can conclude that my choice to pursue higher education above all else is not a foolish one because as the aforementioned individuals have shown, it is possible to succeed despite coming from a working-class neighborhood.

If I am fortunate enough to be elected into public office, I hope to use my working-class background to my advantage. I had the honor of knowing Joe Moakley on a personal level and if you didn't know who he was, you would have never guessed he was a congressman. Moakley was always willing to help the people in his district. I believe this can be credited to his upbringing, where people relied so much on others. Everyone helped each other out. Moakley's upbringing also influenced his decisions on the national level. When dealing with issues such as health care and welfare reform, I am sure Moakley did not forget his childhood, growing up in the South Boston housing projects.

There may be subliminal reasons why I want to pursue law school and politics. If you asked me why, I would tell you that I want to get into politics someday and I feel a good law background will make me a better politician. I believe this to be the true reason why I wish to become a lawyer, but there may be others. In her essay "My Image Struggles in Capitalist Society," SUNY-Oneonta student Anna Schlosser states

> "the media does not show favorable images of the working class" (Newman 283). Al Bundy, the character from *Married with Children*, and Homer, the character from *The Simpsons*, are just two examples of how badly the working class male is portrayed

The movie *Affluenza* showed us the power that marketing and advertising has on people. The media has always portrayed occupations such as physicians, lawyers, and banking as occupations endowed with **social capital**. The show *Roseanne* represented my life more so than a show like the *West Wing* ever did, but it is the characters in the *West Wing* that I want to emulate. It is possible that my career decisions have been persuaded by media influence, whether I knew it or not. In his work, *Class, Status, Party,* Max Weber describes **social stratification** as the way "different jobs are treated as superior or inferior to one another…based on reputation and wealth and expressed in a rank order of social status" (Farganis 123). In American society, we are judged by the type of work we do. For example, your local garbage man could be very kind and very smart. Perhaps he has had prior success in the banking industry or holds a master's degree. When comparing him to a lawyer or a doctor, we automatically assume that the doctor or lawyer is smarter, richer, and more successful than the garbage man. Even if this particular garbage man proves this theory untrue, it will not stop us from characterizing the next garbage man we meet the same way.

My goal of becoming a lawyer has nothing to do with money, but I cannot say that it has nothing to do with personal ambition. When I am finished with school, I want to be able to look back proudly at my success and look forward to my future. However, the more successful I get, the more potential trouble there may be. The amount of success a person has may present certain opportunities that were not previously available to that person. For example, Martha Stewart would not have been involved with an inside-trading scandal had she pursued another career. Martha Stewart came from a modest middle-class background and probably never imagined she would be as successful as she became. However, she also probably never imagined herself being involved in anything illegal. However, her status has changed tremendously since that during her childhood. Ralf Dahrendorf writes "the greater people's personal chances of leaving their class---in other words, the greater the degree of '**intergenerational mobility**'---the less likely they are to identify actively with it" (Wallace and Wolf 125).

If I am successful in becoming a lawyer, I must avoid these circumstances. Otherwise, I am just insulting the loved ones who helped get me there. In his film, *Roger and Me*, Michael Moore shows the irresponsibility of large corporations. The film showed how corporations, such as GM, make decisions that have terrible consequences for many people. GM chose to save money and increase profits when they moved their factory from Flint, MI. However, the majority of Flint residents were employed in some form or another by GM. Therefore, GM had a responsibility to ensure the well-being of the people of Flint. After all, it was GM that created the jobs in the first place. The people of Flint provided a great service to the GM Company. However, none of that meant anything to the GM executives. GM brought the town of Flint together by creating a work environment that became part of the community. Everyone was involved with GM in some form or another. This created a distinct **social class**. However, when GM decided to leave Flint, it created many struggles for its citizens. This is what Georg Simmel referred to as the "**web of conflict**," which points to "the cross-cutting allegiances that can both bind a society together as well as generate struggles and confrontations" (Farganis p.131).

Morrie Schwartz was also critical of today's American society. Morrie stated that "the culture we have does not make people feel good about themselves. We're teaching the wrong things. And you have to be strong and say that if the culture doesn't work, don't buy it" (Albom p.34). This holds true in my life. My family and peers have accepted a certain way of life. I have decided that this life does not work for me, so I don't "buy it." However, this is not to say that my community's culture is bad in anyway. I merely say that it is not right for me. Morrie's statement also holds true for the macro-society. In the film *Super Size Me*, Morgan Spurlock shows the tremendous health risks involved with consuming McDonald's food. Spurlock showed how McDonald's food is loaded with sugar, salt, fat, and grease. All those ingredients lead to a meal that is high in fat, calories, and cholesterol. McDonald's is a world-wide conglomerate, with restaurants in almost every country in the world. It is not like they don't have the money to create a healthier menu, they just choose not to. Spurlock's interview with Eric Schlosser, author of *Fast Food Nation*, was especially frightening. Schlosser points out how McDonald's uses meat from various different parts of various different cows. He also told how McDonald's slaughter houses are so jam packed with animals, that the animals are forced to live in their own excrement. Meanwhile, pediatric obesity and diabetes is on the rise. Schlosser mentioned the In & Out Burger food chain in California. Although In & Out does not serve the healthiest food, they use fresh potatoes for their French fries and grade A beef for their burgers. They also provide health care and vacation time for their workers---something McDonald's does not. Like GM, McDonald's has shown tremendous corporate irresponsibility.

I now feel as though my career goals contrast my upbringing. I was raised to help others and give to those less fortunate. Simmel discussed the **small town life** in which people "rest upon more deeply felt and emotional relationships." Although my hometown of Dorchester is right in the heart of the city of Boston, we still share the characteristics of the small town. The people in my neighborhood care for one another and do whatever they can to help each other out. I sometimes feel like a stranger because I tend to look after my own interests rather than others in my community. This isolates me somewhat from my community. I see myself finishing school in a few years and starting a life in public service. Once I start that life, I see my friends, family, and community accepting my decision to stick with education. I see myself as becoming successful in the work I do. What I strive for more than anything else in my life is to be successful. However, I want to be successful in public service and to do that I have to have certain educational goals achieved. My ambitions are not monetary, but rather personal. It has been a dream of mine to someday run for office and I want to pursue that dream. A man's success is not shaped by the size of his wallet, but rather by the amount of good he does in the world. The good I want to do is in the community I grew up in. This is how I see myself, but I am not sure if the forces working against me are too strong to prevent me from attaining such goals.

There are certain things I must do to ensure that my educational goals stay on track. First, I must understand my family's and friends' point of view and accept it. By accepting their opinions, I am not taking their advice, but rather understanding the reasons why they give it. After all, when it's all said and done, they will be the ones by my side whether I succeed or not. Morrie Schwartz said "the most important thing in life is to learn how to give out love and let it come in" (Albom 52). Fortunately, this is not a problem I have to face. Secondly, I must learn to accept and deal with the criticism I receive. I can not let outside forces distract me from my goals, however. This is difficult because the people criticizing me are the ones I care about most; however, I must do this in order to succeed. Thirdly, I must be persistent in achieving my goals. In the end, I am the one who paves the road to my future. I am solely responsible for my decisions. I cannot let the negativity stop me from my ultimate goal. Because once that goal is achieved, I can start to give back to the community I love.

BIBLIOGRAPHY

Ahmed, Ayan. *The Complexity of Naïve Acceptance of Socially Manipulated Beliefs*. Journal of Self-Knowledge Vol. II, No.2, Fall 2003/Spring 2004.

Albom, Mitch. *Tuesday's with Morrie*. Doubleday Dell Publishing Inc, 1997.

Farganis, James (ed.). *Readings in Social Theory: The Classical tradition to Post-Modernism*. Fourth edition. McGraw Hill College Division, 1999.

Marx, Karl. *Critique of Hegel's Philosophy of Right*. 1843. http://www.marxists.org/archive/marx/works/1843/critique-hpr/

Newman, David M. *Sociology: Exploring the Architecture of Everyday Life*. 4th ed, California: Pine Forge Press, 2002.

Roper, Annie. "From Alienation to Exploration: Breaking Free from the Iron Cages of My Life." *Human Architecture: Journal of the Sociology of Self-Knowledge*, Vol. II, No. 2, Fall 2003/Spring 2004.

Schlosser, Anna. (2003) "My Image Struggles in Capitalist Society." *Human Architecture: Journal of the Sociology of Self-Knowledge*. Vol. II, Issue 2, Fall/Spring.

Wallace, Ruth A. & Wolf, Alison. *Contemporary Sociological Theory: Expanding the Classical Tradition*. Fifth edition. New Jersey: Prentice Hall, 1999.

A Family of Neglect and "Dysfunction"
Personal Blames or Structural Constraints?

L. Z.

University of Massachusetts Boston

Abstract: Using various sociological concepts and perspectives, in this article the author presents a case study of a family where the personal troubles of parents (substance abuse and alcoholism) translate into neglect for the children's well being. The impact of parents' addiction on their own career, employment situation, and parenting duties are contrasted with the children's efforts at finding alternative ways of doing family with others, and providing for themselves to make ends meet, at the expense of their educational and career outcomes.

In her article "Confessions of a Maineiac: The Family, Academia, and Modernity," Macalester College student Jessica Sawyer writes that the **family** is "intended as a place to enrich children, so they are then able to leave and reach their full potentials"(195). While this may be society's expectation of what a family must be, and even the definition for many families in many social settings, it is only a faint hope of what could have been for the Stewart[1] family. Sharon, Mark, and children Katie, Alex and Chris form the Stewart family. Over the course of their lives they have struggled with many difficult situations. With a mother so addicted to heroin that it was the only thing she truly cared about and a drug-addicted alcoholic for a father,

---

[1] Family and personal names used in this article have been modified to maintain privacy.

the three Stewart children could only pretend and wish that their family could function like other families.

Patricia Hill Collins states in her article, "It's All in the Family: Intersections of Gender, Race, and Nation," that families in our society are

> ... expected to socialize their members into an appropriate set of 'family values' that simultaneously reinforce the hierarchy within the assumed unity of interest symbolized by the family and lay the foundation for many social hierarchies. (158)

The specific hierarchies that Collins suggests are those of gender, age, wealth, and sexuality. These hierarchies exist inside of the family and are comparable to similar

---

L. Z. is an undergraduate student at UMass Boston, majoring in Criminal Justice. She wrote this paper while enrolled in the course Soc. 242: "Sociology of the Family," taught by Anna Beckwith (Lecturer of Sociology at UMass Boston) during the Spring 2007 semester.

hierarchies in our society. Collins continues to say that hierarchy "in this sense becomes 'naturalized' because it is associated with seemingly 'natural' processes of the family" (Collins 158). There is little room in the Stewart family to create any type of solid hierarchy, however, as each member operates as an individual unit, providing for and relying only upon themselves.

In their article "Kinscripts," Carol Stack and Linda Burton present a personal account by a man named Henry who believes that, "[s]omeone in my family must be at the helm. Someone has to be there to make sure the next generation has a start. Right now, we are a family of co-dependents. We need each other" (409). Mostly when the children were younger, but even so now, Katie, Alex and Chris in the Stewart family also needed someone to be there for them, to "take the helm" and give them enough direction and support to give them a start in life. In most families this is where **mothering** and **fathering** takes place. The adults, being the mother and father of a family, assume the role of running the family and taking care of the children and home. However, in the Stewart family, since Sharon and Mark were so overwhelmed by their own lives, addictions, and problems, they were unable to help their children at all. As a result, Katie, Alex, and Chris have been left to fend for themselves.

To truly understand the situation that the Stewart family is in, I think it is important to consider the background of each member of the household. To begin with, Sharon Stewart was as of three months ago, a recovering heroin addict. In the early 1970s, when Sharon was thirteen years old she began stealing her mother's Valium---which had been prescribed to ease symptoms of menopause---and her life pretty much went downhill from there. Since then she has lived a life of lying and stealing to feed her addiction. Sharon seems to have no morals when it comes to getting what she wants. She has sunk low enough as to steal jewelry that had been passed down to her sister and even stealing the pain medication her husband had been prescribed just days after a painful back operation.

Sharon has had frequent run-ins with the law but her most recent, and worst, came last year. She had gotten a job as a personal care assistant for a ninety six year old woman, whose family basically wanted nothing to do with her. After the woman passed away it was revealed that Sharon had been stealing items from her home, as well as forging checks from the woman, essentially clearing out her rather substantial bank account. As a result of this, Sharon was sentenced to six months in jail. Since being released over the summer, she has been at a drug rehabilitation home trying to beat her addiction to heroin.

The theme of secrets and lies in the movie *TransAmerica* is similar to Sharon's situation. In the movie, Bree is about to have an operation to officially make her body that of a woman. Bree deals with secrets and lies as she does not initially tell her son that she was his father, instead choosing to lie and say that she worked for a church. Furthermore, when talking to her therapist after learning she had a son, Bree told the therapist everything had been worked out, when in fact it had not. The therapist did not believe this and I think, deep down, neither did Bree. While the exact situations of Bree and Sharon are incomparable, the fact that they harbor secrets and lies can be related.

For many years Sharon denied that she had a problem with drugs, and would lie to anyone who suggested that she did. She has been in rehabilitation four times and every time she left before she was truly ready. Sharon would say she was ready to leave; however, her counselors would say otherwise, knowing that she would turn right back to drugs upon being released. Furthermore, when she was back on drugs and the signs were obvious, she would become enraged at anyone who suggested she needed help, and deny she was back to using drugs. Therefore, even though the situations may be different, the central theme of lying is evident in that of Bree's and Sharon's situations and behaviors.

While Sharon offers little to her children there is also no support or structure that comes from her husband either. He is a drug addicted, alcoholic that is more consistent in showing up to drink in the local bar than showing up to his job. On occasion he has been known to stumble home from the bar and begin to verbally abuse any one of his kids that crosses his path. He commonly chooses Katie as his target for his verbal attacks, tearing her down for anything from the fact that she dropped out of school, to his disgust that she cannot find a better job than making sandwiches at Subway, which is ironic because at least she consistently shows up to work, unlike her father. Mark every now and then tries to "make up" for is behavior by making empty promises to his victims, such as promising a car to Katie. He knows that he can barely afford food for the family to eat, yet alone a car; however, he makes these promises to have his family view him in a better light than when he is abusive.

Society's **family ideal** expects parents to provide a loving and safe environment for their children to reside in. In "It's Late At Night, And I'm Screaming At My Kids Again," author Christopher Scanlan, like Mark, also invokes terror in his family by taking out his anger and frustration in the form of screaming at his family. However, Scanlan, unlike Mark, understands that what he is doing is detrimental to his family and makes an effort to change his behavior. He recognizes this when he states that "I don't want my children to remember me…as this looming, frightened man" and attempts to mend the problem by recording his thoughts and frustrations in a "Temper Log," where he can monitor his behavior (Scanlan 304). By doing this, Scanlan is internalizing society's standards of **parenting** and also behaving the way he knows he should. I believe that Mark recognizes that his behavior is inappropriate, which is exemplified in the way he makes big promises to his family. However, unlike Scanlan and many in our society, he does not know how to harness his anger and addictions in a way that will allow him to function on a normal level with his family.

Katie is the oldest child and after a troubled childhood dropped out of school at the beginning of her freshman year of high school. Currently she is pregnant and spending the majority of her time at her boyfriend's family's apartment where she now lives. The middle child, Alex, never seemed to fit in with her family as she was an extremely gifted student who was the only one of her siblings that consistently went to school. However, she dropped out of school her sophomore year and has recently become involved with a group of kids known for causing trouble. The youngest child, Chris dropped out of school after the eighth grade and was a troubled boy growing up, often trying to light the walls of his apartment on fire. He was involved with the murder of a homeless man in 2004, but since he was only present at the murder and not directly involved, was sentenced to six months in a group home. The last time I talked to him he was nervous because "some kids from the projects" were supposedly looking to "kill" him.

In "Child Abuse in Context: An Historian's Perspective," John Demos defines **child abuse** as "physical force, applied intentionally, so as to inflict substantial" injury to a child (655). Demos continues to say that "neglect---the failure to provide for the central needs of the child" is not included in the definition of abuse (655). In my view, the definition of abuse cannot be broken down to simply mean physical abuse. Neglect causes children's physical needs to go unmet in terms of lack of proper nutrition, suitable clothing for changing weather conditions, and hygiene needs. In terms of emotional needs, children can be verbally berated or ignored, either of which can cause numerous psychological problems for a child. As far as I'm concerned, I would imagine the scars from feeling unwanted or being constantly screamed at will last long after the bruises from physical abuse have faded.

The three children have been neglected in many ways over the years; however, one area that stands out is that they have never been to the doctor for anything except emergencies or dental work. The reason for this is that the family does not have health insurance and cannot afford to pay for doctor's visits, therefore putting the children's health in danger. All have crooked teeth, Alex and Chris are missing teeth, and Chris severely chipped a tooth in an accident when he was younger, one which has never been fixed. In addition, one winter when the children were still in school, their lack of proper winter clothing alarmed a teacher, prompting one of many visits from the Department of Social Services (DDS) to the family's apartment. The lack of dental hygiene has caused their physical health to suffer and as a result I feel that it can be classified as abuse.

In an example of emotional neglect, I can remember a then-fourteen year old Chris crying, and saying that he had nobody that cares for him, after a relative of mine had to post his bail money after he had been arrested. Sharon was nowhere to be found at this time and Mark was apparently at the bar while their son was attempting to contact them from the police department, leaving my mom to collect Chris and take him home. The feeling of not being cared for seemed to be more painful than any physical abuse Chris could have endured at that time.

While Katie, Alex, and Chris have not taken the traditional route of graduating from high school, considering college, and participating in things like sports or extracurricular activities like many children in our society do, they do seem to attempt to make the best of their situation. As a result of their father's inconsistency in going to work and their mother's habit of using all available money for drugs, money was often hard to come by. While the children were younger, they often had to rely on others to scrape by. For instance, my mother would frequently drop a week's worth of food by their home and my uncle Mike tried to make sure they had enough, suitable clothing to wear. Once Katie, Alex and Chris grew older, they quickly became tired of often not having electricity or a phone line, a result of the bills not having been paid.

Since the three children had all dropped out of school, they had plenty of time to work, to supply money for themselves and each other. Katie had her job at Subway, Chris was employed by Blockbuster video, and Alex at a convenience store. The three worked, as Immanuel Wallerstein states in "Households as an Institution of the World-Economy," "not for the individual but the **household**," meaning that each child worked to be able to promote a better situation to their family members and home (243). Furthermore, they were able to "pool income coming from multiple sources in order to ensure their individual and collective reproduction and well-being" and contribute to the family economy (244). Basically the three children worked to be able to pool their money to be able to afford food and occasionally take care of issues such as not having electricity. Clearly their efforts could not make any significant changes, but they did what they could.

While the children were able to afford food once they were old enough to work, when they were young there were many times when there would be no food at all in their home. I can remember countless occasions when my mother would get a phone call from one of the children, often calling from the pay phone on the corner of their street because they didn't have a working phone line in the home, to say that there wasn't a single thing to eat in the home and they were starving. As a result, to keep the children from being malnourished, at one point my mother would drive the forty five minutes it takes to get to the Stewarts' apartment, once a week, in order to bring them food. My mother did this because the Stewart children are family. Even if we do not see and interact with them as a normal functioning family would, we are still related and therefore as members of their extended family need to take care of them if their immediate family does not.

In "Affluence and Poverty in Feeding the Family," Marjorie Devault observes a "disturbing" fact that "income differences mean considerable variation in the amounts and kinds of food consumed" by families (171). She continues to note that "a significant group of people continue to experience hunger and malnutrition" (Devault 171). While most families who experience hunger and malnutrition in our society do so because of being in a single-parent situation or have parents that work at minimum wage paying jobs, the Stewarts are in this situation because of the selfishness and addictions of Mark and Sharon.

Mark is the co-owner of a construction company that he runs with his brother which allows him to have an irregular work schedule without getting fired. His brother is a wealthy man, which would lead one to imagine that if Mark actually worked a normal schedule he would be able to sufficiently provide for his family. Mark is able to take off so much time from work because his brother and other members of his family make up for the work that Mark misses. I do not know why his brother puts up with this but I would surmise that it has to do with the fact that they are family, and his brother may not want to discipline or fire him. Since Mark would often go for weeks without a single day of work, it sometimes happens that there is no money to buy food during the times he would not work. To further this situation, Mark spends a significant amount of money that he does earn on drugs and specifically alcohol.

Sharon's behavior make the family's financial situation even worse. Since she comes across as a friendly and outgoing person, she is often hired for jobs as employers assume that she will be a decent worker based on her personality. However, she does not last more than a few weeks before she begins stealing from her employers, resulting in her termination from these jobs. She also has been known to frequently ask family and friends for money to buy food for her children. The people that she asks for money, would for a while give her enough money to provide food for a week, with no questions asked. However, once after a couple of years it was revealed that Sharon took the money that people gave her, and spent it on drugs. So while people like my mother and uncle Mike thought Mark and Sharon were helping their children by providing food for them, instead they were fueling Sharon's addictions.

Sharon's and Mark's working situation and commitment to supplying for their family sharply differ from the majority of other parents in society. While most parents start a family to take care of it, Sharon and Mark have done the opposite of what is expected of them by barely working and paying little attention to their children. Anita Ilta Garey, in "Constructing Motherhood on the Night Shift: 'Working Mothers' as 'Stay at Home Moms'" describes how many women with children under the age of fourteen work the night shift. Garey states that

> working the night shift allows employed women with children to construct a definition of 'working mother' that preserves the dominant cultural ideal of a 'traditional' family form in which the mother is

at home during the day. (710)

The women that work these shifts basically have two full-time jobs, caring for their children during the day to maintain the ideal of a traditional stay at home mother, while earning an income for her family at night. Garey explains that mothers working the night shift are "able to emulate non employed mothers in their availability to participate in children's school and extracurricular activities"(714). One mother explains how working at night allows her to bring her daughter to karate and dance classes, saying that if she worked days her daughter would miss out because her mother would not be around to take her (Garey 714). These mothers work hard to be able to provide both time and money for their children.

The level of poverty the Stewarts have experienced is much lower than most could ever imagine. As a result the children have been forced to fend for themselves. While they are able to provide for themselves as of now, their jobs may not be enough in the future. Since none of the children graduated from high school, their job opportunities will be restricted to minimum wage paying jobs. Once the children are grown adults, they will have to provide a shelter, food, and necessities for themselves, all on a low salary. Collins writes that "[f]amilies use wealth to create opportunities, secure a desired standard of living, and pass their social class status to their children" (167). This has proven true for this family. Sharon and Mark have "passed their social class status to their children," which is not one to be desired. Like their parents, Katie, Alex, and Chris will most likely have to struggle to make ends meet for the rest of their lives. Katie may feel this strain earlier than her other siblings as she is now pregnant. She will now have to pay for her own necessities while also covering the expenses of another human being, all on her salary from working at Subway.

In their article "The Anti-Social Family," Michèle Barrett and Mary McIntosh state that "most boys will live out their lives in the same class and even in the same section of it [as their father's]; most girls will marry a man in a situation very similar to their own father's" (219). Since Katie, Alex, and Chris have little education and no current plans to change their level of schooling, they are and most likely will continue to live in the same class as their father. Similarly, since the children hang around with friends that are much like themselves, it is most likely that the girls will marry a man in the same financial situation as themselves and their father. This is because the type of men they have been around all their lives, poor and uneducated, is the only type they have ever known. A world of a higher social class and more opportunities is unknown to them, so all three children have nothing to strive for as they do not know that it is attainable to them or even exists.

In "Time Squeeze: The Extra Month of Work," Juliet Schor discusses how "**time squeeze**" has become a major issue with today's families and households. Schor believes that as a result of members of families and households working more and longer hours, the time that individuals have to spend with their families is limited. Some factors that influence families working more is the desire to provide for one's family, in addition to trying to "keep up" with those in their social class. Furthermore, Schor states that women are the "most visible group" that is affected by the "time squeeze." This is because women often have double the responsibilities by having to care for the family while maintaining a job to provide income. It is described that "many working mothers live a life of perpetual motion, effectively holding down two full-time jobs." The author continues on to describe a typical day of a working mother. The day begins with the mother doing some housework, preparing the children for school, and going to work, only to come back home to have to clean, cook, and take care of the children (Schor 115).

This theory is somewhat applies to the responsibilities of the children in the Stewart family. As previously discussed, the two parents in the family contribute little to the well being of the family, so the children provide what is needed for themselves, participating in **domestic labor**. The children often felt the "time squeeze" when they were younger and still in school. In the children's situation I believe school can be substituted for work, as school is the child's equivalent to work as they spend the majority of their day there, like an adult does with work. Like Schor's example of a working mother who does housework, gets the children ready for school, goes to work, and comes home to clean, cook, and take care of the children, the Stewart children would often act in a similar day. For instance, all three children would go to school and do housework. However, I think the greatest strain was placed on the girls, Katie and Alex. Since Katie was the oldest she often felt responsible for taking care of her brother and sister. Similarly, Alex felt responsible for taking care of her siblings as she always put others before herself. While Chris would help, he would do little of the cleaning and as he was the younger child, approximately eight years old at the time, there was little he could do to help with cooking.

Many times, Katie would wake up early to make sure that Alex and Chris had clothes to wear to school as well as to make lunch for the three of them with whatever food she could find in the home. Before heading off to school, Katie and Alex would try to find something to prepare for breakfast for the three, even though they often went without breakfast because of the lack of food. Once the three got home from school, Katie and Alex would try to clean up as much as possible before all three children would try to find or prepare dinner. After dinner, Katie would try to help Alex, and Alex would try to help Chris with homework. However, as there was no parental figure making sure that homework got done, most of the time Katie's and Chris's did not. The two had never liked school so homework got completed probably only a couple of times a week, unless Alex, the more studious one, tried to make the other two complete their homework.

While these activities may not be as intense as those of a working mother, they come pretty close considering it is three children doing the work, not an adult. These children took on a great deal of responsibility, which most children would not even have to think about doing. Instead of engaging in normal childhood activities like sports or playing with friends after school, these children were given the responsibility of having to "fill in" for their often absent parents. As a result, a "time squeeze" was placed on the amount of time the children had doing normal childhood activities, as well as the time they had to spend together when not engaged in "responsible activities" like cleaning and cooking.

While the exact situations for each are much different, while reading "Mothering From a Distance: Emotions, Gender, and Intergenerational Reactions in Filipino Transnational Families" by Rhacel Salazar Parrenas, I found the motivations behind the individuals reported in the article and those of Sharon in her current situation to be very similar. Sharon's recent effort to provide for her children draws bleak comparison to the efforts of the Filipina women. While Sharon has put her needs before everyone else for most of her life, since finishing her prison sentence and entering her rehabilitation home she has mentioned how she feels remorse for not being able to provide for her children in the way other mothers care for their children. As a result, in an attempt to "start over" and begin supporting her children any way she can, Sharon got a job close to her rehabilitation home. She works the maximum amount of hours a week that her program will allow her and with the exception of buying herself a pack of cigarettes a week, she sends the rest of her earnings to be split among the three children. In the article, Parrenas states that in order for many Filipina women to provide for their families, an increasing number are "mothering from a distance," and leaving their children behind in the Philippines while they "take advantage of the greater labor market opportunities in other countries" (404). These women leave everything they have to go to work to provide the best life they can for their children.

Parrenas says that the "pain of family separation creates various feelings, including helplessness, regret and guilt for mothers and loneliness, vulnerability, and insecurity for children" (405). While the situations that have caused mother and children to separate are much different in the Filipina mother's situation than Sharon's, all mothers seem to be working in their situations because they care about their children and want them to live comfortable lives, even though for Sharon's children it may be a little late for that.

The Stewart family is similar to that of the Binghamton University student Rena Dangerfield's as reported in her essay, "Mom and Dad's Waltz: A Dance of Love and Sacrifice," where she describes how "unfortunately, our home, with the privacy afforded it, was a dangerous place" (64). Dangerfield grew up in an impoverished home where her father was an alcoholic that abused her mother. As a result, times at home were seldom happy for Dangerfield and her siblings. Things were so bad at her home that they also interfered with her ability to form bonds with others outside of her blood family. She recalled how her and her sister were viewed as "daughters of the town drunk," resulting in their being frequently excluded from social situations and "none of [their] friends were allowed in [their] house" (Dangerfield 64).

While the Stewart children have been able to form bonds with others, as is shown in the significant amount of time they spend with those in their non-biological families, others in their community look down upon and assume things about them solely based on their home life. For instance, the neighbor's that Alex spends so much time with will not allow their children to spend any time at Alex's home, which is why she spends so much time at theirs. Furthermore, Alex, who is an intelligent girl who is never disrespectful, was often singled out by teachers and administrators at her school because of her family's reputation. For instance, one year, on one of the first days of school, Alex's teacher made a comment to the effect that just because Alex's family was so out of control did not mean that that type of behavior would be allowed by her. This teacher clearly did not know Alex as she never got in trouble at school, yet the teacher assumed Alex was just like the rest of her family. By stereotyping Alex based on her family's background, the teacher was not allowing her to live up to her full potential which will not help her in getting out of her current situation.

It is very obvious that Katie, Alex, and Chris do not receive much care or positive attention from their parents as their **nuclear family**. As a result, the three have turned elsewhere to find support and a feeling of being wanted from their **chosen families**, those people that are like family to them, even though they are not biologically related. Katie lives at her boyfriend's home and his mother treats Katie as her own. Alex spends most of her time at a neighbor's apartment, which she has gone to since she was young. In addition, Chris seems to have formed a type of family among his friends, most of whom are in somewhat similar situations with their own biological families. These individuals provide food, a place to spend the night, and even clothes for the Stewart children. As well, the children even frequently celebrate holidays with the members of these families.

These types of "families" that the Stewarts have formed compare to what Katrina Wegar, in "Adoption and Kinship," studied. She noted in her article that "the concept of **kin** was not exclusively reserved for biological relatives but could include close friends as well" in the groups of individuals she observed (42). Furthermore, she stated that "familial relationships are nourished and sustained by the accumulation of thousands of daily acts of support and care" (42). As a result, while the families that the Stewarts have formed may not be conventional, at least they are a place of comfort and support that otherwise the children would not have.

I find that Martha Minow in "Redefining Families: Who's In and Who's Out" presents a perfect argument for the Stewarts' situation. Her argument "emphasizes not any particular definition of family, but instead, the interests of the child…[because] those interests, above all, are what must take center stage" (Minow 16). Basically, she does not think it matters what defines a family as long as the needs of the child are met. In the Stewarts' situation, their "families" may not fall into society's typical definition of a family, yet their needs are being met by their "families," and that is all that matters.

While the Stewarts do consider their non-biological families to be the only real family they have in their lives, my mother still tries hard to help the children with whatever they need and to include them in family gatherings and events. For instance, when a couple of years ago Alex told my mom that she wanted to get her GED, my mom drove her to the school to sign up, paid for her, and bought her books, only to have Alex decide that she really wasn't ready to go back to school. Furthermore, she makes sure the children know about every family gathering and offers to pick them up and drive them home. My mother says that she does this because they are family, and especially because it is what her mother would want her to do. Her mother would always say that family never gives up on and always helps out family. These beliefs were instilled to her by her parents who always said that it was the "Greek way" to help out family, that it was an obligation that family members should be happy to undertake. As a result, my mom has put in so much effort to help the Stewart family because she knows it is the right thing to do, but even more so because it is what her Greek ancestors' culture expects of her.

While the concept of family does not apply normally to the Stewarts, neither does their home. During the years that the Stewarts lived in their apartment they were often late paying the rent and sometimes would not pay at all. Mark's brother was their landlord so he allowed them significant leeway in paying rent. However, there were many times that he threatened to evict them, until he finally did last year. During the time they lived at this apartment, the conditions inside the home were often repulsive. The family owned two dogs that were so vicious they were not allowed outside; as a result they often would relieve themselves inside the house. Many times, nobody would bother to pick up after the dogs. There was dirt covering every inch of the apartment and the heater did not work properly. In addition, for a period of about a year the family had no door to their apartment, so anybody could basically just walk in. In "It's All in the Family: Intersection of Gender, Race, and Nation," Patricia Hill Collins suggests that "'**homes**' provide spaces of privacy and security for families, races, and nation-states, they serve as sanctuaries for group members…these homes represent idealized, privatized spaces where members can feel at ease" (161). When thinking of the physical condition of the Stewarts' apartment, combined with the emotional misery that the family must live with, it seems that their "home" is anything but a sanctuary.

Even though growing up was tough for Katie, Alex and Chris---and I don't think anyone would blame them for harboring some resentment for their parents---the three don't seem to have any ill feelings at all. While the children seem to be indifferent to Mark, not overly caring for him but not hating him either, the three all have a mutual admiration and love for their mother. No matter what anyone says about her, all three will quickly jump to her defense, even if their reasonings make no sense. Furthermore, all three would drop anything they were doing just to see their mother for a second.

The actions of Katie, Alex, and Chris seem to be defined by Collins's view that "even when family members lack merit, they are entitled to benefits simply because they belong" (165). Collins continues on, saying that family members often feel that they are "responsible for members of their families" and as a result will "routinely help their family members by babysitting, lending money, helping relatives find employment or caring for the elderly" (165). While Sharon did not really provide much of anything for her children while they were growing up, they still feel obligated and more than willing to help their mother now. The children do this by supporting her with her treatment for drug abuse and recently by helping her find a new apartment, and even lending her money to buy furniture and supplies for it. While Katie, Alex, and Chris do not have to help their mother, they do simply because she is their mother.

While the children support their mother simply because she is their mother, Mark does not support his children just because they are his children. When Mark found out that Katie was pregnant, he told her that she would have to find another place to live. As Katie had no other options and spends enough of her time there anyway, she moved in with her boyfriend's family. In one apartment will now reside, Katie, her boyfriend, his mother and brother, his brother's girlfriend, their two children, and Katie's daughter once she is born. Katie obviously would not have enough money to rent her own apartment so her only choice is to live there. Similarly, her boyfriend's brother also lives at the apartment to save money.

These situations are reminiscent of the situations depicted in Judith Seltzer's article "Families Formed Outside of Marriage." Seltzer writes that "**cohabitation** remains more common among those with less education and for whom economic resources are more constrained" (234). The boyfriend's family can be classified as poor since the only income comes from minimum wage paying jobs from the boyfriend and his brother, in addition to a small amount of disability money that the mother gets from having a respiratory problem. It is also significant to note that no one other than the mother in this apartment graduated from high school. If any one of those individuals had completed high school and maybe gone to college and had a higher paying job they may not be in the situation they are in, needing to cohabitate because their resources are "more constrained" than individuals that have finished school and gone on to higher education.

When Katie called to tell my mother that she was pregnant, my mom asked Katie what the current working situation was for her and her boyfriend. She did this because she knew that the income from the two of them would pretty much be the only means of support for the child, my mother most likely being the only outside source that would be contributing to the financial wellbeing of the baby. Katie replied that she would continue working at Subway and her boyfriend was in the process of finding a second job to be able to support the baby. Katie told my mom that one of her aunts was very upset about the pregnancy, saying that it was a disgrace that the baby was being born into such a situation, where the couple is unmarried, poor, and unable to find work other than minimum wage paying jobs. The aunt said that the baby would end up living the same life that Katie has.

Katie admitted to my mom that she knew she wasn't in the best situation to have a baby; however, she thought everything would be alright. She said that having had the family life that she did growing up, she wanted to make sure her baby's life was better than that. This desire to provide a life as good as is possible for her child is illustrated in a passage quoted in Denise Segura's "Working At Motherhood." The quote by a single mother states that she's always wanted a family because she thinks "it was more like I didn't have a family-type home when I was growing up. I didn't have a mother and a father and the kids all together in the same household all happy" (Segura 732). I think Katie probably feels the same. While she did not intentionally try to get pregnant, she wants to try and create the type of family life now that she has always wanted and never had.

As a result, the members of the Stewart family have thus far lived a non-traditional, neglected life. The parents do not act as parents, therefore leaving the children to raise themselves. Consequently, the children have just scraped by in providing for themselves and in doing so have pretty much sentenced themselves to living the same quality of life as they grow older. Since they have little education they will have little job opportunities and little opportunity to find a better situation for themselves in the world. Therefore, Sharon and Mark Stewart have passed on their poor quality of life to their undeserving children, who were never given a chance to have better than their parents.

While one may blame Sharon and Mark for the situation passed on to their children, sociologically it would be logical to also ask if Sharon and Mark were themselves products of similar familial or other social circumstances, and what this may tell us about social structural supports or constraints that make such familial and personal troubles public issues for many families across the nation and the world. This, however, should await another opportunity for further analysis.

BIBLIOGRAPHY

Barrett, Michèle, and Mary McIntosh. 1982. "The Anti-Social Family." Pp. 219-229 in *Families in the U.S.: Kinships and Domestic Politics*, edited by Karen V. Hansen and Anita Ilta Garey. Philadelphia, PA: Temple University Press.

Collins, Patricia Hill. "It's All in the Family: Intersection of Gender, Race, and Nation." Pp.156-176 in Uma Narayan & Sandra Harding (eds.), *Decentering the Center* Bloomington: Indiana University Press, 2000.

Dangerfield, Rena. "Mom and Dad's Waltz: A Dance of Love and Sacrifice." *Human Architecture: Journal of the Sociology of Self-Knowledge*, vol. 1, Issue 2, 62-66.

Demos, John. 1986. "Child Abuse in Context" An Historian's Perspective." Pp.651-667 in *Families in the U.S.: Kinships and Domestic Politics*, edited by Hansen and Garey. Philadelphia, PA: Temple University Press.

Devault, Marjorie.1991. "Affluence and Poverty in Feeding the Family." Pp. 171-187 in *Families in the U.S.: Kinships and Domestic Politics*, edited by Hansen and Garey. Philadelphia, PA: Temple University Press.

Garey, Anita Ilta. 1995. "Constructing Motherhood on the Night Shift: 'Working Mothers' as 'Stay-at-Home Moms'." Pp.709-726 in *Families in the U.S.: Kinships and Domestic Politics*, edited by Hansen and Garey. Philadelphia, PA: Temple University Press.

Minow, Martha. 1991. "Redefining Families: Who's In and Who's Out?" Pp.7-17 in *Families in the U.S.: Kinships and Domestic Politics*, edited by Hansen and Garey. Philadelphia, PA: Temple University Press.

Parrenas, Rhacel Salazar. "Mothering From a

Distance: Emotions, Gender, an Intergenerational Relations in Filipino Transnational Families." In Susan J. Ferguson (ed), *Shifting The Center: Understanding Contemporary Families*, Third Edition, Boston: McGraw-Hill, 2007, Pp.404-415.

Sawyer, Jessica. "Confessions of a Maine-iac: The Family, Academia, and Modernity." Pp. 193-203 in *Human Architecture*, Vol III, Nos 1&2, Fall04/Spring '05.

Scanlan, Christopher. "It's Late At Night, And I'm Screaming At My Kids Again: A Father Confronts His Rage." Pp.301-305 in Estelle Disch, *Reconstructing Gender: A Multicultural Anthology*, Second Edition. Mountain View, CA: Mayfield Publ. Co., 2000).

Schor, Juliet B. "Time Squeeze: The Extra Month of Work." Pp.113-130 in *Families in the U.S.: Kinships and Domestic Politics*, edited by Hansen and Garey. Philadelphia, PA: Temple University Press.

Segura, Denise A. 1994. "Working at Motherhood: Chicana and Mexican Immigrant Mothers and Employment." Pp.727-744 in *Families in the U.S.: Kinships and Domestic Politics*, edited by Hansen and Garey. Philadelphia, PA: Temple University Press.

Seltzer, Judith. "Families Formed Outside of Marriage." Pp. 252-250 in Susan J. Ferguson (ed.) *Shifting the Center, Understanding Contemporary Families*, Third Edition, Boston: McGraw-Hill, 2007.

Stack, Carol, and Linda Burton. "Kinscripts." Pp.405-417 in *Families in the U.S.: Kinships and Domestic Politics*, edited by Hansen and Garey. Philadelphia, PA: Temple University Press.

Wallerstein, Immanuel. "Households as an Institution of the World-Economy." Pp.234-252. *The Essential Wallerstein*. New York: New Press Books, 2000.

Wegar, Katarina. "Adoption and Kinship." Pp. 41-51 in *Families in the U.S.: Kinships and Domestic Politics*, edited by Hansen and Garey. Philadelphia, PA: Temple University Press.

"TransAmerica." Dir. Duncan Tucker. Weinstein Company and IFC Films, 2005.

Exiting the Self-Destructive Highway
A Sociological Path Back to A Future Career

Paul Connor

University of Massachusetts Boston

paul.connor001@umb.edu

Abstract: Lucky for me the date is 2007, because trust me when I say I would not have written these words, and you would not be reading them, if it was 2006 or prior. Why? Well, many times—at least many times that I can actually recall in my past feeble attempts at college—whenever a final paper was due, or any type of final project was assigned, I would just quit the class. Some might call it just plain old laziness and back then I probably would have agreed. Now, though, looking back, I think it had more to do with my being afraid of not just failing, but scared of actually doing something to get ahead. That's how I lived almost my entire adulthood; it seemed I would deliberately do things to derail any progress in my life. The problem with that, however, is that I may have thought for a time I was only hurting myself but now I realize I was also hurting all the people who loved and cared about me as well. Using various sociological concepts and theories, in this essay I explore the reasons for my self-destructive behavior of substance abuse while growing up, and explain how I have sought to exit the path in favor of more fulfilling educational and career plans.

Lucky for me the date is 2007, because trust me when I say I would not have written these words, and you would not be reading them, if it was 2006 or prior. Why? Well, many times—at least many times that I can actually recall in my past feeble attempts at college—whenever a final paper was due, or any type of final project was assigned, I would just quit the class. Some might call it just plain old laziness and back then I probably would have agreed. Now, though, looking back, I think it had more to do with my being afraid of not just failing, but scared of actually doing something to get ahead. That's how I lived almost my entire adulthood; it seemed I would deliberately do things to derail any progress in my life. The problem with that, however, is that I may have thought for a time I was only hurting myself but now I realize I was also hurting all the people who loved and cared about me as well.

My thinking became so warped you could say I behaved in the polar opposite of how the theories on rational choice conventionally claim humans behave. **Rational Choice Theory** assumes that "people are rational and base their actions on what they perceive to be the most effective means to their goals" (Wallace & Wolf 303). Looking back and thinking about all my past decisions and behaviors, never did I act with any rationale or with any particular focus towards my future. George Homans's term

---

Paul Connor is an undergraduate student at UMass Boston, majoring in Sociology. He wrote this paper while enrolled in the course Soc. 341-3: "Elements of Sociological Theories," instructed by Mohammad H. Tamdgidi (Assistant Professor of Sociology at UMass Boston) during the Spring 2007 semester.

elementary social behavior—which means "behavior that appears and reappears whether or not people plan on its doing so" (Wallace & Wolf 315)—can best describe the manner in which I lived during my young adulthood. The behaviors that kept appearing in my life were behaviors that led to my own gratification. They appeared often.

Moving out of my parents' house and gaining my freedom all my parents could do was watch in horror. The only time I finished a semester at school was when my father used what Homans called **the value proposition** that is "the more valuable to a person is the result of his action, the more likely he is to perform the action;" my parents actually would have to bribe me to go back and then stay in school. Once when they bought me a car and I didn't finish the semester. I think they decided that they had enough and I was on my own when it came to school.

Several times I tried to go back on my own. I enrolled so many times I made a habit of it. In my previous half-hearted attempts at school I would make it to the end of the semester and just stop showing up—not every time, but enough times. I got to the point that I just expected to fail. I expected to fail not only in school but to fail in life as well. People I knew from high school were doing the same thing so I didn't think there was too much of a **stigma** involved with not succeeding.

My expectations for myself were low, thus my self-esteem was low as well. One thing I found that helped raise the way I felt was to drown my sorrows in substance abuse. This went on for most of my young life. At the age of 29 I decided enough was enough and it was time to turn my life around. I had had enough of the way I was living and for the sake of my then-fiancé and for myself I wanted to change. I needed to change.

While some people in this day and age are addicted to material things like big, huge plasma televisions, nice cars, fancy clothes, and other meaningless possessions, I never had any need for most of these things at any time in my life. As shown in the film *Affluenza* our society is largely made up of people who are very passionate about accumulating material wealth. There were times that I wanted some of these things, but I spent so much time, energy, and money on my hard-living ways that I had no time for any of it. At the time I usually got by with the basic necessities and more often than not didn't even really care.

Looking back is something I do often. I've learned that it is the only way to move forward and not make the same mistakes again. For this paper I think I need to go all the way back to high-school, to the beginning of my substance abuse, to really comprehend why I've been so self-destructive my entire adult life.

High-School

I always promised myself in my early teens that I wouldn't ever pick up the bottle because of someone close to me who battled with alcoholism; I stayed with this for a long period. I don't know if the first time I remember getting drunk with a friend was because I really enjoyed it or if I just liked the feeling of saying I got drunk to all my other friends. Either way it became part of my life. Being on the football team and just trying to fit in, I really couldn't avoid it. My getting drunk was a **symbol**, "the stimulus whose response is given in advance" (Wallace & Wolf 211). I was symbolically telling the other players that I was part of the team. I was joyous on the outside because I had waited longer than most and got a certain amount of ribbing for not ever trying it sooner. Now I could finally say that I drank. I wish I could say it was the last time but the main reason I can't is best described by Charles Horton Cooley's concept, **the looking glass self.** The way I imagined how my classmates saw me and the way I imagined they judged me left me feeling very alone inside. Yes I played football, basketball, and baseball, but I didn't have any real friends and just went out for the teams to fit in. I do remember feeling a certain amount of guilt when it became a regular thing but my feelings of belonging even just a little bit far outweighed them.

Goffman's concept of **impression management** can best describe my high school years. I certainly tried to guide and control the impression my peers formed of me by following what everyone else was doing. Everyday I made sure to wear my football or basketball jackets depending on the weather. They were my **personal fronts**. The only place I considered my **back region** was my bedroom. I didn't even want my parents to see how unhappy I was. Since everyone else during my senior year was binge drinking almost every night, that meant I was as well and since the next logical step for everybody else was to smoke, I did that too. I look back on those years and while part of my recovery is to try to have no regrets I do wish I hadn't tried so hard to **associate** with people who were doing things that weren't any good for me and in the end weren't really my friends at all.

THE OLD COLLEGE TRY

Leaving high school I definitely thought going away to college would be life changing for me. Even though I was not purposefully conducting what Herbert Blumer calls research **exploration**, the concept can sum up how I felt to leave home and go off to school. I was engaging in "a close and comprehensive acquaintance with a sphere of social life which was unfamiliar and hence unknown" (Wallace & Wolf 228) to me. I thought leaving my town and the classmates I tagged along with for so many years would be good for me. The four years I spent in high school felt like one long process of **self-indication**, meaning that I never felt like anyone was really listening to me, that I was just conversing with myself. I thought with college things might be different.

One night after being there for only a short while I ended up alienating every single person on my floor which had roughly seven or eight people living together on it. I got severely intoxicated and got into a physical altercation with just about every one living there. I vaguely remember calling my father in a drunken state after the incident and begging him to come get me. My father drove all the way to my school which was in another state just to console me. He didn't want to but I made him take me home. For a very long time afterwards I felt like a **sociopath** and a very selfish person in my father's looking glass eyes.

My father never once pushed me for answers on why my attempt at going away to college failed but it wasn't for the lack of his not caring about me or his not caring about my education. He and my mother always stressed the value of a good education to my sister and me. I think he realized I was extremely embarrassed by what had happened at the school and he didn't want to embarrass me any further. Just recently, however, we sat down for the first time and talked about what had happened and why I really left that particular school. To delve more into the matter I would have to relate it to the concept of **ethnomethodology**.

Harold Garfinkel, as restated by Wallace and Wolf, defines ethnomethodology as the method "of making sense of everyday activities," of "how people make sense of their everyday activities," (Wallace & Wolf 269). Looking back at my behavior then amid my friends, I think that I felt then that by drinking and being rowdy with my new "friends" they would not only embrace me but find me funny and completely normal. What I didn't realize then, and not until years later, was that I should have been doing the exact opposite. I should have stayed away from the alcohol and tried to stay as low-key as possible. My **stock of knowledge** then of what went on at college was limited to what I had heard about it from my high-school classmates and the stories they told me about the college parties either they or their siblings went to and how they couldn't wait to go to college themselves to be free of their parents and to party it up. In no uncertain terms did I actually think that I was going to learn something; I was going to meet girls, have fun, and be free of my parents.

In the end it may have taken me over 10 years but with the help of sobriety I was finally able to sit down with my dad and give him a full **account** of what had actually transpired and relayed to him the events that occurred and why I was in such a rush to leave that college. I never realized that he harbored almost as much guilt about it as I did because he had put some of the blame on himself for taking me home that day and feeling somewhat responsible for my not wanting to return after the fact. After we talked about it, though, I think we both got some much needed closure on the issue. I just only wish that we had spoken about it sooner so that he knew that I felt solely responsible for whatever stupid things that I've done—especially that one.

DRIFTING

Looking back, for several years I really felt like I had just drifted through life. Not really going anywhere but never feeling I was in one place for very long either. I did things that I'm not proud of, but some were things that I justified at the time as helping to pay the bills. My behavior during this time could be described by Robert Merton's **Theory of Deviance**. If we follow Merton's typology of deviant behavior, in the United States where "monetary success is highly valued and the legitimate means to it are unavailable for many our society should have a lot of deviance" (Wallace & Wolf 55). I, sadly, fell into to this category. My **dysfunctional** way of thinking led me to believe that engaging in deviant behavior was the only way I wanted to be living. To me it was the American Dream; but it was just my American "Dream." I thought I was being my own boss, making my own hours, making enough money to pay whatever bills that I had to pay, and the number one thing for me was that I almost always had something to help me escape reality and keep me feeling euphoric. Another thing that I thought was great about not having a steady job was that I didn't have to deal with any type of **bureaucracy** telling me what to do and when to do it. I thought this was great because I was never good at taking orders even if it was sound advice that might point me in the right direction.

I can almost identify with the last holdout juror in the film *Twelve Angry Men*, in a twisted sort of way. If I was in a room with five people having a discussion on any type of subject I more often than not would turn it into some kind of heated debate. Just as the juror probably felt cornered, I would almost force people including my friends to try and back me up against a wall with my sometimes outrageous views on the world. I think I became so combative on purpose, or perhaps became so subconsciously, so that it would be easier for the people around me to care less about me and my problems.

The only **manifest function** such a behavior served—i.e., functions involving "consequences that people expect" (Wallace & Wolf 51)—was to supposedly help me have a good time. My life revolved around nothing and no one, except the substances that kept me going. Sometimes I wanted to change and other times I thought I was just living the good life. Neil Smelser's take on the concept of **ambivalence** sums up how I felt about my life at the time after living this way for several years. "As quoted by Wallace and Wolf, according to Smelser "the nature of ambivalence is to hold *opposing affective orientations* toward the same person, object, or symbol. Further, in the words of Wallace and Wolf, "In applying the notion of ambivalence Smelser refers to phenomena such as death and separation, retirement, and moving away from a community" (Wallace & Wolf 60). Smelser also says that the form of dependency may vary. Feeling ambivalent, I was afraid of separating myself from the substances that helped get me through the day. After living the way that I had for so long I often thought about cleansing my body of these chemicals and moving on from the toxic lifestyle I had been living for all those years but I didn't realize until it was too late that it wouldn't be as easy as I had thought. My ambivalence stemmed from the part of me who wanted to keep doing the things I was doing and the part of me who wanted to clean up and straighten out.

A passage from Toni Cade Bambara, quoted in Avery Gordon's book, *Keeping Good Time,* describes it all for me, "So used to being unwhole and unwell, one forgot what its was to walk upright and see clearly, breathe easily, think better than was taught, be better than one was programmed to believe" (Gordon 200). This is what became of me, I had become so used to being a broken down man at the age of 25 that I all but gave up on myself. I felt "unwhole," and "unwell." I needed help but didn't know how or even whom to ask for it.

THE NEXT STEP

Using C. Wright Mills' **sociological imagination**, which involves the ability to relate my personal realities to the larger social structures, I often wondered at the time if my feelings and actions were normal. It took me a long time to realize I had a substance abuse problem, and even longer to make the distinction that my **personal troubles** could even be related to a **public issue**. Mills makes the distinction between the two and his definitions of both are what make me believe that my problem although very personal to me is part of a very public one. There is another passage in *Keeping Good Time* that struck a chord with me, "People all over the world and in unprecedented numbers are struggling in all kinds of ways in the streets, on their farms, in their communities and schools for a sustainable existence" (Gordon 116). I honestly was oblivious to the fact that there were many people out there like me that were struggling with anything, including the substances that I was struggling with. My **alienation** from society in every way led me down a path where I was only concerned with myself; I had no concern for the people I loved or for anyone else's well-being but my own. One could characterize me back then as having a very **blasé attitude**—i.e., as people who are "in boundless pursuit of pleasure, to the point where they become disinterested" (Farganis 132). I was only interested in myself and gradually it I became only interested in where and when the next feeling of euphoria came from.

MULTIPLE PERSONALITIES

I never thought I had a problem because I wasn't like this twenty-four hours a day, I became pretty good at hiding my ever growing dependency on substances. I could be one way when I had to see my family and then another way when I was out looking for the next good time. I had several of these personas, one for work, one for my parents when I would go by their house every few weeks to let them know I was alive, and my favorite one at the time was the one for when I was out drinking. Only after viewing the movie *Multiple Personality: The Search for Deadly Memories* (HBO) did I become keenly aware of something. The movie obviously showed the extreme side of the mental illness and, while not to the extent of the cases portrayed, I think everybody has multiple sides to their personalities. What I've become aware of was the several personalities that came out in me quite frequently. Not to the extent of the three people the film portrayed, and not because of any horrible thing that happened to me during childhood, I now realize how different I could be in the double-life that I was leading. Looking back on this I think the time I finally realized it was time to clean my life up was when the side of me that was very self-destructive completely took over and became the sole personality that I lived with.

Where Do I Fit Into the World?

One thing on my road to recovery that I have struggled with is answering the question: after all the years of wasted time and energy spent chasing something that was never there in the first place, now that I'm free and clear of those demons (or at least now that I have got a hold on my demons) where do I fit into the bigger picture of life? Where exactly can I find a place and contribute to society? Where do I fit into the world?

While I was wasting my twenty something years old life away most people my age were training and preparing themselves for promotions and better things; at least, the people who I ended up wanting to be like were. I wanted to get a good job and support my wife but knew I didn't yet have the tools or skills required to make it in today's job market. In this age of **globalization** where "large corporations dominate the globe" (Wallace & Wolf 179), no respectable company was going to hire me on my life skills or the associate's degree that I somehow managed to get when I was younger.

I was nervous but I decided it was time to go back and finish what I started. I needed to go back and attain the skills I would need to be employed in one of those jobs I knew I wasn't still qualified for. I not only promised my parents but myself as well to follow up that route and make the effort. As the anonymous author of "Hooped Dreams: Internal Growth, External Stagnation, and One Man's Search for Work" said, "It involves fits and starts, sometimes it takes two steps forward, other times three steps back" (4). I felt like I'd taken enough steps backwards and that going back to really finish school would be a huge step forward for me. I also thought that now was my time to start contributing something towards a society that I had for long shunned so as to be alone and stay introverted caught in my own realities and addictions.

James McHugh's "It's Worth Living in the World" (2003), even its very title, was very inspirational for me. I picked his essay to read because the title caught my eye, then reading into it I found out that James was a homosexual. At first, I just didn't think I could relate to him. While James's main issue was different than mine he still dealt with most of the same struggles, fears, and emotions as I had. He also handled life situations the way I did: "I was alone, I avoided those around me, but I still wasn't happy when I pushed everyone away either" (1). This statement made me reminisce about the way I used to be. The last stage of my substance abuse was when I got to the point where I pushed everyone away and just wanted to be alone with the substance of my choice at the time. Opening up when it came to my journey through sobriety was at times painful and difficult and at other times wondrous and simple. Something Morrie told Mitch in *Tuesdays with Morrie* deeply resonated with me. He said to him "When we're infants we need others to survive, when we're dying we need others to survive, and in between we need others to survive." That was a lesson that I had learned the hard way, but it was a lesson learned none the less. I was ashamed of the problems I was dealing with and the thought of asking for help to me was out of the question. The problem was that I had a very beautiful, loving girlfriend who didn't like the way I was living and I wanted to spend the rest of my life with her. Even in the haze and fogginess of my life I knew I wanted this and that if I did lose her it would lead me down the path of never being able to change my life. Morrie was right; in between we do need others to survive.

Something that I had procrastinated about for a long time, probably longer than most, was what I did want to get my degree in when I finally did finish. I've worked in restaurants for years as a waiter and as a bartender I had to engage more than a waiter in **emotional labor**—which is "the management of feeling to create a publicly observable facial and bodily display; emotional labor is sold for a wage" (Wallace & Wolf 250). I didn't want to leave my fate in the hands of someone who could fire me on a whim and/or pick up and move the company elsewhere like we saw in Michael Moore's film *The Big One* where in the movie it is all about the big corporation stomping on and taking advantage of the little guy. At first I thought when I entered my first semester at UMass Boston I would major in business management because of all my restaurant experience. I decided halfway through that first semester that it probably would be best if I majored in something else because I was stuck with what Arlie Huchschild called a strain of **emotive dissonance** which is "the struggle to maintain a difference between feeling and feigning" (Wallace & Wolf 251) from working in restaurants and bars for so long.

My father was a teacher, my grandfather was a teacher, and my uncle Paul who I am named after was a teacher. I was never comfortable in front of large groups of people and I just never thought that it was for me to become a teacher. Even though growing up the thought of my becoming a teacher felt awkward to me, I thought it was a profession held in great esteem and I was proud of my father. I have been blessed with some degree of what Pierre Bourdieu calls **cultural capital** from my parents. Bourdieu says that in the educational context, "those from privileged homes have the attitudes and knowledge, especially cultural knowledge that make the education system a comfortable, familiar sort of place in which they can succeed easily" (Wallace & Wolf 113). I think that in my generation there is a strong trend whereby everyone believes that they have a destiny to become part of the **power elite,** that is "those who hold dominate positions in political, military, and economic institutions" (Wallace & Wolf 107). However, I think not everyone has to be a millionaire off of the website that they sold for a bunch of money. In the age of reality television and personal websites everybody seems to want their fifteen minutes of fame even if it means selling yourself out. I'm not judging anybody because I know what it feels like to sell out the values you were raised with.

Leaving those feelings behind and no longer looking for any great social **status** I have decided that I would like to teach in some capacity and in fact came to the conclusion that I owed it not only to myself but more so to the society I live in to give back. For years I not only didn't contribute anything I actually worked against it and I was not only hurting myself but I was helping others hurt themselves along the way. I thought that by helping to counsel others about the dangers of drugs and alcohol and the impact they have on one's life I would be rectifying some of my past errors while contributing to the betterment of society.

TODAY

I was looking forward this semester to

working on this paper, the opposite of what Harold Muriaty said in his essay titled "My Life So Far: A Work in Progress." Harold started his paper saying he had been dreading it for so long and begun to worry as it got later and later. Well, I wasn't dreading doing this paper and in fact I was quite looking forward to it. While I was writing it, though, I became keenly aware of the extremely personal feelings I was actually putting on paper. I didn't know if I would be embarrassed that a professor I held in high-esteem and respected was going to be reading and grading my account of my emotional and spiritual reawakening. Then I thought of something Morrie Schwartz said to Mitch Albom in *Tuesdays with Morrie*. A little wave is moving up and down and a big wave says to him why it looked so sad? The little wave says sadly that what's the point of being happy when we're all going to just crash onto the rock? The big wave then tells the little wave to not be so sad about that because it is not just a little wave, but a part of the ocean. The lesson I got from that was everybody in life sometimes crashes and it's part of life, but one has to see this as part of the bigger picture of world's troubles and promises. I'm not embarrassed by the person I used to be because I've taken the things I've done, the missteps and mistakes, and learned and grown from them and like Morrie said, can now feel that I am part of a bigger life of people in public who have similarly experienced troubles such as mine.

Today I'm happy to say I've been on the road to recovery for the last two years and been completely clean and sober for one full year. I took baby steps at first and then decided it was all or nothing. My girlfriend is now my wife and along with just celebrating my one year anniversary of sobriety we just celebrated our one year anniversary of marriage. Life is better now, but I am constantly reminding myself of my past. I am neither embarrassed nor ashamed of what my life was like before I became sober, I have no regrets about the past, only hopes for the future. I've turned my self–destructive tendencies into more positive and hopeful ones, by not only getting sober but also by reflecting on why I was so destructive to myself—realizing through exercises such as this paper that I do deserve to succeed in life and to be happy doing it.

REFERENCES

Farganis, James. (2004). *Readings in Social Theory: The Classic Tradition to Post-Modernism*. 4th Ed. New York: McGraw-Hill, 2004

McHugh, James. (2003) "It's Worth Living in the World." *Human Architecture: Journal of the Sociology of Self-Knowledge*. Vol. II, Issue 1, Spring

Anonymous. (2004/2005) "Hooped Dreams: Internal Growth, External Stagnation, and One Man's Search for Work." *Human Architecture: Journal of the Sociology of Self-Knowledge*. Vol. III, Issue 1 & 2, Fall 2004/Spring 2005.

Harold Muriaty (2004/2005) "My Life So Far: A "Work" in Progress." *Human Architecture: Journal of the Sociology of Self-Knowledge*. Vol. III, Issues 1 & 2, Fall 2004/ Spring 2005

Wallace, Ruth and Alison Wolf. 2006. *Contemporary Sociological Theory: Expanding the Classical Tradition*. 6th Ed. New Jersey: Prentice Hall.

Gordon, Avery F. *Keeping Good Time: Reflections On Knowledge, Power And People*. Boulder, Colorado: Paradigm Publishers, 2004

Films:

"Multiple Personalities" (1992). HBO Home Box Office.

"Tuesday with Morrie" (1999). Touchstone.

"Affluenza" (1997). KCTS-Seattle and Oregon Public Broadcasting.

"Twelve Angry Men" (1957) MGM.

Beginnings

Arie Kupferwasser

Creative Art Therapist

arie8k@rcn.com

Abstract: Not once in my life did I seriously think I might one day become a therapist. The idea might have existed as a joke within me, as friends and acquaintances had always come to me with their problems, telling me how gifted a listener I was. Some had even suggested, over the years, that I'd make a great therapist. *Cute,* I'd always thought, *but I don't think so.* So, my choice to become a therapist---which I barely trusted at all---came as a surprise, the realness of which I did not believe until I was encircled within it. With nothing to reference but two months of experience at Sloan-Kettering and a feeling that I was ready for my life to change, I interviewed at the two biggest and nearest schools, was accepted into one of them, and braced myself, as though lifting off for another planet. I had no idea at all what on earth I was doing or where it would leave me, and only vague speculation as to why I was choosing this path. It felt crazy to me, diving right into uncharted waters. And it would take some time before I learned to integrate that nothing could have been saner than the risk of a life without guarantees.

What's the Point?

If we knew the point,
Would we forfeit the line, the wave, the form,
The formless?
Would we miss the points
That disappear into the magic of
The pointless?

Every story begins somewhere, sometime; this one, at a time in my life when I was emerging from a dark ocean that was calm enough to keep me afloat and furious enough to draw me under whenever hope cracked a smile. I didn't yet know it, but I was finding my way towards change, initiating a shift in landscape that would alter my life completely. What I did know was that I had become fed up with despair, pissed off enough to do something about it, and gentle enough to appreciate my efforts without knowing where they might lead me, or if they would lead me anywhere at all.

I was twenty-seven years old, living with the family export business that my grandfather had begun and my mother had inherited. Me in the bedroom, a self-imposed confinement, surrounded by the jarring sounds of office tedium: the popping typewriter my mother still used; the softer computer keys made manic by her onslaughts of speed, punctuated by little blips of silence; the chatty business calls with well-known suppliers and customers overseas; the banal discussions with a friend she had employed to help her with the cutting

---

Arie Kupferwasser, ATR-BC, LCAT, is a New York State licensed Creative Arts Therapist in private practice, having received his M.P.S. from Pratt Institute. He also teaches "Creative Arts as Experiential Group Process" modules at BlueStone Institute and is a freelance artist, writer, and editor.

and arrangement of textile fabric samples; the chopping sound of that heavy-duty cutting machine. It all seemed so crass and loud, always way too early in the morning for such sudden sounds. Or too late in the evening. My folks lived three stories below and my mother made her own hours, so she was in and out of the apartment as she pleased. Even after I'd asked her to check in with me evenings before she came upstairs, it was difficult for me to insist on privacy. But then, I'd been working in the family business too, for four years, ever since I'd returned from college. Against my will and wishes, it had somehow become the only life I could manage to patch together.

My grandfather, whom I loved dearly and whose judgment I had come to trust over the years since his death, had named the company after me in 1973. Ariel. The same name he imagined as my own when I was still in my mother's womb. The rarely voiced but well-understood family myth was that exporting textiles was my destiny, should I fail to find another. And not knowing what else to do with myself, I had become caught in that narrative, even though nothing could have interested me less than exporting and textiles.

Coming out of college, all of my hopes had been wrapped up in writing a novel I began to envision during my last year in school. When I moved back home, amidst confused ideas about what was supposed to happen next in my life, I typed out one chapter after another, stuck within a loop of ceaseless editing, revising, and refining. I took notes on themes and characters and scenes with no destination in sight and little drive for publishing. My initial intention for college had been primarily to develop my identity as an artist, since making images had been my greatest joy from the age of six, but I had managed instead to shut down that part of me. So I held on to writing, my other great love, as if it were the lifesaver keeping me afloat. It was the only thing I knew for sure that I wanted to do.

When I began to work for the export company, I justified it as a way to earn my keep while I followed my true passion. I had no intention at all of making it my life's work. But as time passed, the unspoken story that had begun to linger within my psyche, supported by my parents' incessant questioning of intent, was that my written efforts were an invalid pursuit, since I was unwilling to apply them towards a practical vision. Through my parents' eyes, the export company was a more realistic aspiration, and as I spent greater hours learning the business, unaware that I was acquiring their lens as my own, my dreams of writing a book slowly fizzled into the bluntness of my bland life, till I could hardly discern one day from another.

Putting a spin on a growing feeling that I had been letting myself down, I entertained the possibility that my grandfather had wisely laid down a path I might follow, whose joys, though still hidden from me, I would one day unveil. From time to time, I would reapply myself toward this desperate hope, as if trying to save a marriage that was sour from the start. I even went so far as to take a course in exporting, hoping that I might transform the company into something that better suited my interests. It was the most god-awful boring topic I could possibly imagine, but I clung to my dim and misguided faith that something would eventually click for me and light the way. Soon, having banished the writer within me as well as the artist, I was next in line to inherit the business if I could somehow find it within me to embrace the years ahead of learning how to promote, buy, and sell. But I couldn't.

It was no secret that I couldn't stand the work. And my mother was at a loss to inspire any interest in me, which, I'm sure, saddened her some. Yet, there I was, reduced to an image of adulthood I'd hated to witness as a child: the money game; the anti-creative act; the calculation of profit; the buying of someone else's goods for cheap and the selling of them for a little less cheap. I knew such work had accounted for the comforts I enjoyed, and that, for my grandparents, a proclivity for business had been the stuff of life itself, but I had also known, even as a child, that I would want something different for myself when I grew up. But when would I grow up? Stuck within a life that was seemingly unfolding without my say, I felt utterly snuffed out and shut down.

By the time I had become a dulled and despondent twenty-seven year-old, I entered into a relationship with Shoshana, a woman I had known in college. Her father had recently died and she was living in The Bronx, in an apartment that she and her sister had inherited from him. Shoshana recognized my hopelessness and, unlike my friends and family, she unapologetically looked me in the eye and called it what it was. Her own harrowing and seemingly bottomless mourning process also stood as a stark mirror for my despair. No longer was the depth of my suffering held preciously in secret. And, more importantly, no longer was I suspended in a net of seclusion. My slumbering soul had been awakened through a rusty empathy that often terrified me, as I witnessed her suffering from such closeness I could feel the breath of it on me.

The awkwardness of forming intimacy so near to my mother's livelihood and her father's memory compelled me to imagine possibilities of a different life, but I did not yet know how to make a living outside of the export company. Shoshana challenged me to revive my imagination, provocatively engaging me in a manner that was also gentle and kind. The first thing I learned through our friendship was that if I wanted change to happen, I had to place myself in situations that were new and unforeseen. I had sworn off academia from the moment I'd received a bachelor's degree, yet I found myself craving a return to the classroom---not for the sake of another degree, or for any pursuit of future aims, but just for the indulgence of interest and curiosity. This feeling surprised me. What surprised me even more was that I felt no urge to return to the art room, which had been the reluctant thread throughout my college experience. I had yearned for a return to the creative roots that had given form to my youth, but at this moment such things felt laden with suffering and hurt, and so I gravitated towards classes in which I did not feel so heavily invested.

I enrolled at a local city university in courses on African-American history, Latino heritage in New York City, and the history of Jews living under Christian and Islamic empires. I received credit for these classes, but with no avenue of application, and for the first time in my life, I felt as if I was learning simply for the joy of learning. And it was a wonderful feeling, because I had been living in fear of the classroom since my earliest years in school, having associated it with humiliation, shame, vulnerability, and rage. Finally, I was learning how to be a student on my own terms; a *real* student, eye-to-eye with my teachers in a zone of mutual respect.

During this time, as Shoshana and I dreamt of possibilities for the both of our lives as best we were able, trudging through the muddle, she suggested on a tip from a friend that I investigate art therapy. I had heard the phrase "art therapy" somewhere random in my memory and I remembered having written it off as a ridiculous idea. I had never much cared for the field of psychology and my few sessions with a therapist during my college years had seemed anything but therapeutic. But at this time in my life I was willing to recognize that my cynicism had only shut doors before I got to see the stuff on the other side of them. In reality, I knew nothing about art therapy, or about psychology for that matter. I decided to learn.

I read bits here and there about the field, but I knew, with the help of Shoshana's wisdom and encouragement, that real learning would only come through experience. So, with little idea how to find places where I might volunteer, I picked up a Yellow Pages and called as many medical facilities as I could handle in a day, deciding that I'd stop at the first place that invited me to visit an art therapy department. That place was Sloan-Kettering Cancer Center, a highly regarded facility not too far from where I lived. It did not have an art therapy department, but it did have something called a recreation therapy department, which employed two art therapists. Upon hearing the words "recreation" and "therapy" linked together, my cynic monster popped its head, but I understood that it was only my fear of the unknown trying to talk me out of this venture. I had never worked in a setting even remotely like that of a cancer center and I had no idea how I would feel entering through its doors.

Much to my surprise, I felt at ease. I had decided that, if it felt right, I would quit the export business and volunteer at the hospital as if it were a full-time job, so that I'd have something to put on my résumé. If I liked the experience, I would apply to some graduate programs. All of these ideas scared the hell out of me, but I did my best to keep focus simply on what was in front of me. In short time, I found that I enjoyed the activities that took place around the recreation room, as well as the personalities that showed up there; and I learned, with a yet greater sense of revelation, that I felt extremely comfortable among people who suffered from severe illness, facing their own mortality. In fact, I felt *more* at home, *more* connected than I did with many of my family and friends. Several of them would ask me, "Don't you find it depressing?" I told them; on the contrary, I found it inspiring.

I knew very little about cancer. My mother's friend who'd worked with us in the office had recently died from cancer. Very suddenly. All I knew about it was that it had rapidly spread throughout many organs in her body and claimed her life within four months. Shoshana's father had also died from cancer. In fact, he had spent some time at Sloan-Kettering, while his malignancy had advanced. Through Shoshana's accounts, I learned how heartrending it is to watch a loved one die slowly, feeling powerless to do anything but offer love as best you can, even while you feel as though your efforts are never enough. She had lived with him and taken care of him throughout his ordeal, doing all she could to preserve his sense of dignity, and still she felt oftentimes as if she had failed him.

What I understood about cancer came through bits of others' experiences. I'd never spent time in direct contact with a person suffering from cancer. Quickly, I learned that I didn't need to know anything about it; I only needed to know what was in someone's heart and what was in my own. I only needed to spend time being present, giving my attention, and opening myself up, the way a flower blooms, true to its own nature and not merely as a matter of choice. I only needed to show up. The rest would take care of itself. I had no idea about it at the time, but that was the first lesson I would learn about the meaning of therapy---one which I would have to learn over and over to this very day.

Not once in my life did I seriously think I might one day become a therapist. The idea might have existed as a joke within me, as friends and acquaintances had always come to me with their problems, telling me how gifted a listener I was. Some had even suggested, over the years, that I'd make a great therapist. *Cute*, I'd always thought, *but I don't think so*. So, my choice to become a therapist---which I barely trusted at all---came as a surprise, the realness of which I did not believe until I was encircled within it. With nothing to reference but two months of experience at Sloan-Kettering and a feeling that I was ready for my life to change, I interviewed at the two biggest and nearest schools, was accepted into one of them, and braced myself, as though lifting off for another planet. I had no idea at all what on earth I was doing or where it would leave me, and only vague speculation as to why I was choosing this path. It felt crazy to me, diving right into uncharted waters. And it would take some time before I learned to integrate that nothing could have been saner than the risk of a life without guarantees.

From the Cover Artist

Arie Kupferwasser

I entitled my recent exhibit in New York City, in which *The Mirror* (cover art) appeared, *Practicing How to Dream*. Most of my work for this showing materialized between the winter of 2004 and the summer of 2005. During this time, I also began a private practice as an art therapist, left behind the institutional settings of nursing homes and hospitals in which I had been working, and allowed myself, after longer than a decade's length hiatus, to be wholly immersed in the process of artmaking that had so deeply enriched my childhood, adolescence, and college years. The work shown represented a time of great joy and triumph in my life and a rediscovery of essence. Although I had never worked extensively with oil pastels, it seemed to be the material particularly suited to allow me a sense of boundlessness, spontaneity, and intuition---all qualities counter to how I approached art in my earlier years.

My current process and method is largely, with a few exceptions, an exercise of the imagination at play, in which I approach the blank page with nothing in mind, allow for an image to form, and work until I recognize what I am doing. At the point of recognition, a struggle begins as the intellect wants to take over and shape what is on the page. In making these pieces, I discovered that a tyrannical intellect is really nothing but a child frightened of the dark, of the unknown. I was able to navigate spaces that were undefined, mysterious, and yet uncannily familiar by working with great speed and making choices---such as what color to use or where to make a mark---before I could consciously recognize my decisions. In that sense, I trusted my body to decide and move ahead of my intellect, which produced a dream state relatively free from judgment.

While producing this work, I have been seeking to understand more clearly how spiritual, ecstatic, and mystical orientations of experience relate with those of mundane, worldly, and day-to-day quality. My hope is that it inspires a similar contemplation in others…

Contact Information:

Arie Kupferwasser
210 W. 89th St.
New York, NY 10024
(917) 941-2406
arie8k@rcn.com

www.ingramcontent.com/pod-product-compliance
Lightning Source LLC
Chambersburg PA
CBHW080401030426
42334CB00024B/2961